Compliance and Ethics in Law Firms

Other titles available from Law Society Publishing:

Solicitors' Accounts Manual, 13th edition
Solicitors Regulation Authority

SRA Handbook
Solicitors Regulation Authority

The Solicitor's Handbook 2015
Andrew Hopper QC and Gregory Treverton-Jones QC

Titles from Law Society Publishing can be ordered from all good bookshops or direct (telephone 0370 850 1422, email **lawsociety@prolog.uk.com** or visit our online shop at **bookshop.lawsociety.org.uk**).

COMPLIANCE AND ETHICS IN LAW FIRMS

A Guide for Legal Support Staff

Tracey Calvert

The Law Society

ISBN-13: 978-1-78446-034-1

Published in 2015 by the Law Society
113 Chancery Lane, London WC2A 1PL

Typeset by Columns Design XML Ltd, Reading
Printed by Hobbs the Printers Ltd, Totton, Hants

The paper used for the text pages of this book is FSC® certified. FSC (the Forest Stewardship Council®) is an international network to promote responsible management of the world's forests.

FSC
www.fsc.org
MIX
Paper from responsible sources
FSC® C020438

Contents

Preface

One of the more common pieces of feedback I receive when I visit law firms, or deliver training on ethics, is relief that the topic is not as dry as the audience had expected it to be. Nothing could be further from the truth! Professional ethics throws up many different conundrums to be analysed and resolved and does make for an interesting life.

Working in a legal environment creates a variety of practical challenges which need to be answered with the correct regulatory and ethical response. For example, can we act for a particular client? What do we need to tell the client about the services we offer? Is the client asking us to do something which is inappropriate? Should we be challenging inappropriate behaviour in the workplace? All these questions require an ethical response.

These are challenges which must be understood by the managers and compliance officers in the law firm. They are expected to create a working environment in which there is proper governance and reporting lines, zero tolerance of mavericks or unprofessional behaviour, and the means to ensure that all colleagues work in an ethical way. The additional challenge is to ensure that they understand what these ethical behaviours are. For example, how do you explain confidentiality or duties to the court to colleagues who are not themselves solicitors?

Non-solicitor colleagues also need to understand the weight of regulation which is part and parcel of working in an SRA-authorised law firm. This is necessary both to ensure that they are personally safe from disciplinary scrutiny and also to ensure that they are not a weak link that may jeopardise the firm's authorised status.

I hope that this book will help shed light on some of these challenges. It is intended both to assist the managers wanting to ensure the right level of understanding of core duties and values in their business, and as also a reference book that can be read by anyone in the law firm wanting to understand what makes their workplace different.

I would like to take this opportunity to thank friends and colleagues with whom I have enjoyed many an ethical debate over the years, and from whom I have learned so much, in particular Helen Carr, Pearl Moses, Bronwen Still and Kirsty Swann. I would also like to thank Janet Noble of Law Society Publishing for her support and patience.

Tracey Calvert
September 2015

Table of cases

Table of statutes

Table of statutory instruments

Table of Law Society rules

Abbreviations

ABS	alternative business structure
AR	approved regulator
CDD	customer due diligence
CILEx	Chartered Institute of Legal Executives
CIPA	Chartered Institute of Patent Attorneys
COFA	compliance officer for finance and administration
COLP	compliance officer for legal practice
FATF	Financial Action Task Force
FCA	Financial Conduct Authority
FPO	Financial Services and Markets Act 2000 (Financial Promotion) Order 2001
FSMA	Financial Services and Markets Act 2000
HMRC	Her Majesty's Revenue and Customs
IB	indicative behaviour
ICO	Information Commissioner's Office
ITMA	Institute of Trade Mark Attorneys
LA	licensing authority
LeO	Legal Ombudsman
LSB	Legal Services Board
LSA	Legal Services Act 2007
MDP	multi-disciplinary practice
MLR	Money Laundering Regulations 2007
MLRO	money laundering reporting officer
NCA	National Crime Agency
OLC	Office for Legal Complaints
OFR	outcomes-focused regulation
PFR	SRA Practice Framework Rules 2011
POCA	Proceeds of Crime Act 2002
REL	registered European lawyer
RFL	registered foreign lawyer
SAR	suspicious activity report
SDT	Solicitors Disciplinary Tribunal
SRA	Solicitors Regulation Authority

CHAPTER 1

Introduction

1.1 INTRODUCTION

There has never been a more exciting and dynamic time to work in the legal services industry. Solicitors in the twenty-first century have far more opportunities to provide services in a creative way and non-solicitors are able to have very successful and interesting careers in this environment. The traditional image of a solicitor dictating letters to his secretary, with the support of articled clerks and outdoor clerks, is fading rapidly. Instead, law firms are expected to be run in the same way as any other business.

This means that solicitors work alongside a number of colleagues who have probably joined them not because they want to be solicitors themselves but because they want to add their own skills and expertise to successful businesses. The modern law firm sees solicitors working alongside lawyers qualified in other jurisdictions or home-grown but trained through a different regulatory system, paralegals providing a variety of fee-earning roles, support staff providing far more than secretarial services, human resources and marketing experts, receptionists, accounts staff, and a back-room team of IT specialists and administration staff. It is not uncommon in some firms for solicitors to be in the minority.

One of the common features which binds all the different people in the firm together is the need to act ethically and to understand the requirements of professional conduct which must be displayed. In other words, to understand what acceptable behaviour looks like in a law firm and to be able to deliver services in this way. This requires an understanding of what it means to work in a regulated business.

Law firms are subject to external regulation. The majority of law firms in England and Wales are authorised and regulated by the Solicitors Regulation Authority (SRA). The SRA has powers to be able to influence what happens in a law firm in order to ensure, ultimately, that the right behaviours are demonstrated and that clients receive an appropriate service and the reputation of the profession as a whole survives untarnished. The SRA expects everyone working in the law firm to understand what it needs to see.

It takes at least six years to become a solicitor. During that time, aspiring lawyers spend a substantial amount of time at college and in law firms learning legal skills.

By the time that they are admitted to the roll of solicitors, and they are working in practice, the expectation is that they will be competent. One of the hallmarks of being competent is the ability to act ethically and to understand the requirements of professional conduct, or professional ethics as it is sometimes also described. Many new lawyers struggle with this idea, so it is hardly surprising that, for those of us who have not had the benefit of a formal legal training, but are nonetheless working in a law firm and therefore bound to behave in the same way as the solicitors, this may all seem a little bewildering at times.

1.2 PROFESSIONAL CONDUCT/ETHICS

A standard definition of the phrase 'professional conduct/ethics' is that this means the professionally acceptable standards of personal and business values. The crux of the matter is that the legal profession – and by that we do not simply mean solicitors and other lawyers but absolutely everyone connected with them in the provision of legal services – is distinguishable from a lot of other businesses by the fact that it is heavily regulated and this regulated relationship means that there are ethical behaviours which must be displayed at all times. It is important to know how to behave.

Most lawyers enter the profession because they have an understanding of fairness and a belief in upholding the law and they want to make a difference in some way. Being a good lawyer is more than this, though; after all, applying the law correctly but acting unethically is a bad combination. Skills and knowledge must be combined with an understanding of the correct way to behave.

The form of ethical behaviour in a law firm is not just down to individuals and their personal code of morality. After all, this could result in a decision to accept instructions to act for a client in a matter without having the skills or knowledge to act in the client's best interests because the individual thinks he will try his best to look after the client and that is acceptable. It isn't. It is not even down to the law firm owners or managers to make decisions about how everyone in their firm will behave. This could result in commercial decisions about such things as arrangements with third parties for the introduction of clients which mean that the firm's independence is compromised. This would be wrong too.

Both individual and firm-driven professional conduct could result in a lot of inconsistency and that would not be good for the reputation of the profession. Law firm clients must have the confidence that they will receive a safe and consistent service irrespective of which law firm they instruct and this cannot be left to luck or chance or to the law firms themselves. So, how we all behave if we are qualified solicitors, or if we are employed in a law firm which is authorised and regulated by the SRA, is pre-decided by the regulator who has the important role of setting and monitoring our ethical behaviour. The regulator has a variety of statutory and non-statutory sources of ethics at its disposal and must now intertwine this with a consideration of the regulatory objectives in the Legal Services Act 2007 to create behavioural requirements which are non-negotiable.

1.3 CONCLUSION

The Principles, outcomes, rules and regulations which control our ethical behaviour are contained in the SRA Handbook. In the following chapters we will look in more detail at the parts of the Handbook which are essential reading for everyone working in the firm. Everyone working in a law firm needs to understand the repercussions for themselves and their firms in not understanding professional conduct requirements and what it takes to ensure that they are a safe pair of ethical hands.

CHAPTER 2

The regulatory landscape

2.1 INTRODUCTION

There have been more changes in the legal services market in the past decade than had been the case for a good amount of time before that. In fact, the developments of the last few years have been described as a quiet revolution with the winner being the client, or 'consumer', as the politicians and others would like us to describe the people to whom we provide legal services.

What we have seen is clients once again becoming the focus of what we do. This may seem an odd statement to make but it cannot be denied that there were some firms at the turn of the century in which client considerations were not high on the agenda when thinking about the business and how it operated.

With this change of heart and direction, business models have changed, and non-solicitors are also winners in the new scheme of things. There are now opportunities for unqualified individuals to own law firms and to be in business with solicitors. The opportunities also filter down to the roles of unqualified people working in law firms. We have legal apprentices, paralegals, and lawyers qualified through alternative routes (such as licensed conveyancers, legal executives, barristers and foreign-qualified lawyers) all working in law firms which are authorised and regulated by the SRA. In addition the modern law firm also employs a variety of support staff to provide assistance with office and administration duties, human resources and even, in some firms, marketing. A law firm is far more than just the solicitor headcount.

However, these opportunities come with the responsibilities attached to working in a regulated industry. Non-solicitors will be expected to behave in the same way as their solicitor colleagues and respond to the same regulatory and legal compliance obligations.

For all these reasons, it is important to understand what has happened in the legal services industry in the past few years and the effect that the changes have on non-solicitors working in law firms.

2.2 THE LEGAL SERVICES ACT 2007

The starting point is the Legal Services Act 2007, which came into force on 20 October 2007. This law was the consequence of a very thorough 'root and branch' review of the regulation of legal services at the start of the century which culminated in a report known as the Review of the Regulatory Framework for Legal Services in England and Wales, authored by Sir David Clementi. At this time the feeling was that there was insufficient competition in the marketplace (for example, solicitors could only be in business with other solicitors and they were subject to very tight restrictions on investment in those businesses), that clients often received inappropriate levels of service, and that the professional institutions which regulated and represented lawyers were not coming up to scratch and were sometimes too complex and inconsistent in approach.

Sir David Clementi had been asked to do two things: first to consider and advise on a regulatory framework which would promote competition, innovation and the public and consumer interest and, secondly, to recommend a regulatory framework. His report contained a number of far-reaching recommendations, as follows:

- The establishment of a legal services regulator to oversee the regulatory bodies (described as front-line regulators or bodies) with direct responsibilities for service providers.
- Statutory objectives and regulatory powers to be given to the legal services regulator.
- The front-line regulators to split and separate regulation from representation.
- The investigation of consumer (client) complaints to be removed from the front-line bodies and to become the responsibility of one independent body which would be answerable to the legal services regulator.
- The establishment of alternative business structures.

All of these recommendations require some explanation.

2.3 THE LEGAL SERVICES BOARD

The Legal Services Board (LSB) is the independent organisation which is responsible for overseeing the regulation of all lawyers in England and Wales. This means that it is not simply concerned with solicitors but is also casting a watchful eye over other providers of legal services such as barristers, legal executives and licensed conveyancers. It states that its goal is to 'reform and modernise the legal services market place by putting the interests of consumers at the heart of the system, reflecting the objectives of the statute that created us, the Legal Services Act 2007.' The LSB does not have a direct relationship with solicitors and other lawyers but instead has a role in overseeing regulation through a group of approved regulators. The approved regulators have the direct 'hands-on' relationship with regulated individuals while the LSB ensures that they make rules and regulations and regulate their members in compliance with a set of values known as regulatory objectives.

2.4 REGULATORY OBJECTIVES, PROFESSIONAL PRINCIPLES AND RESERVED LEGAL ACTIVITIES

Because of the criticisms aimed at regulation, and the feeling that it was a little confusing and over complicated, the Legal Services Act 2007 lists a set of values which must be adopted and promoted by approved regulators when making rules to deal with the profession which they regulate. The LSB sits behind this to ensure that this is happening.

The regulatory objectives are in s.1(1) of the Legal Services Act 2007:

(a) protecting and promoting the public interest;
(b) supporting the constitutional principle of the rule of law;
(c) improving access to justice;
(d) protecting and promoting the interests of consumers;
(e) promoting competition in the provision of services known as reserved legal activities;
(f) encouraging an independent, strong, diverse and effective legal profession;
(g) increasing public understanding of the citizen's legal rights and duties;
(h) promoting and maintaining adherence to the professional principles.

The 'professional principles' (s.1(3)) are:

(a) that authorised persons should act with independence and integrity,
(b) that authorised persons should maintain proper standards of work,
(c) that authorised persons should act in the best interests of their clients,
(d) that persons who exercise before any court a right of audience, or conduct litigation in relation to proceedings in any court, by virtue of being authorised persons should comply with their duty to the court to act with independence in the interests of justice, and
(e) that the affairs of clients should be kept confidential.

The professional principles which are mentioned in the Legal Services Act apply to 'authorised persons', in other words people who can carry on certain legal activities (known as reserved legal activities) because they are qualified and legally entitled to do so. Qualified persons includes solicitors with practising certificates.

The reserved legal activities (s.12(1)) are:

(a) the exercise of a right of audience;
(b) the conduct of litigation;
(c) reserved instrument activities;
(d) probate activities;
(e) notarial activities;
(f) the administration of oaths.

It is important to understand these regulatory objectives and professional principles because these are the behaviours which are used to test us to make sure that we are fit and safe to provide services. Lots of the terms – such as 'public interest' in the regulatory objectives and 'integrity' in the professional principles – appear regularly in the SRA's regulatory language.

2.5 APPROVED REGULATORS

The LSB shares responsibilities for applying the regulatory objectives with the approved regulators of the legal profession. It is the approved regulators which directly regulate lawyers practising in England and Wales to provide reserved legal activities. Some of the approved regulators are also described as licensing authorities. This means that they are able to license alternative business structures to provide reserved legal activities to members of the public. In this way, those licensing authorities are supporting the specific regulatory objective which relates to the promotion of competition.

Table 2.1 is a list of the approved regulators reproduced from the LSB's website. The table also shows whether the approved regulator is also a licensing authority and the reserved legal activities it is entitled to regulate.

Table 2.1 Approved regulators

Profession	Approved regulators (representative body)	Independent regulatory body	Approved regulator (AR) Licensing authority (LA)	Reserved legal activities regulated
Solicitors	Law Society	Solicitors Regulation Authority	AR LA	• The exercise of right of audience • The conduct of litigation • Reserved instrument activities • Probate activities • The administration of oaths
Barristers	Bar Council	Bar Standards Board	AR	• The exercise of right of audience • The conduct of litigation • Reserved instrument activities • Probate activities • The administration of oaths

Profession	Approved regulators (representative body)	Independent regulatory body	Approved regulator (AR) Licensing authority (LA)	Reserved legal activities regulated
Legal Executives	Chartered Institute of Legal Executives	CILEx Regulation	AR	• The exercise of right of audience • The conduct of litigation • Reserved instrument activities • Probate activities • The administration of oaths
Licensed Conveyancers	Council for Licensed Conveyancers (regulatory body for Licensed Conveyancers, no representative body)		AR LA	• Reserved instrument activities • Probate activities • The administration of oaths
Patent Attorneys Trade Mark Attorneys	Chartered Institute of Patent Attorneys (CIPA) Institute of Trade Mark Attorneys (ITMA)	Intellectual Property Regulation Board (Regulatory body for both CIPA and ITMA)	AR LA	• The exercise of right of audience • The conduct of litigation • Reserved instrument activities • The administration of oaths
Costs Lawyers	Association of Costs Lawyers	Costs Lawyer Standards Board	AR	• The exercise of right of audience • The conduct of litigation • The administration of oaths
Notaries	Master of the Faculties (regulatory body for Notaries, no representative body)		AR	• Reserved instrument activities • Probate activities • Notarial Activities • The administration of oaths

Profession	Approved regulators (representative body)	Independent regulatory body	Approved regulator (AR) Licensing authority (LA)	Reserved legal activities regulated
Chartered Accountants	Institute of Chartered Accountants in England and Wales There is no separate regulatory body; all decisions relating to legal activities are delegated to the independently chaired Probate Committee		AR LA	• Probate

2.6 SEPARATION OF REPRESENTATION AND REGULATION

The Legal Services Act contains a requirement that professional bodies separate their governance arrangements into regulatory and representative functions. This was to address the criticism that there was inconsistency and over-complexity in the existing state of affairs. Representation focuses on the promotion of the members' interests while the regulation function is designed to ensure that the public are protected when they receive legal services from this membership.

In terms of the solicitors' profession in England and Wales, the Law Society of England and Wales is constitutionally the regulatory body but it has given that role to the SRA and instead focuses on the representation of its membership.

2.7 THE OFFICE FOR LEGAL COMPLAINTS

Traditionally, professional bodies not only represented and regulated their members but they also investigated consumer complaints about the services provided by these members. This led to criticisms that such a service was not sufficiently independent. The Legal Services Act created a system in which the handling of consumer complaints was taken away from the professional bodies and given to an independent complaints handling organisation known as the Office for Legal Complaints (OLC) which is led by the Legal Ombudsman (LeO). This organisation handles complaints in respect of services offered by all lawyers although and, as maybe expected, the vast majority relate to solicitors purely because solicitors are the largest single group of service providers. The OLC has wide-ranging powers to investigate consumer complaints and to provide remedies to clients who have suffered poor service.

2.8 ALTERNATIVE BUSINESS STRUCTURES

To address the criticism that there was a lack of competition in the marketplace and the way in which solicitors could practice was overly restrictive, the Legal Services Act establishes alternative business structures (ABSs) that enable different types of lawyers and non-lawyers to manage and own legal businesses providing reserved legal activities to consumers. ABSs must be authorised by a licensing body. The SRA is a licensing body and considers applications from a range of ABS applicants. This is a varied market; some ABSs come about because a traditional law firm wants to invite non-solicitor employees to become part of its management and ownership structure, others are a merger of law firms and industry groups, and others are in-house legal teams (i.e. teams of lawyers working for non-solicitor employers in the private and public sector) who want to form a law firm with external investment. A common requirement is that all ABSs must comply with the rules of their regulator in the same way as traditional law firms.

2.9 THE EFFECT OF THESE CHANGES ON THE SRA

The requirements of the Legal Services Act meant that the Law Society of England and Wales had to separate its representative and regulatory functions. The Law Society represents solicitors in England and Wales. It does this in a number of ways; for example it negotiates and lobbies with regulatory bodies and the government and other institutions on behalf of its membership; it offers training and advice services and guidance; and it generally seeks to promote the profession both within England and Wales and internationally. It works within a framework known as the Law Society Group. The Solicitors Regulation Authority is part of the Law Society Group and is the independent regulatory body for solicitors as well as for the majority of law firms in England and Wales and all those working within such firms.

On its website, the SRA says:

> Our purpose is to protect the public by ensuring that solicitors meet high standards, and by acting when risks are identified.

It does this in a number of ways, i.e. by:

- ensuring that certain standards are met in terms of the training undertaken by prospective lawyers;
- issuing practising certificates;
- authorising law firms (including sole practitioner law firms) to carry out reserved legal activities;
- setting standards of behaviour for solicitors and for everyone working in a law firm authorised by it or connected with a law firm authorised by it;
- supervision of individuals and law firms; and
- using disciplinary and enforcement powers to ensure the public is protected.

In total the SRA regulates more than 130,000 solicitors in England and Wales and authorises about 10,500 law firms. The number of additional people which come within the SRA's regulatory powers is not known, but will include everyone working in a law firm regardless of their job title or what they do and also everyone who has an ownership interest in a law firm.

The SRA is an approved regulator and that means that it must regulate in accordance with the regulatory objectives in the Legal Services Act 2007. It does this through a publication known as the SRA Handbook which was launched in October 2011.

The contents of the Handbook is the SRA's toolkit of Principles, outcomes, rules and regulations to ensure that it can regulate in accordance with the regulatory objectives. It is approved by the LSB. The SRA says:

> The SRA Handbook sets out the standards and requirements we expect our regulated community to achieve and observe, for the benefit of the clients they serve and in the public interest.

It is primarily an online resource available on the SRA website, **www.sra.org.uk**. Printed versions are available to buy from the Law Society bookshop (**www.lawsociety.org.uk/bookshop**). Care needs to be taken when considering a regulatory requirement, as the Handbook is updated at regular intervals and the current version will be the one that is published online. This sets out the history of changes which may also prove to be useful information.

In order to adapt to regulatory requirements which support the regulatory objectives, the SRA has changed its approach to regulation and is now an outcomes-focused, risk-based and entity-based regulator. These are terms which must be understood by everyone working in a law firm which is authorised and regulated by the SRA.

2.9.1 Outcomes-focused regulation (OFR)

The Solicitors Regulation Authority implemented outcomes-focused regulation with the launch of the SRA Handbook in October 2011. The SRA says (Regulatory Risk Framework 2014):

> Outcomes-focused regulation means that our goal is to ensure that those we regulate deliver the right outcomes for the public, in line with the intent of the regulatory objectives.

In this way, OFR was a move away from the prior rules-based approach to regulation to one that focuses on high-level outcomes to govern practice and the quality of outcomes for clients. Outcomes appear in two ways in the Handbook: first, in the individual rules and requirements to introduce and explain the purpose of what follows and, secondly, in the SRA Code of Conduct 2011, which sets out ethical standards that the SRA expects of practices and practitioners and the outcomes that the SRA expects them to achieve for their clients.

Outcomes-focused regulation is one of the reasons why there have been a lot of changes in recent years in the way that law firms operate. The SRA expects law firms to consider how best to achieve outcomes-focused requirements in its particular circumstances and take into account the type of clients which receive services from the firm, the type of work, and even the people within the firm and introduce systems and processes which will suit their environment.

Many practitioners have been critical and concerned about how OFR works in practice and preferred the detailed requirements of more traditional regulation which gave them a certain and detailed method of compliance and a lot more guidance from the regulator. OFR certainly places extra responsibilities on the managers and owners of the law firm (the partners, directors or members) for having suitable arrangements in place to ensure compliance. It also means that the arrangements must cover the work carried on by everyone in the firm and every individual must understand which policies, procedures and requirements apply to them. When OFR works as intended, it is designed to ensure that the firm has a framework which will allow it to decide the best ways of delivering an ethical service without being dictated to about its methods of compliance.

2.9.2 Risk-based regulation

Risk-based regulation has also required law firms, and individuals working within law firms, to reconsider what they do. The SRA says:

> Risk-based regulation means that risks to us acting compatibly with the regulatory objectives are assessed in terms of their probability and the impact of any harm they cause to desired outcomes, before action is taken. This approach ensures that regulatory activities and resources are prioritised and applied proportionately.

In other words, both the SRA and everyone it regulates has to consider what events could occur which would create obstacles to meeting the regulatory objectives, what would be the impact on the SRA, the regulated individual and the reputation of the profession, and what could be done to minimise the impact.

This introduces another new concept – 'proportionality'. What is the appropriate response to a risk event and the sensible use of resources to address it? Is it appropriate to react in the same way to a relatively minor breach (such as information about the firm's regulated status dropping off the website on a temporary basis) with something of greater consequence (such as a manager or employee stealing client money)? In other words, the consequences of some risk events justify both the SRA and law firms focusing more resources on risk prevention in some areas rather than others.

The SRA does expect law firms to identify what constitutes a major risk in the practice and to react appropriately with risk registers, policies and training. Risk will be determined by a number of factors such as the type of work, the type of client, even the type of firm and who is employed in it. For example, a large

City-based form with many international offices and clients will identify risks which are unquestionably going to be different to a small high-street practice in a market town.

However, and unlike the application of OFR where the SRA expects law firms to identify their own methods of compliance, a lot more guidance about risk-based regulation is available. For example, the SRA publishes the document Risk Outlook (**www.sra.org.uk/risk/outlook/risk-outlook-spring-2015-update.page**), which provides an interpretation of the key issues and trends in the provision of legal services and the legal services market and describes what the SRA considers to be the obstacles to fulfilling the regulatory objectives. It keeps this document updated so that current risk priorities are identified and emerging trends highlighted. For example, in the Risk Outlook Spring 2015 Update, the SRA identified the following as key risks with the implication that these risks should also be considered by individuals working in law firms:

- misuse of money or assets, and poor controls providing opportunities for financial misconduct;
- money laundering;
- the threats from bogus law firms and bogus lawyers;
- the lack of a diverse and representative profession;
- poor standards of service to consumers.

Other emerging priorities were identified in connection with the risks attached to information security weaknesses and cybercrime and the threats attached to the duties of independence and upholding the rule of law when acting in litigation. The SRA keeps law firms informed about new scams, identity fraud and the like through news items and updates on its website.

Again, this style of regulation requires law firms to be proactive and work on their own risk management strategies. Individual law firms need to consider the likelihood of a risk event happening in their business and put in place measures to deal with this. Many firms now have an internal risk register or, in other words, a document to record their own consideration of what could happen in the law firm and what systems and procedures will be appropriate in terms of risk prevention. This will largely be the responsibility of the law firm managers, and those colleagues in a risk and compliance role, but there will be an expectation that everyone in the business will play their part in keeping the business safe. In other words, risk management requires everyone to understand what the risks are and to be actively engaged in making sure that the risks are kept in mind when working in the business.

2.9.3 Entity-based regulation

The third feature of the SRA's post-2011 style of regulation is described as entity-based regulation but it can also be called firm-based regulation. The SRA actually started to work in this way before the launch of the SRA Handbook but the

Handbook makes the purpose of this type of regulation clearer. In changes introduced in 2009, the SRA was allowed to regulate law firms as well as the solicitors within them and have powers to impose sanctions on non-solicitor managers and employees of regulated firms.

For solicitors, this change has meant that it is now a more complex process to register a law firm. They now must overcome a number of hurdles before they are granted authorised status and able legally to provide reserved legal activities and other services to the public. There are also a lot more conditions attached to the continuing authorisation of the business such as the need to demonstrate appropriate systems and processes to ensure compliance with Handbook requirements, effective governance, and proper risk management. These systems and processes must take into account what everyone in the firm is doing and not just what the solicitors are doing.

For non-managers, regardless of role, the impact of entity-based regulation is significant. The SRA requires everyone in the entity to comply with the various Principles, outcomes and other obligations in the Handbook and it has supervisory, enforcement and disciplinary powers which it can use against any individual employed in the business. This is a very important fact to bear in mind when working in a law firm.

2.10 AUTHORISATION, SUPERVISION AND ENFORCEMENT

Mention of supervision introduces another important feature of the relationship with the SRA which everyone in a law firm must take into account. This requires an understanding of how the SRA structures itself internally. Because the SRA regulates in the public interest and in accordance with the regulatory objectives in the Legal Services Act 2007, its work now focuses on three main areas; authorisation, supervision and enforcement.

2.10.1 Authorisation

We have already touched on authorisation. The SRA's authorisation department not only deals with practising certificate applications from solicitors, but it also considers applications from new firms (or entities to describe them properly) which are seeking authorisation to provide reserved legal activities. This SRA department must consider whether it is safe to grant an entity this status, and what the impact would be on the public and in meeting the regulatory objectives. Applicants have to provide a great deal of information to the regulator including business plans and descriptions of how risk will be managed. The SRA has the power to authorise, or refuse authorisation, and also to allow authorisation subject to conditions being met.

2.10.2 Supervision

The consideration will also be concerned with assessing how safe it will be for a member of the public to receive legal services from a law firm. The SRA's supervision responsibilities are closely connected with this type of consideration. By analysing and assessing the risks posed by different law firms, the SRA works out an appropriate and proportionate supervisory response. With some firms, where the risks are judged to be high, the SRA has the option to assign a regulatory manager to the firm. This will be an individual SRA employee who will work with the firm and provide a one-to-one service to ensure that risks are managed appropriately.

The majority of firms are not in a regulatory manager relationship with the SRA, and supervision is largely desk-based and with fewer regular visits by the regulator to the firm's offices. Desk-based supervision has created a number of changes which have a bearing on everyone in the law firm. The SRA expects openness and transparency and a way of working in which the firm tells it what it needs to know about what is happening in business, in particular where this relates to material breaches of the SRA Handbook and events which are not compatible with the regulatory objectives.

Because of this need for openness and risk management, firms must have compliance officers in place as a term of their initial and continuing authorisation. These compliance officers are usually the interface between the business and the regulator.

In additional to this communication channel, the SRA Handbook also includes a requirement that anyone working in a law firm must notify the SRA of anything about themselves which is relevant to the regulator (such as a serious failure to comply with Handbook requirements) and also must report serious misconduct by any person or firm authorised by the SRA or any employee of an authorised firm.

2.10.3 Enforcement

Enforcement is also another priority function of the regulator. The enforcement function has been modernised of late to make it more appropriate for the style of regulation we are working with. We have already mentioned that the SRA now has powers of enforcement which can be used in respect of non-solicitors where this is in the public interest. There are a number of examples of non-solicitors having orders made against them to prevent their employment in authorised law firms except with the SRA's permission.

However, the focus of the enforcement department is geared to working more positively with individuals and law firms wherever this is possible. The SRA has a number of powers, including the use of regulatory settlement agreements and written rebukes, to deal with compliance issues where there is the possibility of dealing with a regulatory breach and moving on with lessons learned about what has happened. In fact, the SRA has stated on the record that it wants to work with law firms which have shown a commitment to outcomes-focused, risk-based and entity-based recognition. The flip-side of this is that the SRA now has increased fining powers and a range of disciplinary measure it can use against individuals and firms not prepared to co-operate and work with it.

2.11 PARTICULAR COMPLIANCE ROLES IN LAW FIRMS

All of the above means that the modern law firm is likely to have a more obvious compliance culture than was previously the case, and that the compliance culture extends to everyone in the business rather than just the solicitors. There are some key players with this way of working and it is important to understand their various roles and how everyone else in the firm should work with them to keep the business safe and ethical.

2.11.1 The managers

Solicitors can provide legal services in a variety of different types of entity or firm. Commonly, this will be as a sole practitioner or sole trader (albeit sometimes with a number of employees), in a partnership, or in a corporate business such as a limited liability partnership or a company. The precise form is usually decided on a consideration of a number of things such as financial circumstances, taxation considerations and similar.

When talking about managers, the SRA means the following:

- a member of an LLP;
- a director of a company;
- a partner in a partnership; or
- in relation to any other body, a member of its governing body.

The managers of a law firm must be approved by the SRA. Because of entity-based regulation, and the need for the whole firm to comply with the requirements in the SRA Handbook, there are a number of requirements on the managers to ensure that there is effective governance of the firm. In other words, the managers will need to lead the firm in an ethical way and will need to demonstrate strong leadership and clear responsibilities and reporting lines.

2.11.2 Compliance officer for legal practice

It is a condition of authorisation that every law firm which is authorised and regulated by the SRA must have a compliance officer for legal practice (COLP).

The COLP must be a lawyer and a manager or employee in the law firm. In SRA terms, a lawyer means a member of one of the following professions, entitled to practise as such:

- the profession of solicitor, barrister or advocate of the UK;
- a profession whose members are authorised to carry on legal activities by an approved regulator other than the SRA (for example, a Chartered Legal Executive);
- an Establishment Directive profession other than a UK profession;
- a legal profession which has been approved by the SRA for the purpose of recognised bodies in England and Wales; and
- any other regulated legal profession specified by the SRA for the purpose of this definition.

The COLP must volunteer for the role and must be approved by the SRA and will have needed to satisfy the regulator through a complicated application process that they are a suitable person to undertake the job in hand. This is because they have personal obligations to ensure that certain things happen in the firm. They are required to take all reasonable steps to:

- ensure the authorised body, its managers and employees comply with all terms and conditions of its authorisation (except any obligations imposed under the SRA Accounts Rules 2011);
- ensure the authorised body complies with relevant statutory obligations;
- record any failure to comply with authorisation or statutory obligations and make such records available to the SRA;
- report any material failure (either taken on its own or as part of a pattern of failures) to the SRA as soon as reasonably practical. Licensed bodies (ABS firms) must, in accordance with the Legal Services Act 2007, also report non-material breaches.

In practice, the effect of this is that there will be systems and processes in the firm designed to support compliance with the terms of authorisation and demonstrate that the Handbook requirements are being met. Where this does not happen, the COLP will record the breach and decide whether or not this needs to be brought to the attention of the SRA because it is material in nature. Because of this responsibility, and because COLPs could be subject to disciplinary proceedings if they failed in their duties, they must be satisfied that they are told about anything of a breach-like nature and many firms have internal reporting mechanisms which they expect everyone to follow.

The SRA say that the COLP role is essential to the success of outcomes-focused regulation.

2.11.3 Compliance officer for finance and administration

The compliance officer for finance and administration (COFA) is also a required role because it is also a condition of authorisation. Again, this role must be taken by a manager or employee in the firm. However, unlike the COLP position, this role holder does not need to be a lawyer and many COFAs are in fact non-solicitor practice managers or similar. The SRA suggests that COFAs should have sufficient seniority in the business to fulfil their personal obligations which are to take all reasonable steps to:

- ensure that the authorised body, its employees and managers, comply with any obligations imposed under the SRA Accounts Rules 2011;
- keep a record of any failure to comply and make this record available to the SRA;
- report any material failure (either taken on its own or as part of a pattern of failures) to the SRA as soon as reasonably practical. ABS firms must, in accordance with the Legal Services Act 2007, also report non-material breaches.

At first sight, and because the COFA's duties relate to the Accounts Rules, this appears to be of little relevance to many people in the firm. In fact, when the roles went live in January 2013 much of the focus was on the COLP role. However, it would be dangerous to ignore the significance of the COFA role particularly as misuse of money and assets is one of the SRA's current risk priorities and the SRA sees a link between this and non-compliance with the Accounts Rules.

The COFA must make sure that client money is safe and that draws a lot of people working in the law firm to the role holder's attention and not just members of the accounts team or the managers and solicitors. Anyone who handles client money may do something, or not do something, which creates a recordable breach and even possibly the need to report to the SRA.

2.11.4 Money laundering reporting officer

We have already observed that money laundering is a priority risk for the SRA. Criminals like to be able to use law firms to launder their criminal property; we can add respectability to what they are doing, we disguise the fact that money is dirty, and quite frankly we can perform legal activities which they cannot. Individuals and law firms which are targeted by such criminals often find that they commit criminal offences themselves and that they have breached SRA Handbook requirements and are therefore subject to disciplinary action.

It may come as a surprise therefore to know that not every law firm is required to have a money laundering reporting officer (MLRO). This depends on whether the firm must comply with the Money Laundering Regulations 2007 because of the type of work which is performed for clients. Firms which only provide legal advice and litigation services, will writing and criminal work are not obliged to comply with the Regulations and appoint an MLRO. All other firms which can broadly be described as undertaking transactional work for their clients are bound to, and therefore must, appoint an MLRO.

The MLRO's duty is to ensure that knowledge or suspicion of money laundering is disclosed to the law enforcement agencies (currently the National Crime Agency (NCA)) in a timely fashion. This is known as suspicious activity reporting and failure to disclose is a criminal offence. Everyone in the firm has a role to play in ensuring that they remain vigilant for any warning signs that the firm is being used for money laundering purposes and that they report their concerns to the MLRO. It is essential that everyone knows the MLRO's identity and understands how to discuss concerns with that individual.

In firms which do not have an MLRO, it is still necessary to consider the risks attached to breaking laws such as the Proceeds of Crime Act 2002 and the Terrorism Act 2000 (which apply to us all) and the impact that this would have on the individual and the firm in terms of the relationship with the SRA. In such businesses, it is important to understand the person with whom concerns should be shared. There is more information about money laundering in chapter 10 of this book.

CHAPTER 3

The SRA Handbook

3.1 INTRODUCTION

It is because of entity-based regulation that everyone working in an SRA-authorised law firm must have a good knowledge of regulation and what behaviours are expected of them personally. However, it would be risky to leave to individual choice a decision as important as how you should behave while working in a law firm. Instead, the behaviours which we are all expected to demonstrate are decided by the SRA and justified by them on the basis of the regulatory objectives.

These requirements are contained in a set of materials collectively known as the SRA Handbook. We will now look at its content in more detail.

3.2 PURPOSE OF THE SRA HANDBOOK

The SRA Handbook was launched in October 2011 and at the time the SRA said that: 'this will bring together all the SRA's regulatory requirements into a single, coherent structure that underpins the regulation of solicitors, law firms and alternative business structure.' It was the result of a very thorough review of the regulator's rules and regulations which were updated to reflect the requirements of the Legal Services Act 2007 and the modern-style of legal services provision.

It is a web-based resource and can be read on the SRA website, **www.sra.org.uk**. It has been through a number of revisions since its launch, with two or three versions being published each year as a response to changes in law or following SRA policy decisions. The SRA expects law firm managers and employees to use the most up-to-date version and therefore there is a need to refer to the website and to make sure that the firm's policies and processes remain in line with the latest edition of the Handbook.

3.3 STRUCTURE OF THE SRA HANDBOOK

The Handbook is broken down into different sections as shown in **Table 3.1**.

Table 3.1 Structure of the SRA Handbook

Section heading	Contents of section	Objectives
Principles	SRA Principles 2011, the 10 principles of conduct which underpin all aspects of practice	These define the fundamental ethical and professional standards which the SRA expects of all firms and individuals regulated by the SRA
Code of Conduct	SRA Code of Conduct 2011	Contains outcomes relating to professional conduct which when achieved are designed to benefit clients and the public at large
Accounts Rules	SRA Accounts Rules 2011	Set of rules designed to protect client money when it is held by a law firm
Authorisation and Practising Requirements	SRA Practice Framework Rules 2011 SRA Authorisation Rules for Legal Services Bodies and Licensable Bodies 2011 SRA Practising Regulations 2011 Solicitors Keeping of the Roll Regulations 2011 SRA Training Regulations (currently the 2014 Qualification and Provider Regulations and 2011 CPD Regulations) SRA Admission Regulations 2011 SRA Qualified Lawyers Transfer Scheme Regulations 2011 SRA Higher Rights of Audience Regulations 2011 SRA Quality Assurance Scheme for Advocates (Crime) Regulations 2013 SRA Suitability Test 2011	These sets of rules and regulations include key requirements for the training and admission of solicitors and in respect of certain advocacy roles which they may wish to fulfil. These will not be relevant to non-solicitors within the firm. However, the Authorisation Rules will be relevant as they relate to the setting up and continuing authorisation of law firms and set out conditions for some role holders which can include roles held by non-solicitors (for example, as owner/manager of the firm or in a compliance role)

Section heading	Contents of section	Objectives
Client Protection	SRA Indemnity Insurance Rules 2013 SRA Indemnity (Enactment) Rules 2012 and the SRA Indemnity Rules 2012 SRA Compensation Fund Rules 2011 SRA Intervention Powers (Statutory Trust) Rules 2011	This section of the Handbook contains rules designed to ensure financial protection for clients of law firms by making requirements relating to compulsory professional indemnity insurance and for solicitors to make payments to the SRA Compensation Fund
Discipline and Costs Recovery	SRA Disciplinary Procedure Rules 2011 SRA Cost of Investigations Regulations 2011	This section contains regulations, etc. relating to the SRA's disciplinary and costs recovery powers
Overseas Rules	SRA Overseas Rules 2013	These rules are the Handbook requirements and behaviours which must be met when solicitors are working overseas on a permanent basis (e.g. practising outside of England and Wales)
Specialist Services	SRA Property Selling Rules 2011 SRA Financial Services (Scope) Rules 2001 SRA Financial Services (Conduct of Business) Rules 2001 SRA European Cross-border Practice Rules 2011 SRA Insolvency Practice Rules 2012	These behaviours must be demonstrated only when certain services, such as property selling/estate agency services, are being provided through the authorised law firm
Glossary	SRA Handbook Glossary 2012	All the italicised words and phrases in the rest of the Handbook have specific meanings which are listed in this section

3.4 AN OVERVIEW OF THE SRA HANDBOOK

Some parts of the SRA Handbook simply cannot be ignored as they describe the basic standards of behaviour which the SRA expects everyone in the law firm to know and to follow. These are found in the SRA Authorisation Rules for Legal

Services Bodies and Licensable Bodies 2011 (the Authorisation Rules), the SRA Principles 2011 (the Principles), the SRA Code of Conduct 2011 (the Code) and the SRA Accounts Rules 2011 (the Accounts Rules). They are all essential reading.

The Authorisation Rules have already been mentioned in passing. Authorisation is one of the SRA's strongest methods of making sure that it regulates in the public interest and that only safe legal services providers can offer legal advice and assistance to the public using the SRA badge. For this reason, the Authorisation Rules contain very complex requirements which must be satisfied by anyone wishing to set up a new firm and impose very strict conditions which must be met by existing firms which wish to remain authorised. This includes the need to comply with the SRA Handbook. An important message for everyone to understand is that the authorised firm is only as safe as its weakest link and that could be anyone in any role in circumstances where they do anything in breach of Handbook requirements.

The Principles and Code describe professional conduct – or ethical behaviours – which must be achieved by everyone in the law firm. These are essential knowledge because they are the starting point for having a good relationship with the regulator and clients and, indeed, anyone else with whom we have dealings. The Accounts Rules are designed to ensure that when client money is held by the law firm, the SRA and the public have confidence that it is held safely.

These sets of rules are described in greater detail elsewhere in this book.

Everything else in the Handbook cannot be ignored but needs to be considered in the context of what the firm does, the services it provides, or the situation in which individuals find themselves. Many firms have made arrangements, at manager and compliance officer level, to review the Handbook contents to ensure that where necessary there are appropriate systems and procedures in place to support compliance. This is likely to be covered in various policies in the firm's office manual. If in any doubt as to how to behave, then advice should be sought from the compliance officers and senior colleagues.

3.5 COMPLIANCE WITH THE SRA HANDBOOK

Compliance with the SRA Handbook is therefore a condition of authorisation as is the recording and reporting of breaches by the COLP and COFA. Here, there is a distinction made between non-material and material breaches. All breaches must be recorded, but in the case of non-ABS firms these records do not need to be submitted to the SRA as a routine event. However, all material breaches must be reported to the SRA in a timely manner. The SRA has reflected on what they mean by 'timely' and suggest that it means straight away and it is not the case that a report can be delayed until after a solution has been found to deal with whatever has happened.

There are two obstacles to complying with this requirement: first, there is not a Handbook definition of the phrase 'material breach' and, secondly, the ability to fulfil the reporting requirement is dependent on the compliance officers being made aware of such events in their business. Most compliance officers are not telepathic!

Many firms have done a lot of work to develop and support the growth of an internal compliance culture and this has been spurred on by the need for such recording and reporting to happen.

The closest the SRA comes to explaining what is meant by material breaches is in the form of guidance notes to the Authorisation Rules. In these notes, which are not mandatory, the SRA suggests that compliance officers should consider the following features of a breach occurrence:

- the detriment, or risk of detriment, to clients;
- the extent of any risk of loss of confidence in the firm or in the provision of legal services;
- the scale of the issue;
- the overall impact on the firm, its clients and third parties.

Since the publication of the SRA Handbook in 2011, we have had further indicators from the regulator in the form of advice given at conferences and in speeches. For example, the SRA has asked compliance officers to consider the following:

- Would you feel you were being transparent with the SRA if you didn't disclose something?
- A good rule of thumb to adopt is that if you are not certain about materiality it is worth letting the SRA know.
- Well-run firms should be able to use their own judgment about what constitutes a breach or a serious risk.
- Bear in mind that if a COLP/COFA is wondering if something is material then it probably is.

The SRA has also started to issue warning notices, case studies and other risk reports which include examples of good and poor practice. In many firms, the compliance officers monitor these sources of help to ensure that they are up to speed with SRA thinking.

However, what we do not have is a ready-made list of material and non-material failures to use as a guide. This means that compliance officers will be making some significant decisions about the need to communicate with the SRA and will need their colleagues to be open and accountable to help them with their judgment calls.

In addition, the COLP and COFA will need to keep appropriate records of failures in compliance to fulfil a number of obligations:

- to monitor overall compliance with obligations;
- to assess the effectiveness of the firm's systems;
- to be able to decide when the need has arisen to report breaches which are material because they form a pattern.

3.6 RECORDING BREACHES

The SRA has not told compliance officers how they should record breaches and many different methods have been developed. Some firms have a formal recording and notification system, some have computerised methods connected to case management systems, while others rely on colleagues to volunteer information on a need-to-know basis. It is important that everyone in the firm knows what is expected of them in this regard and whom they should be talking to if they have any compliance queries or need to record a breach event.

3.7 CONCLUSION

The main message that can be given about this style of regulation is that it includes the need for everyone to understand the importance of accepting that the SRA Handbook is a necessary part of their working lives because they are employed in an SRA-authorised business. The SRA expects law firms to be open and accountable in respect of compliance matters, particularly when something has gone awry and risk management needs to take place. In turn, law firm managers and compliance officers will only be satisfied that this is the case if they have the confidence that everyone in the firm is comfortable with the role they are performing and understand how they are expected to behave.

CHAPTER 4

The SRA Principles 2011

4.1 INTRODUCTION

The SRA Handbook is available on the SRA website, **www.sra.org.uk**. This electronic format means that its size is hard to gauge but the printed edition, available annually from Law Society Publishing, runs to almost 600 pages.

We have seen that not all of these 600 pages of regulatory requirements are needed on a daily basis. However, as mentioned in the previous chapter, some of the content is essential reading and knowledge for everyone in the law firm regardless of the role they play in the business. This is because some parts of the Handbook contain requirements about how to behave, and what must be demonstrated, and getting these requirements wrong can have serious consequences not only for the individuals concerned but also for their colleagues and the business itself.

This essential knowledge includes an understanding of the SRA Principles 2011 (the Principles) which some say is all that is actually needed from the SRA to understand how to behave. This is because, in the SRA's own words:

> The Principles embody the key ethical requirements on firms and individuals who are involved in the provision of legal services. You should always have regard to the Principles and use them as your starting point when faced with an ethical dilemma.

4.2 THE PRINCIPLES

There are 10 principles in the SRA Principles 2011, as follows:

> You must:
>
> 1 uphold the rule of law and the proper administration of justice;
> 2 act with integrity;
> 3 not allow your independence to be compromised;
> 4 act in the best interests of each *client*;
> 5 provide a proper standard of service to your *clients*;
> 6 behave in a way that maintains the trust the public places in you and in the provision of legal services;
> 7 comply with your legal and regulatory obligations and deal with your regulators and ombudsmen in an open, timely and co-operative manner;

8 run your business or carry out your role in the business effectively and in accordance with proper governance and sound financial and risk management principles;
9 run your business or carry out your role in the business in a way that encourages equality of opportunity and respect for diversity; and
10 protect *client* money and *assets*.

An important point to make at the outset is that when words and phrases are printed in italics in the SRA Handbook, they are defined terms which are included in the SRA Handbook Glossary 2012. In the Principles, 'client' and 'assets' are italicised defined terms. The word 'client' means the person for whom you act and, where the context permits, includes prospective and former clients. Obviously this can be an individual or a group of individuals or any type of legal body such as a company, charity or trust or similar. The word 'assets' is defined to include money, documents, wills, deeds, investments and other property.

The Principles apply to 'you' if you are a manager (i.e. a partner in a partnership, a member of a limited liability partnership or a director of a company) or employee in an SRA-authorised law firm. They are compulsory behaviours which must be achieved. This means that they are non-negotiable and not achieving a principle may have disciplinary consequences for the individual concerned. Having said that, not all the Principles will apply in all circumstances and the individual will need to decide which ones are appropriate in any particular scenario. Sometimes when considering the various Principles, it may be apparent that there are conflicts between them and if that is the case the right behaviour to follow is based on a decision about which principle best serves and protects the public interest regulatory objective.

For example, if you were in court and you knew that your client was lying and therefore deceiving or misleading the court, your ethical dilemma would be whether to stand by and allow this to happen. It could even be argued that by doing this you were acting in the best interests of the client and achieving Principle 4. However, by behaving in this way, there would be questions over whether you were acting in a way which was consistent with upholding the rule of law and the proper administration of justice as required by Principle 1. In other words, there is a conflict between two of the Principles and a decision has to be made about which behaviour should be prioritised. Bearing in mind the public interest objectives, it would be necessary to prioritise Principle 1 and take action to ensure that you are not supporting your client's behaviour in court.

In more detail, the following points should be taken into account:

4.2.1 Principle 1 – you must uphold the rule of law and the proper administration of justice

Broadly, the term 'rule of law' describes the legal principle that law should govern a nation as opposed to government taking the form of arbitrary decisions of individuals. Every citizen must be subject to the law of the land.

Bearing in mind that a solicitor's complete title is 'solicitor of the senior courts of England and Wales', and that the regulatory objectives include the requirement to support the constitutional principles of the rule of law, this principle reinforces the position that individuals have obligations to the court and also to third parties with whom they have dealings on behalf of their clients.

4.2.2 Principle 2 – you must act with integrity

The SRA does not define integrity. In the absence of an SRA explanation, it is sensible to rely on the dictionary meaning, which is: 'the quality of being honest and having strong moral principles.'

The narrative to Principle 2 describes the behaviour as personal integrity and that this quality is central to the role of being the client's 'trusted adviser'. An individual to whom the principle applies must also demonstrate personal integrity when dealing with the court, other lawyers and the public.

In practical terms this will mean that, notwithstanding any pressures placed on you by others, whether they are the client or your work colleagues or third parties, you must always act in a way that demonstrates this characteristic and shows that you have personal integrity qualities.

In the office environment this may mean that you would need to challenge inappropriate behaviour. If you were asked to do something which compromised your personal integrity then this would need to be addressed. For example, if a client or another colleague asked you to act as a witness to a document in improper circumstances (such as being asked to provide witness services in the absence of the person whose signature you are supposed to be witnessing) or to back date a legal document or similar, then it would be wrong to follow such instructions as this would call into question your duty of integrity.

4.2.3 Principle 3 – you must not allow your independence to be compromised

Unlike Principle 2, the SRA does explain how it interprets this word by stating: '"Independence" means your own and your firm's independence, and not merely your ability to give independent advice to a client.' In other words, it would be wrong to be in any situation where you were not able to act in an unconstrained way. For example, Principle 3 and your duty of independence would be challenged if you were under pressure from a client or even a third party (perhaps a business which introduced a lot of work to you) to behave in a certain way which you knew was improper.

4.2.4 Principle 4 – you must act in the best interests of each client

This means that you must act in good faith and be able to do your best for your clients. Again, it is useful to consider dictionary definitions of good faith which include: 'the honest intent to act without taking an unfair advantage over another person or to fulfil a promise to act' and 'to act with sincerity and good intent'.

This principle will be particularly relevant when deciding whether it is appropriate to accept instructions and in considering what the client is trusting you to do on his or her behalf. Is there a conflict of interest which prevents you from acting in the client's best interests? Is there any question over whether you have the skills or the time to act in the client's best interest? Will you be breaching confidentiality in anything you do or, alternatively, do you have any difficulties in disclosing material information to a current client?

Consider the position if you were in a support role and providing services to a fee earner in the matrimonial department. The fee earner is acting for a gentleman in a divorce and his wife is your sister. Would you feel confident that you could personally act in your shortly to be ex-brother-in-law's best interests and not disclose any confidential information to your sister? Anything less than the ability to consider the client's best interests regardless of any other peripheral issue means that you may not be able to demonstrate you are achieving Principle 4.

4.2.5 Principle 5 – you must provide a proper standard of service to your clients

Developing the theme of competence, this principle applies specifically to the services you provide to clients and this is directly connected with client care duties. It is designed to ensure that clients receive a consistently safe – or proper – level of service from their legal service provider regardless of who that person may be.

This principle relates to the individual service provider's level of competence or legal skills. It also requires the service provider (i.e. you) to think about individual clients and ensure that services are provided in a way that suits that particular client's circumstances. This means that you would always want to bear in mind whether your client is vulnerable or has some particular needs which must be taken into account.

This also means that you need to consider whether it is appropriate to accept instructions so that in this way Principle 5 is very closely connected with Principle 4 and the duty to act in each client's best interests. For example, if you were a family law specialist and undertook no other type of legal work, but had an approach to accept instructions from a client who wanted to buy a company, it is going to be difficult to show that in these circumstances that you have the competence or skills set to provide a proper standard of service.

For solicitors in the business, this principle is reinforced through the need for them to demonstrate that they are also complying with SRA requirements relating to their continuing competence and a reference document called the Competence Standard. For non-solicitors, the question to be asked is whether you have had sufficient training to undertake your specific role in the business.

What the SRA is not attempting to introduce through this principle is any requirement to be excellent, as strange as that statement may seem; the reference to 'proper' is in many ways a direction about the lowest acceptable level of fitness or aptitude which is acceptable. Excellence is something which firms can strive to achieve once they have achieved a 'proper' standard of service. What you will need to understand is the value-added business or commercial strategies with which your firm wants to top up this principle and be satisfied that you are able to support the business in achieving this extra service element. The SRA would not necessarily be interested in such extras unless they caused ethical dilemmas by misleading publicity or the like.

4.2.6 Principle 6 – you must behave in a way that maintains the trust the public places in you and in the provision of legal services

It has often been said that a client's trust in his or her solicitor is one of the most important and essential features of the relationship and Principle 6 supports this value. The SRA says:

> Members of the public should be able to place their trust in you. Any behaviour either within or outside your professional practice which undermines this trust damages not only you, but also the ability of the legal profession as a whole to serve society.

For solicitors, registered European lawyers (RELs) and registered foreign lawyers (RFLs) and certain other lawyers, Principle 6 is a lifelong obligation and will apply to activities outside of the law firm and not just something which arises solely in respect of the services which they provide in the law firm to their clients.

4.2.7 Principle 7: You must comply with your legal and regulatory obligations and deal with your regulators and ombudsmen in an open, timely and co-operative manner

This principle supports the SRA's style of operation and the current focus of regulation. In effect it requires a partnership between the regulator and solicitors and everyone else to whom the SRA Handbook applies. There is an expectation that there will be timely communication of events, facts and anything else which the regulator needs to know about you, your firm and other regulated people in order to achieve the regulatory objectives:

- Is there anything about you which the regulator needs to know because this has a bearing on your ability to provide services to your clients?
- Have you done something which could be classed as a serious breach or failing in terms of SRA Handbook requirements?
- Have you concerns about anyone else in the firm or in respect of whom you have had dealings on behalf of a client of the firm?
- Is there anything about the firm which you feel that the SRA should be made aware of?

- Is the SRA asking questions of you about yourself or anything to do with the business in which you are employed?

While whistle-blowing of this nature may feel uncomfortable, it is important to understand that this is part of the bigger picture of safe regulation, and regulation which is designed to ensure that the reputation of the profession of which you are a part remains strong.

4.2.8 Principle 8: You must run your business or carry out your role in the business effectively and in accordance with proper governance and sound financial and risk management principles

At first sight this principle may not seem to be relevant to anyone other than the managers of the law firm because of its description of business, governance and risk management. Nothing could be further than the truth. Principle 8 is addressed to all members of the firm, and the phrase 'carry out your role' means that the key to successful application is to understand what part each individual plays in ensuring a collectively proper response.

This is because this principle goes to the heart of risk-based regulation and is applied to the whole entity and addresses the following issues: How safe is the business? How well run is it so that clients' interests are properly served?

Successfully achieving this principle means that the law firm must be well run, with managers ensuring that there is clear and effective governance at senior levels and that every member of the firm understands to whom they should report, whom they supervise and who supervises them, who has specific roles in terms of compliance and other key functions (such as the money laundering reporting officer, the quality representative in firms providing legal aid and legal help with the Specialist Quality Mark accreditation, the person who handles complaints and deals with negligence matters and similar).

Principle 8 also triggers the need for every firm to identify risks in terms of financial matters and also in being able to comply with regulatory and legal obligations. In practice, this means that managers, and senior compliance role holders, ought to assess the risks in the firm, complete risk registers, ensure that there are ways to monitor the risk scores and try to reduce the likelihood of a risk event occurring. While the initiative will start at this level, it needs to be communicated to everyone in the business with information about the part which individuals are expected to play in keeping the firm safe. To take one example, anyone who has responsibilities in terms of supervising others (whether this is in respect of a fee-earning or other role) needs to understand what they should be monitoring and what concerns should be discussed with others in the firm.

4.2.9 Principle 9: You must run your business or carry out your role in the business in a way that encourages equality of opportunity and respect for diversity

The phrasing of this principle is very similar to Principle 8, so that everyone is required to consider their role in the business and ensure that they apply an appropriate and proportionate role in encouraging equality and diversity.

This principle directly links to the regulatory objectives designed to ensure that there is an improvement in access to justice and encouragement of an independent, strong, diverse and effective legal profession. Indirectly, this principle supports compliance with equality legislation such as the Equality Act 2010.

Most law firms have documented statements and procedures about how equality and diversity will be demonstrated in action. These are usually prepared by the managers and senior compliance colleagues. Often, in larger firms, human resources departments have a role to play too. However, this principle, and those internal documents, must be used by everyone in the business in terms of their role in recruitment and interview processes, internal progression, internal working relationships, and in respect of dealings with and on behalf of clients.

Applying this principle in practice means that it may be necessary to challenge inappropriate behaviour or instructions. For example, doing nothing in circumstances where you are part of an interview panel with a colleague who refuses to shortlist a certain type of candidate on the basis of a gender or race decision is not acceptable. Similarly, neither is it acceptable to act on a client's instructions which are discriminatory for whatever reason.

4.2.10 Principle 10: You must protect client money and assets

The significance of law firms being able to hold client money should not be underestimated. This is not possible in some other legal professions in the world and the fact that we can do so is not without critics.

Being able to ask clients for money on account of costs and similar, and receiving money on behalf of clients, is a huge responsibility and doing this in a risk-free way goes to the heart of the confidence which clients and others have in the solicitor's profession in England and Wales. When this duty goes wrong, there are a number of significant repercussions in terms of the detriment to the client, the disciplinary consequences for wrongdoers and their firms, and for the reputation of the SRA and the profession.

Principle 10 is designed to deliver a strong message to solicitors, to everyone working in a law firm, to clients and to the public at large that holding client money safely is a key concern. The SRA says in its guidance to this principle:

> This Principle goes to the heart of the duty to act in the best interests of your clients. You should play your part in e.g. protecting money, documents or other property belonging to your clients which has been entrusted to you or your firm.

To continue the theme that the Principles apply to everyone, the duty to ensure compliance with Principle 10 does not rest only with the managers, the COFA, or the accounts team. With reference to the specific duty to 'protect client money', it is essential that anyone who has any role in handling and holding client money knows what is required of them to keep themselves and the firm safe. This means that someone working in reception must understand the firm's requirements in terms of the receipt of monies from clients over the counter and anyone with responsibilities in terms of mail delivered to the firm must understand the need to deal with client cheques safely.

In terms of assets, we have already explained that this is a defined SRA Handbook term and means not only client money but also documents, wills, deeds, investments and other property which belong to a client but which have been entrusted to the firm. In this way, anyone receiving such property, or perhaps dealing with a client's matter, must ensure that they play their role in keeping original documents safe and secure. Losing such property will amount to a breach of this principle and in addition may create adverse publicity for the firm and give rise to a negligence claim or a complaint which the firm will be required to address.

4.3 CONCLUSION

The SRA will consider whether there has been a breach of the Principles when investigating the behaviour of a solicitor or anyone else working within the law firm. The disciplinary response will be proportionate and designed to ensure an appropriate response to the risks posed by an event.

There have been a number of examples of solicitors and non-solicitors being investigated by the SRA and being unable to practise, or work in a law firm, as a consequence of a breach of one or more of the Principles.

Complying with the Principles is a fundamental requirement and the behaviours which are described are non-negotiable because they sum up the essence of what it means to be a solicitor, or part of an authorised firm, providing legal services to the public and providing such services in a way which supports the trust and confidence which clients and the public at large should be able to expect from us. That this is not just empty words or meaningless statements is demonstrated by reported disciplinary findings against both solicitors and non-solicitors.

CHAPTER 5

Understanding outcomes-focused regulation

5.1 INTRODUCTION

One of the most radical changes that solicitors have had to grapple with in recent times relates to alterations in the way professional conduct obligations are expressed. Previously professional conduct behaviour was explained in terms of rules and guidance and was very detailed and prescriptive in nature. However, with the introduction of the SRA Handbook in 2011, a new version of the Code of Conduct was issued which was based on outcomes rather than rules. This change in language set the scene for the changes brought about by outcomes-focused regulation.

5.2 PRINCIPLES

Although the Principles are described as the guiding lights of ethical behaviour, they are very high level and broad in content. The SRA Code of Conduct 2011 adds some flesh to the bones of these high-level principles by explaining the professional conduct behaviours which must be displayed in a variety of scenarios which are commonplace and familiar in law firms. Complying with the behavioural requirements in the Code is likely to assist with a demonstration that the relevant Principles have been achieved.

As a starting point, we need to understand the language of the Code if we are to apply the conduct requirements successfully to what we do in the law firm. The most important point to note is that rules of conduct were replaced in 2011 with outcomes in order to support and reinforce outcomes-focused regulation. The overview to the Code says:

> Outcomes-focused regulation concentrates on providing positive outcomes which when achieved will benefit and protect *clients* and the public. The SRA Code of Conduct (the Code) sets out our outcomes-focused conduct requirements so that you can consider how best to achieve the right outcomes for your *clients* taking into account the way that your

firm works and its *client* base. The Code is underpinned by effective, risk-based supervision and enforcement.

5.3 OUTCOMES

The outcomes are mandatory, by which we mean that they are compulsory and must be achieved. Breaching, or not achieving, an outcome will be a disciplinary issue. Like the Principles, and most of the rest of the SRA Handbook, the outcomes apply to solicitors plus all other employees within SRA-authorised and regulated law firms.

Whereas rules of conduct in a bygone age were drafted to be very detailed and precise, outcomes are more high level and broadly drafted. Because of this style it can sometimes be difficult to work out what needs to be done to prove that an outcome has been achieved. The nature of outcomes is such that there are gaps which must be filled by the person or the firm with a consideration about how they will demonstrate that they are doing the right thing.

This is in contrast with the rules which the outcomes replaced, which explained exactly how the individual and firm had to demonstrate that the obligations had been fulfilled. Whereas, an old-style rule would include the method for compliance (for example, by requiring solicitors to send a letter to their clients in order to demonstrate conduct obligations in respect of client care had been satisfied), outcomes are drafted so that the person or the firm needing to demonstrate compliance must assess for themselves how this will be achieved. This goes to the heart of outcomes-focused regulation: when working out a method of compliance, the individual must consider the needs of different clients (so that for client care, an individual client's needs and circumstances must be taken into account when deciding upon the best method of communication of important information relating to the instructions and the services provided and this is not always going to be through a detailed letter).

5.4 INDICATIVE BEHAVIOURS

This means that there is very little guidance in the Code which again is in contrast to previous styles of regulation where the detailed rules of conduct were usually accompanied by copious amounts of guidance. Instead of detailed guidance, the outcomes (O) in the Code are accompanied by a series of statements which are called indicative behaviours (IBs) which are examples of behaviour likely to demonstrate that an outcome either has been achieved or has not been achieved.

It is not compulsory to comply with an indicative behaviour and the SRA states that the examples of behaviour which have been included in the Code are not mandatory. In fact, the SRA says that they do not represent a complete list of behaviours and that there may be other ways of demonstrating that an outcome has been achieved, so that simply adopting an indicative behaviour may not always be appropriate. The SRA says:

> We encourage *firms* to consider how they can best achieve the outcomes, taking into account the nature of the *firm*, the particular circumstances of the matter and, crucially, the needs of their particular *clients*.

In practice this has meant that since 2011 many firms have taken the time to reflect on their fundamental and distinctive characteristics and qualities and developed internal systems and processes designed to ensure that the outcomes can be achieved in a consistent and safe fashion. This piece of work is largely going to be the responsibility of the managers and compliance officers. However, it would not be wise to assume that this means that what the managers are doing is not relevant to other members of the firm. Everyone else in the firm must ensure that they understand what outcomes are relevant to them, because of the role they play and because of the firm's and clients' characteristics, and what systems and procedures they must follow. In some firms, not following an internal system is a disciplinary matter in that it is a condition of employment to comply.

5.5 STRUCTURE OF THE SRA CODE OF CONDUCT 2011

Being familiar with the structure of the Code will also support compliance. It is a fairly brief document, divided into five sections. The sections contain chapters of broadly grouped, similar conduct requirements. **Table 5.1** illustrates this point.

5.6 RELEVANCE OF OUTCOMES

It is not the case that all outcomes will be relevant simply because an individual is employed in a law firm and another exercise which needs to be undertaken is to decide which outcomes apply to which people or roles within the firm. For example, the outcomes in chapter 5 (Your client and the court) do not need to be considered by individuals who do not undertake court-related litigation or advocacy work or support the fee earners doing such work. However, outcomes in other chapters will be relevant to everyone simply because of the fact that we are employed within an SRA-authorised firm. For example, the chapters which include outcomes relating to client care, conflicts of interest and confidentiality and disclosure duties cannot be ignored as it is essential to achieve such outcomes in respect of all clients irrespective of the type of services delivered or role performed.

These chapters and conduct outcomes are explained in detail in the following sections of this book.

Table 5.1 Structure of the Code

Section heading	**Contents of section**	**Brief explanation**
Section 1 – You and your client	Chapter 1 – Client care Chapter 2 – Equality and diversity Chapter 3 – Conflicts of interests Chapter 4 – Confidentiality and disclosure Chapter 5 – Your client and the court Chapter 6 – Your client and introductions to third parties	Professional conduct behaviours with a connection to the relationship between you, the firm and the client are grouped together in this section of the SRA Handbook. It is here that the answers to some essential questions about the relationship are provided, such as: What do I need to tell the client about my services? Can I accept instructions to act for a client? What duties do I owe current and former clients? What duties do I owe the court? What do I need to consider before I recommend my client uses a third party service-provider?
Section 2 – You and your business	Chapter 7 – Management of your business Chapter 8 – Publicity Chapter 9 – Fee sharing and referrals	The conduct behaviours in this section relate to how the business is run and publicised, and how work can be generated in an ethical way. Here you find the correct conduct response to such questions as: What are the risks which supervision processes should address? Can I cold-call prospective new clients? Can I pay someone to introduce a new client to me?
Section 3 – You and your regulator	Chapter 10 – You and your regulator	This section and chapter reinforces and supports the SRA's style of risk-based regulation with notification and reporting outcomes and the outcome to be co-operative.

Section heading	Contents of section	Brief explanation
Section 4 – You and others	Chapter 11 – Relations with third parties Chapter 12 – Separate businesses	This section groups together outcomes which relate to how we deal with third parties and also what we can do as spare-time, non-SRA authorised activities. The outcomes deal with such ethical topics as the giving of undertakings and dealing with unrepresented third parties.
Section 5 – Application, waivers and interpretation	Chapter 13 – Application and waivers provisions Chapter 13A – Practice overseas Chapter 14 – Interpretation Chapter 15 – Transitional provisions	This is largely the 'housekeeping' section of the Code. This includes a section to describe when and to whom the Code is applied and includes a later addition to the Code in terms of application provisions arising when an individual is temporarily overseas, such as when they may visit a client overseas (which in this context means anywhere in the world except England and Wales).

CHAPTER 6

The SRA Code of Conduct 2011 – essentials for all staff

6.1 CLIENT CARE

With an understanding of the regulatory objectives of the Legal Services Act 2007, and knowing the importance of making the client/consumer the focus of everything we do, it is perhaps not surprising that the first and biggest chapter in the Code describes client care outcomes which must be achieved.

The staring point in knowing how to behave is identifying your client correctly, which is sometimes easier said than done. The client will be the person or the legal entity (a trust, company or similar) whose position is altered by the services you provide. This is clear enough when an individual client instructs the firm to act on his or her behalf, as would be the case where clients instruct the matrimonial department in respect of divorce proceedings. The individual instructing the firm will obtain a divorce with the law firm's assistance and is obviously the client to whom client care behaviours must be displayed. Life becomes more complicated by the addition of a paying party (i.e. someone other than the client paying your legal fees) who must not assume that this gives him or her any entitlement to be considered the client, or where instructions are received from joint clients (with the need to consider all clients when acting on instructions and giving legal advice) and where the client is not a human being but a legal entity such as a trust and a voice is needed to give instructions in respect of the entity (such as directors of a company giving instructions on behalf of the company which is the client in these circumstances).

Professional conduct outcomes in the SRA Code of Conduct 2011 chapter are directed to the correctly identified client and they are designed to ensure that the relevant SRA Principles are achieved. The following are particularly relevant in this context:

- Principle 2 – 'you must act with integrity'.
- Principle 3 – 'you must not allow your independence to be compromised'.
- Principle 4 – 'you must act in the best interests of each client'.
- Principle 5 – 'you must provide a proper standard of service to your clients'.

- Principle 6 – 'you must behave in a way that maintains the trust the public places in you and in the provision of legal services'.

The conduct outcomes which follow are broadly divided into four subject areas: providing clients with information about the service which they will receive and considering proper service standards, costs issues; complaints handling, and behaviours which must be displayed when deciding whether to act, refuse to act or end the relationship with the client.

In more detail, the following points should be noted:

6.1.1 Service standards

The first outcome in the Code is outcome 1.1 and the requirement that 'you treat your clients fairly'.

What this actually means is not defined, but the clues from other outcomes in the Code and the indicative behaviours all provide a guide that we should be thinking about the services we can provide to the client and how these will be delivered. There are certain questions which fee earners and support staff should ask themselves when thinking about service standards. Very importantly, it is necessary to be confident that you are in a position to provide a proper standard of service both because you have the time and resources to do so and also because you have the knowledge and competence to carry out the client's instructions. It would be improper to accept instructions if you did not feel that this was the case.

Other outcomes coming under this service standard heading and which must be achieved include the following:

O(1.2) you provide services to your *clients* in a manner which protects their interests in their matter, subject to the proper administration of justice;

...

O(1.4) you have the resources, skills and procedures to carry out your *clients'* instructions;

...

O(1.5) the service you provide to *clients* is competent, delivered in a timely manner and takes account of your *clients'* needs and circumstances;

In other words, the key concerns are whether you are able to act in the client's best interests and deliver a proper standard of service. The indicative behaviours which the SRA uses to show how these requirements may be achieved (or not achieved, as the case may be) include the following:

IB(1.1) agreeing an appropriate level of service with your *client*, for example the type and frequency of communications;

IB(1.2) explaining your responsibilities and those of the *client*;

IB(1.3) ensuring that the *client* is told, in writing, the name and status of the person(s) dealing with the matter and the name and status of the person responsible for its overall supervision;

IB(1.4) explaining any arrangements, such as fee sharing or *referral arrangements*, which are relevant to the *client's* instructions;

IB(1.5) explaining any limitations or conditions on what you can do for the *client*, for example, because of the way the *client's* matter is funded;

IB(1.6) in taking instructions and during the course of the retainer, having proper regard to your *client's* mental capacity or other vulnerability, such as incapacity or duress;

leading to the following outcome:

O(1.12) *clients* are in a position to make informed decisions about the services they need, how their matter will be handled and the options available to them;

Most firms continue to issue client care letters and terms of business or letters of engagement to clients. Strictly speaking this is not necessary; written client care documentation did not survive the cull of rules in 2011. However, in many ways it makes sense to continue having this evidence of the terms agreed with the client. Anyone in a fee-earning or support role with responsibilities for file opening procedures will want to ensure that they understand what they are expected to discuss with the client and the information which must be delivered to the client. The importance of carefully drawn up attendance notes to record discussions about service standards or misunderstandings or conversations about managing client expectation about what can be done for them are valuable records in the event that there is some subsequent dispute about what you agreed to do.

Because of the need to consider delivering outcomes in a way which takes into account the needs of individual clients, there is now an extra dimension to client care conduct duties. It is not sufficient simply to comply with a client care tick list of information to hand over to the client, although it may be sensible to have such a list as an internal aide memoire to ensure that you have discussed everything which is necessary. Instead, the individual with these responsibilities must reflect on whether the client understands the type of service which they will receive and if they do not, then this fact must be incorporated into the service delivery methods.

These behavioural expectations must be understood by anyone with a client-facing role in the firm, whether this is as a fee earner or a member of support staff or in a 'front of house' position in reception.

In many ways these professional conduct requirements are the starting position for law firms. They are the building blocks upon which the firm can then add extra requirements in terms of the type of service which the firm would like to deliver to its clients to attract business to the firm.

6.1.2 Costs issues

It is probably not going to be a surprise to anyone to know that costs issues, particularly in terms of getting costs conversations with the client wrong, can result in a number of conduct and service provision repercussions. At the end of the day, clients who are shocked by the amount that they are being asked to pay – in terms of their own legal costs, in disbursements and expenses, and sometimes in respect of the other party's costs – have the potential to trigger a great deal of resource-intensive activity in the law firm. This may be in the form of the time and money spent in investigating complaints, having to consider the amount of a bill and possibly needing to negotiate a reduced fee, and sometimes needing to defend a costs position in the courts or with the Legal Ombudsman.

The intention of the costs outcomes in the SRA Code of Conduct 2011 is to ensure that clients are not taken by surprise by the costs element of their relationship with a law firm. This is a good thing to achieve both from the client's and the law firm's point of view.

The outcomes which must be achieved are:

O(1.13) *clients* receive the best possible information, both at the time of engagement and when appropriate as their matter progresses, about the likely overall cost of their matter;

O(1.14) *clients* are informed of their right to challenge or complain about your bill and the circumstances in which they may be liable to pay interest on an unpaid bill;

O(1.15) you properly account to *clients* for any *financial benefit* you receive as a result of your instructions;

Costs issues have often been the subject of court action against law firms and it is perhaps not too wide of the mark to say that, broadly, in such circumstances the courts are likely to treat clients with some sympathy where fees have not been explained adequately. The SRA's indicative behaviours give some pointers about what is likely to amount to acceptable behaviour, so it is useful to bear in mind the following recommendations:

IB(1.13) discussing whether the potential outcomes of the *client's* matter are likely to justify the expense or risk involved, including any risk of having to pay someone else's legal fees;

IB(1.14) clearly explaining your fees and if and when they are likely to change;

IB(1.15) warning about any other payments for which the *client* may be responsible;

IB(1.16) discussing how the *client* will pay, including whether public funding may be available, whether the *client* has insurance that might cover the fees, and whether the fees may be paid by someone else such as a trade union;

IB(1.17) where you are acting for a *client* under a fee arrangement governed by statute, such as a conditional fee agreement, giving the *client* all relevant information relating to that arrangement;

IB(1.18) where you are acting for a publicly funded *client*, explaining how their publicly funded status affects the costs;

IB(1.19) providing the information in a clear and accessible form which is appropriate to the needs and circumstances of the *client*;

IB(1.20) where you receive a *financial benefit* as a result of acting for a *client*, either:

- (a) paying it to the *client*;
- (b) offsetting it against your fees; or
- (c) keeping it only where you can justify keeping it, you have told the *client* the amount of the benefit (or an approximation if you do not know the exact amount) and the *client* has agreed that you can keep it;

IB(1.21) ensuring that *disbursements* included in your bill reflect the actual amount spent or to be spent on behalf of the *client*;

Again, nothing in the Code makes it necessary to provide costs information in writing but on a practical level it would be very unwise not to document the costs discussions with the clients and to record whether extra or different explanation was needed in order to demonstrate that the outcomes had been achieved.

This responsibility for explanation will usually fall to a fee earner but anyone in a support role, or even in a receptionist role, needs to be alert to the possibility that the client has misunderstood the position. This may be apparent through telephone calls or other communication with the client and, where this is believed to be the case, the member of the firm must raise this with the fee earner in order that any confusion can be dealt with at the appropriate time.

6.1.3 Complaints handling

The outcomes in the SRA Code of Conduct 2011 support the role of the Legal Ombudsman as the body which deals with service complaints where these cannot be resolved at firm level (the so-called first tier of complaints handling). Unlike service standards and costs information, where we are not told the form which the communication must take, in this instance we are told that complaints information must be given in writing.

The outcomes which must be achieved are:

O(1.9) *clients* are informed in writing at the outset of their matter of their right to complain and how *complaints* can be made

O(1.10) *clients* are informed in writing, both at the time of engagement and at the conclusion of your *complaints* procedure, of their right to complain to the *Legal Ombudsman*, the time frame for doing so and full details of how to contact the *Legal Ombudsman*

O(1.11) *clients' complaints* are dealt with promptly, fairly, openly and effectively;

You will note that 'complaints' is italicised and is therefore a defined term. It is included in the SRA Handbook Glossary 2012 and means:

> an oral or written expression of dissatisfaction which alleges that the complainant has suffered (or may suffer) financial loss, distress, inconvenience or other detriment.

In other words, a complaint does not just take the form of a stern letter written to a senior member of the firm at the end of the matter or relationship. An 'expression of dissatisfaction' can arise at any point in the matter and may be communicated to a number of people including reception and support staff as well as the fee earner with conduct of the client's matter. Those individuals must be prepared to raise the client's concern with the right person (usually the fee earner themselves or, if necessary, someone more senior) in a prompt way so that the grievance can be dealt with at the appropriate time.

The outcomes do not include the requirement for a complaints procedure or person within the firm with responsibility for investigating complaints, although this is what happens in most businesses. It is important that everyone in the firm understands what they should do, including the systems they must follow and who they should speak to, in the event that they are the manager or employee who receives the complaint information from the client.

The SRA's indicative behaviours give the following suggestions about the type of behaviours which would tend to show that the outcomes had been achieved:

IB(1.22) having a written *complaints* procedure which:

- (a) is brought to *clients'* attention at the outset of the matter;
- (b) is easy for *clients* to use and understand, allowing for *complaints* to be made by any reasonable means;
- (c) is responsive to the needs of individual *clients*, especially those who are vulnerable;
- (d) enables *complaints* to be dealt with promptly and fairly, with decisions based on a sufficient investigation of the circumstances;
- (e) provides for appropriate remedies; and
- (f) does not involve any charges to *clients* for handling their *complaints*;

IB(1.23) provide the *client* with a copy of the *firm's complaints* procedure on request;

IB(1.24) in the event that a *client* makes a *complaint*, providing them with all necessary information concerning the handling of the *complaint*.

6.1.4 Accepting and refusing instructions

There are a number of conduct considerations when deciding whether to act or to refuse to act for a client. We have already mentioned the outcome which relates to having the time and competence to act in the client's best interests. In other words, if as a fee earner you simply do not have any spare capacity because of your current workload, it would be wrong to accept instructions in a new matter.

A further outcome in the Code states: 'when deciding whether to act, or terminate your instructions, you comply with the law and the Code.' In other words, when individuals within the firm decide to accept instructions on behalf of the firm and to represent a particular client they must make the judgment that they are not compromising their ethical position. They must be satisfied that they can comply with the SRA Principles 2011, in particular the duty to uphold the rule of law and the proper administration of justice (Principle 1), act in the best interests of the client (Principle 4) and provide a proper standard of service (Principle 5).

There is no obligation to accept all instructions, or in other words, no 'cab-rank rule' and instructions can be refused simply on the basis that you are not willing to act for a particular client at that point in time. However, it is important to bear in mind that decisions not to act which are based on grounds of discrimination are unlawful and would not be tolerated by the courts or the SRA, and also that the Legal Ombudsman can now investigate complaints from prospective clients. It is sensible to document decisions of this nature where you believe that there is a possibility that you may be asked at some later point to justify the decision not to act.

The decision to act is an important one and ought not be made until all the client inception/file opening checks have been made. This is because ending a relationship before the end of the legal matter in hand is not something which can be done lightly or without a great deal of thought. Simply not getting along with a client is not a sufficiently strong reason to terminate the relationship. This would only be justifiable if there was an overriding conduct justification; such as a breakdown in confidence between the client and the fee earner, or a conflict of interest arising or lack of instructions from the client.

The indicative behaviours again give some help with SRA thinking. In the negative, the following indicative behaviours are in the Code as examples of behaviour which tends to show the outcomes have not been achieved:

IB(1.25) acting for a *client* when instructions are given by someone else, or by only one *client* when you act jointly for others only where you are satisfied that the *person* providing the instructions has the authority to do so on behalf of all of the *clients*;
IB(1.26) ceasing to act for a *client* without good reason and without providing reasonable notice;
IB(1.27) entering into unlawful fee arrangements such as an unlawful contingency fee;
IB(1.28) acting for a *client* when there are reasonable grounds for believing that the instructions are affected by duress or undue influence without satisfying yourself that they represent the *client's* wishes.

6.2 EQUALITY AND DIVERSITY OUTCOMES

There are five outcomes in the SRA Code of Conduct 2011 which describes the professional conduct and ethical behaviours required of everyone working in a SRA-authorised law firm in terms of equality and diversity. These are designed to support Principle 9 and the overarching regulatory objectives in the Legal Services Act 2007.

It is crucial that everyone understands both their employer's and regulator's expectations in this regard. Equality and diversity values must be demonstrated in all our dealings with each other, with clients and the public at large, with managers and employees in other law firms, and all other people and parties with whom we come into contact. The values must be demonstrated not only by fee earners and support staff but also by others with roles as varied as human resources and marketing functions where making an incorrect decision may create a breach of these requirements.

The outcomes are:

O(2.1) you do not discriminate unlawfully, or victimise or harass anyone, in the course of your professional dealings;
O(2.2) you provide services to *clients* in a way that respects diversity;
O(2.3) you make reasonable adjustments to ensure that disabled *clients*, *employees* or *managers* are not placed at a substantial disadvantage compared to those who are not disabled, and you do not pass on the costs of these adjustments to these disabled *clients*, *employees* or *managers*;

O(2.4) your approach to recruitment and employment encourages equality of opportunity and respect for diversity;

O(2.5) *complaints* of discrimination are dealt with promptly, fairly, openly, and effectively.

As with client care outcomes, the requirement to have policies and procedures (and what these will look like) is a decision left for the firm to make. Most firms have a written equality and diversity policy which deals with both internal considerations and dealings with clients and on their behalf with third parties.

The indicative behaviours do include a suggestion that having such a policy will help to demonstrate that the outcomes are being achieved but only in circumstances where the content is appropriate to the size and nature of the firm. It is also suggested that such a policy includes the following:

- a commitment to the principles of equality and diversity and legislative requirements;
- a requirement that all employees and managers comply with the outcomes;
- provisions to encompass your recruitment and interview processes;
- details of how the firm will implement, monitor, evaluate and update the policy;
- details of how the firm will ensure equality in relation to the treatment of employees, managers, clients and third parties instructed in connection with client matters;
- details of how complaints and disciplinary issues are to be dealt with;
- details of the firm's arrangements for workforce diversity monitoring; and
- details of how the firm will communicate the policy to employees, managers and clients.

In the negative, the indicative behaviours suggest that being subject to any court or tribunal decision that you have committed an unlawful act of discrimination or being found to have discriminated unlawfully when accepting or refusing instructions to act for a client, would tend to show that the outcomes have not been achieved.

The reference to unlawful acts is a reference to the Equality Act 2010. It is an offence to discriminate, directly or indirectly, to victimise or harass anyone on the grounds of nine protected characteristics. These are:

- age;
- disability;
- gender reassignment;
- marriage and civil partnership;
- pregnancy and maternity;
- race;
- religion or belief;
- sex; and
- sexual orientation.

Getting equality and diversity wrong has a number of consequences for the legal profession, and not only in respect of the relationship of an individual or a firm with the regulator. Recent examples of cases which have attracted negative publicity for law firms are include in chapter 10 of this book, which describes the legislation in more detail.

6.3 CONFLICTS OF INTEREST

There are many misunderstandings about the extent of the professional conduct behaviours imposed on individuals working in law firms by the SRA in respect of conflicts of interest. Some of these misunderstandings come about because of confusion about what is, in fact, a commercial decision about whether to act in particular circumstances and others arise because of client expectations. In fact, in SRA terms, the position and the extent of the duty is relatively straightforward.

Many readers will be familiar with the process of doing a conflicts check when opening a file for a new client. Sometimes, however, the reason for this is not made clear and it becomes a formulaic exercise where opposing parties' names are checked against a database to see if there is a connection with the matter in hand. In some firms this is considered to be a support or administrative task, in others it becomes the responsibility of the fee earner, and in some firms it is a process in which support and fee-earning capabilities merge. A conflicts search should provide information to help the individual fee earner, and the firm, decide whether it is appropriate to accept instructions to act for a particular client and, if it is decided that this is possible, thereafter it becomes a process of regular monitoring to see whether any problems develop which mean that this original decision needs to change. Whoever undertakes the conflicts search process, the reason for doing it must be clear and there must be adequate knowledge of the decision-making process.

This is because the SRA requires individuals working in law firms to consider whether they have a conflict of interest which prevents them from acting in the best interest of a current client of the firm, i.e. someone who is currently instructing the firm to provide legal services. This definition will include a client with an open file or a client where there is a general file or a long-term retainer, as is sometimes the case with company clients and in respect of matters related to employment law. This understanding that the behaviour applies to all current clients means that it is sensible to close files promptly at the end of a matter and to make it clear to the client that the latest relationship is at an end (or, to express this in a different way, that they are to be regarded as a former client). Some fee earners do not like to make this fact clear to the person that they have been helping but confusion creates unnecessary conduct conundrums.

In terms of conflict of interests, the SRA expects us to consider two issues in respect of current clients. First, whether there is an own interest conflict which would prevent you from acting for them and, secondly, whether there is a situation where the firm is acting for two or more clients and a conflict of interests exists between them. Luckily, we have been provided with SRA Handbook definitions with which to assess each of these conduct dilemmas.

6.3.1 Own interest conflicts

An own interest conflict is defined in the SRA Glossary 2012 (and in the 2007 Code as rule 3.01(2)(b)) as any situation where 'your duty to act in the best interests of any client in relation to a matter conflicts, or there is a significant risk that it may conflict, with your own interests in relation to that or a related matter'. In other words, the question to ask yourself is whether there is anything about you which creates an obstacle to your ability to be able to act in a particular client's best interests. This will be a judgment call. If you decide that this situation exists then you must not act for the client concerned.

The SRA expects firms to have systems in operation to identify own interest conflicts. No clues are given as to what the systems should look like, as this would not be consistent with outcomes-focused regulation and the expectation is that the firm should work this out on the basis of its own characteristics and its client base. However, there is a steer as to what type of circumstances could create an own interest conflict, as outcome 3.2 describes the ability to act in the client's best interest being made more difficult by financial interests in the client's matter, by personal relationships creating difficulties, through your appointment, or a family member's or a colleague's appointment to a public office, commercial relationships and anything about your employment in the firm.

The indicative behaviours provide three examples of situations where it may be difficult to show that you can act in the best interests of a client:

- where you are selling or buying a property, 'lending to or borrowing from a client, unless the client has obtained independent legal advice' (indicative behaviour 3.8);
- 'advising a client to invest in a business in which you have an interest which affects your ability to provide impartial advice' (indicative behaviour 3.9);
- using a power of attorney appointment for personal gain (indicative behaviour 3.10).

Table 6.1 provides examples of the types of own interest scenarios which could develop in different departments of the firm.

Table 6.1 Own interest conflicts

Department	Examples of possible own interest conflicts
Property department	Acting for the purchaser of a property where you, another member of the firm, a family member or a friend is the seller Lending money to or borrowing from clients where you draw up the legal deed or arrange for a legal charge to be placed on their property
Private client department	Drafting a will for a client where you are a beneficiary or another person connected with you is a beneficiary Reaching agreement with the personal representatives of an asset to acquire this asset and to act on the legal requirements
Litigation	Acting for clients taking legal action against an individual or an organisation or a business in which you have an interest, perhaps because you have a public appointment or you are a shareholder etc.
Any department	Acting for another member of the firm in circumstances where this has an impact on the way in which you act

Many other situations may create an own interest conflict. Many firms have a conflicts policy which describes the restrictions which the managers and compliance officers have decided to impose internally to manage the risks associated with breaching this outcome. It is important that if such a policy exists, you are aware of the prohibitions and act in compliance. Regardless of this, or in any event in the absence of this type of policy, every individual in the firm, regardless of what role they play in the business, must always consider whether there is something about them which prevents them from acting in a client's best interest and be prepared to make this known to their colleagues if necessary.

A very interesting decision was made by the Solicitors Disciplinary Tribunal (SDT) in 2015 on the issue of solicitor/client conflict which also included an element of taking unfair advantage contrary to the behaviours expected of solicitors. You will recall that the SDT is an independent tribunal which has the power to adjudicate upon alleged breaches of the rules and regulations applicable to solicitors and their firms, including the SRA Handbook. The SDT handed down a record fine to the solicitor in question. As reported on the SRA website in March 2015, the facts were given in a news release of 25 March 2015 (**www.sra.org.uk/sra/news/press/sdt-record-fine.page**).

Record fine from SDT

Nigel Harvie, who worked at a firm with his name in Oxford, was fined £305,000 by the tribunal ... The previous highest amount was £50,000, handed down to firm Fuglers LLP, while the most an individual has been fined is £40,000.

Mr Harvie was also ordered to pay £37,016.40 costs at the hearing, held at the SDT in Farringdon Street, London, on 24–26 February. In a prosecution brought by the Solicitors Regulation Authority (SRA), the SDT heard Mr Harvie admit that:

- He entered into a financial arrangement with a former client without advising her to take independent advice, and where his own interests conflicted or potentially conflicted with the interests of the former client
- He acted towards his former client in a way that was contrary to his position as solicitor

Mr Harvie denied that he used his position as a solicitor to take unfair advantage for himself or another party, but the SDT upheld this allegation as well.

In return for paying for the care and living costs of a lady, for whom he had acted previously, Mr Harvie acquired ownership of her house. The house was valued at £300,000 in 2005 when the arrangement began and over the next five years, Mr Harvie paid out in the region of £200,000.

The house was never valued again and the arrangement came to an end in 2010 when the former client died. The Land Registry recorded the value of the house at £800,000 in 2012.

The client had declared in her will that her estate should be used to set up a trust fund to help foreign students, but this has not happened. The matter was only discovered when neighbours of the deceased complained to the SRA that her wishes had not been carried out.

Mr Harvie asserted that the deceased lady had only been his client when he prepared her will for her in 2004, and that she was happy with the arrangement. He also claimed the co-executor of her estate was aware of his actions at all times.

In delivering the sanction, the tribunal said they were taking a very serious view of the circumstances of this matter. It also said the public would be appalled by the behaviour of Mr Harvie in taking unfair advantage of his former client and he had done significant harm to the reputation of the profession.

David Middleton, Executive Director for Legal and Enforcement, said:

'The SRA is committed to working with solicitors and firms to raise standards and uphold core professional principles. Solicitors occupy unique positions of trust often on behalf of vulnerable members of the public.

'Mr Harvie abused that trust, and the record level of the fine clearly reflects the seriousness of this betrayal. Although Mr Harvie stated that his former client was happy with the arrangement put in place, he should have ensured that she seek independent advice at the outset because he stood to gain financially and therefore there was a clear conflict of interest.'

Mr Harvie, who stopped practising as a solicitor in 2012, has 21 days from receipt of the SDT's decision to appeal. He has 12 months to pay the fine.

6.3.2 Client conflict

Turning to a consideration of client conflict, the issue is not about your personal position but instead turns on the fact that you have multiple clients and need to be able to act in all their best interests. Client conflict as a professional conduct consideration is defined by the SRA and means:

> any situation where you owe separate duties to act in the best interests of two or more *clients* in relation to the same or related matters, and those duties conflict, or there is a significant risk that those duties may conflict.

In these circumstances, the conflict potential must be assessed in any circumstance where you are acting for more than one client either in a joint retainer, in associated retainers, or on different sides of a transaction and the conduct assessment is whether you can act in the best interests of each of these clients or whether the fact that they have all instructed the firm creates an obstacle to this.

If a client conflict, or a significant risk of such a conflict exists, then you must not act for all of the clients unless the matter falls within one of two limited exceptions. Again, the firm is required to have effective systems to identify such circumstances and which enable the following points to be taken into account:

- Are the clients' interests different?
- Is the ability to give independent advice fettered?
- Is there a need to negotiate?
- Is there an imbalance in bargaining power between the clients?
- Are either of the clients vulnerable so that this would have an impact on the judgment which must be made?

Again, there are a few clues to the SRA's thinking in the form of the indicative behaviours included in the chapter:

- declining to act for clients whose interests are in direct conflict such as claimant and defendant in litigation (indicative behaviour 3.3);
- declining to act for a seller and buyer where a builder is selling to a non-commercial client (indicative behaviour 3.4);
- only acting for clients who are a lender and borrower in respect of mortgage arrangements on certain standard terms (indicative behaviour 3.7);
- not acting for buyer/lessee and seller/lessor in respect of a land transaction (indicative behaviour 3.14).

There are countless other scenarios where there is potential for client conflict in different departments of the firm, as shown in **Table 6.2**.

Table 6.2 Client conflicts

Department	Examples of possible client conflicts
Property department	Acting for family members in respect of a loan arrangement secured on property and needing to negotiate the terms of the charge
Matrimonial department	Acting for both parties in a divorce matter
Family department	Acting for both parents in care proceedings
Criminal department	Acting for co-defendants in criminal proceedings
Employment department	Acting for a company and an employee defending an employment-related or discrimination claim

6.3.3 Written conflict policies

While it is not a strict requirement in the SRA Code of Conduct 2011, many firms have produced a written conflict policy to demonstrate that they are complying with the requirement to have an effective control system. If this exists, it is sensible to understand its content and make sure that you understand whether the firm has imposed any restrictions on acting in particular scenarios and the circumstances which the firm considers create such a high risk that achieving the required outcomes is in danger. For example, many firms which provide conveyancing services set out whether, or in what circumstances, individuals in the firm are permitted to act for both seller and purchaser of a property.

A conflict policy may also deal with the acceptable use of the two outcomes which provide an exception to the default position of not acting in a client conflict. These two exceptions are known as the 'substantially common interest exception' and the 'competing for the same objective exception'. By their very nature they are risky exceptions to use; this is because a client conflict has been identified but the firm decides that it is still appropriate and reasonable to continue acting. This statement alone shows the risks attached to such a decision and many firms state in their conflicts policy whether they are happy for the exceptions to be used and the procedure which mangers and employees will be expected to follow should they wish to carry on in such circumstances.

6.3.4 Substantially common interest exception

The SRA Handbook Glossary 2012 defines a substantially common interest as one which arises in 'a situation where there is a clear common purpose in relation to any matter or a particular aspect of it between the clients and a strong consensus on how it is to be achieved and the client conflict is peripheral to this common purpose'. In other words, two or more clients instruct the firm to act on their behalf and there is a clear and agreed decision about the purpose of the instructions and what the clients want to achieve. This is the 'common purpose' described in the definition. There is no need to negotiate on the major issues, there is no imbalance in bargaining power, and no client displays characteristics of vulnerability. The firm identifies a conflict of interest, but the subject of the conflict is minor – or 'peripheral', to use the SRA language – and does not have a particular bearing on the common purpose.

In such circumstances, the firm can decide that it is reasonable to continue acting and deal with the common purpose and leave the peripheral conflict to one side. Making this decision requires the firm to satisfy a number of conditions which are listed in outcome 3.6 in the Code:

> **O(3.6)** where there is a *client conflict* and the *clients* have a *substantially common interest* in relation to a matter or a particular aspect of it, you only act if:
>
> (a) you have explained the relevant issues and risks to the *clients* and you have a reasonable belief that they understand those issues and risks;
> (b) all the *clients* have given informed consent in writing to you acting;
> (c) you are satisfied that it is reasonable for you to act for all the *clients* and that it is in their best interests; and
> (d) you are satisfied that the benefits to the *clients* of you doing so outweigh the risks.

It is clear that the odds of making an appropriate decision are stacked against the law firm because, after all, a client conflict has been identified and the firm is deciding to continue regardless of this fact. Many firms chose never to use the exception for this reason while others allow it to be used but only in very strictly controlled circumstances which usually involves the COLP being involved in the decision and insisting on very careful monitoring throughout the relationship with the clients.

Of course, the SRA cannot say that it is risky in so many words, but the indicative behaviours which have been added to the Code make this point (indicative behaviours 3.11 and 3.12):

- Acting for two or more clients under the substantially common interest exception when their interests in the end result is not the same is unlikely to demonstrate that the desired outcomes have been met. This addresses an argument that acting for seller/lessor and buyer/lessee of a property could fall within the exception. It does not; in these circumstances there is not a common purpose as one party wants to dispose of an interest in land while the other party wants to make an acquisition
- Acting for two or more clients using this exception where it is unreasonable because the parties have an unequal bargaining power is likely to suggest that the conflict outcomes have not been met. Again, conveyancing examples spring to mind and this example hopefully puts to bed any notion that acting for seller/developer and buyer is a good idea
- Declining to act for clients in reliance of this exception where the clients cannot be represented even-handedly or will be prejudiced by lack of separate representation. This is the type of behaviour which would arise in circumstances

where the private client department is preparing trust deeds for perhaps different generations of a family, identify a peripheral conflict between their interests, but choose not to use substantially common interest exception because of vulnerabilities displayed by one of the clients.

6.3.5 Competing for the same objective exception

Using the 'competing for the same objective exception' is the second alternative to declining to act where there is a client conflict. Here, the SRA defines it as meaning:

> any situation in which two or more *clients* are competing for an 'objective' which, if attained by one *client*, will make that 'objective' unattainable to the other *client* or *clients*, and 'objective' means ... an asset, contract or business opportunity which two or more *clients* are seeking to acquire or recover through a liquidation (or some other form of insolvency process) or by means of an auction or tender process or a bid or offer which is not public.

In this scenario, it is highly unlikely that the clients will know each other's identity unlike the substantially common interest exception where the different clients will know each other because they have instructed the firm for a common purpose. Instead, this is the type of situation in which clients will have separately and independently instructed the firm to act on their behalf in order to acquire a particular interest which can only be acquired by one of them. For example, clients may contact the commercial department for assistance in acquiring a company or bidding in a tender situation for a business contract.

It goes without saying that it is crucial that a firm is able to identify through its conflicts process that this situation is present. Thereafter, it is important to address the risks attached to such a situation and to decide whether it is appropriate, or reasonable, to act for both clients notwithstanding the existence of this conflict. This requires the need to comply with conditions attached to outcome 3.7:

> (a) you have explained the relevant issues and risks to the *clients* and you have a reasonable belief that they understand those issues and risks;
> (b) the *clients* have confirmed in writing that they want you to act, in the knowledge that you act, or may act, for one or more other *clients* who are *competing for the same objective*;
> (c) there is no other *client conflict* in relation to that matter;
> (d) unless the *clients* specifically agree, no individual acts for, or is responsible for the supervision of work done for, more than one of the *clients* in that matter; and
> (e) you are satisfied that it is reasonable for you to act for all the *clients* and that the benefits to the *clients* of you doing so outweigh the risks.

Using the indicative behaviours as the clues to the SRA's views of the risks attached to the exception, it should be noted:

- Declining to act for clients in reliance of this exception where the clients cannot be represented even-handedly or will be prejudiced by lack of separate representation tends to show the correct outcome has been achieved. Perhaps two clients are bidding for the same contract and one is a sole trader and the other is a multi-national business. The differences between the two may mean that it would be difficult to show that the two clients could be treated equally by the firm.

- Only using the exception where both clients are sophisticated. This needs some explanation. The adjective 'sophisticated' is not a defined SRA Handbook term but the accepted view is that this is a client who, or which, is commercially experienced and perhaps has the benefit of an in-house legal team.
- Not using the exception to act for two or more buyers wanting to buy the same residential property. Hopefully, the firm's conflicts processes will identify this occurrence.

6.3.6 The SRA's expectations

In summary, the SRA's professional conduct expectations about conflicts of interest are relatively simple:

- There is a system which enables firms to identify conflicts and to manage the risks.
- An own interest conflict, or a significant risk of an own interest conflict, is identified and the instructions to act are declined.
- Similarly, client conflicts are identified and the firm does not act for all clients except in circumstances where one of the two exceptions is justified.
- The two exceptions are used carefully.

These requirements mean that anyone involved with clients in terms of file opening processes, conflicts searching, or providing fee-earning or support services must be vigilant about SRA requirements and understand the internal processes that the managers and compliance officers introduce. It is important that everyone involved with a client, or a client's matters, remains vigilant because making a decision about conflicts is not a one-off exercise at the beginning of a matter. A conflict could arise at any point in the proceedings.

Any additional requirements will be a matter for the firm to introduce and will be a business decision. This is acceptable as long as the firm's own policies do not contradict the SRA's standard, which must always be the starting point. For example, the firm may make a commercial agreement with a particular client not to act against its interests or for its competitors, or it may make a decision never to act in particular scenarios. Again, it will be necessary to understand these additional conditions and restrictions and be able to follow them.

6.4 CONFIDENTIALITY AND DUTY OF DISCLOSURE

Dealing with conflicts of interest requirements is different from the behaviours expected in terms of confidentially and disclosure, but these are often muddled in the minds of both lawyers and their clients. For example, many clients believe that because a firm has acted for them in the past, the same firm is not permitted to act against their interests as this would be a conflict of interest. This is not true. Provided that the firm, or any individual within the business, does not feel awkward in doing their best for a current client (i.e. takes the view that there is not an own interest conflict), the only duty owed to a former client is one of confidentiality.

6.4.1 Duty of confidentiality

The duty of confidentiality is one of the most exceptional things about being a solicitor or working in a law firm. We are bound to keep client matters confidential and not disclose information about our clients, past or current, without their consent unless there is a legal obligation to say something. This means that clients expect to be able to trust us with information of the most personal, sensitive or commercially secret nature. This creates enormous responsibilities and has an impact on the way we work and how we communicate with others. Nothing which is learnt through working in a law firm can be disclosed unless there is confidence that such a disclosure will not be against the client's wishes or is justified because we are legally obliged to put to one side the client's wishes in order to comply with the law.

In fact, not only is the duty of confidentiality one of the defining characteristics of the profession, it also carries with it an enormous amount of responsibility. The duty does not end when the file is closed: former clients can expect us to keep their matters confidential forever. Even after the death of a client, we need the consent of his or her personal representatives to disclose information on a voluntary basis. Even when we switch law firms, or even leave the profession, we are still bound by the duty.

Getting confidentiality wrong can have a ripple effect of consequences which go far beyond regulatory issues. The circumstances surrounding the revelation that an author called Robert Galbraith was in fact J. K. Rowling is a very recent example of the repercussions of a breach of confidential information. The facts are given in **Example 6.1**.

EXAMPLE 6.1 – J. K. Rowling

J. K. Rowling had instructed a London firm of solicitors, Russells Solicitors, to handle matters relating to the publication of a crime novel she had written using a pseudonym. She specifically did not want to publish a novel using her true identity. Unfortunately, she was outed in the press as the author, amidst much speculation as to how her secret had come to be revealed.

The revelation had originated through the careless talk of one of the partners in the law firm which Rowling had instructed, who had revealed the information about the firm's famous client to his wife's friend, who in turn posted the fact on her Twitter account. The result was a newspaper story which revealed J. K. Rowling's connection with the novel.

Ms Rowling said:

> To say that I am disappointed is an understatement. I had assumed that I could expect total confidentiality from Russells, a reputable professional firm, and I feel very angry that my trust turned out to be misplaced. A tiny number of people knew my pseudonym and it has not been pleasant to wonder for days how a woman whom I had never heard of ... could have found out something that many of my oldest friends did not know.

Russells Solicitors apologised 'unreservedly' but said that the revelation had occurred 'during a private conversation', adding that 'the disclosure was made in confidence to someone he trusted implicitly'.

The firm suffered an extraordinary amount of bad publicity because of the gaffe, which perhaps shows that the damage that can be done by not behaving professionally and not acting in an ethical manner can do more harm than just that of a regulatory nature. Despite the fact that the revelation meant that the book, which had only sold 1,500 copies previously, rapidly escalated 5,000 places up to the top of the Amazon bestseller list, the firm and the partner experienced a number of negative consequences.

The story, and the circumstances behind the revelation, became a global news item, with a number of national and foreign commentators using it as an excuse to discuss the breach of confidentiality and a solicitor's duty of confidentiality to his clients. The firm had to pay Rowling's legal fees and a substantial amount in damages.

The SRA moved swiftly to investigate the breach of SRA Handbook requirements. The partner, Mr Gossage, was issued with a written rebuke and ordered to pay a fine of £1,000. The reason given for the finding was: 'By disclosing confidential information about a client to a third party Mr Gossage has breached Principles 4 and 6 of the SRA Principles 2011 and failed to achieve outcome 4.1 of the SRA Code of Conduct 2011.' In other words, the solicitor was found to have breached the principles of acting in a client's best interest and had not upheld the trust the public placed in him and in the provision of legal services and he had breached the duty of confidentiality by disclosing confidential information without the client's consent. This disciplinary finding is now a matter of public record.

Quite simply, the importance of confidentiality must not be misunderstood by anyone working in a law firm, regardless of their role. It is important to understand what outcomes the SRA expects to see in practice and these are in chapter 4 of the SRA Code of Conduct 2011. First and foremost, the SRA says that you must 'keep the affairs confidential unless disclosure is required or permitted by law or the client consents'. It also is a requirement – or outcome – that requires that 'you have effective systems and controls in place to enable you to identify risks to client confidentiality'.

6.4.2 Confidentiality risk hotspots

Most firms have a confidentiality policy as part of their office systems, which confirms the importance of this duty and describes risk-management processes. The risk hotspots are likely to occur in the following circumstances:

- sending emails to the wrong person;
- sending too much information in an email (for example, attaching an email chain to a communication and disclosing confidential information in error in this way);

- sending letters to the wrong postal address or emails to the wrong email address;
- putting additional information into an envelope by mistake and sending this to the wrong person;
- discussing a client's matter with a third party without the client's consent;
- outsourcing work and not dealing with the confidentiality issues which arise because client information is going outside of the firm;
- discussing client matters in a public place;
- discussing the firm and client matters on a social media site such as Facebook;
- taking work home;
- using unsecure information technology systems;
- not destroying confidential information appropriately;
- not archiving files properly;
- theft from the firm's offices.

6.4.3 Managing confidentiality risks

How a firm manages these risks is not discussed by the SRA. In its indicative behaviours it emphasises that this is something which the firm must assess by stating that: 'your systems and controls for client confidentiality are appropriate to the size and complexity of the firm or in-house practice and the nature of the work undertaken, and enable you to assess all the relevant circumstances' (indicative behaviour 4.1). What is clear is that everyone will need to be confident that they know the part they must play in achieving this outcome, for example:

- receptionists being careful about conversations in public areas of the firm;
- drivers taking care when transporting client information across locations or to archive facilities;
- marketing services providers not overstepping the mark in using client information for publicity purposes;
- support staff dealing with telephone enquiries about a client;
- fee earners ensuring that the client gives consent to disclosure of confidential information where necessary.

Internal policies normally cover these points and also identify high-risk pinch points that may occur in the firm, with directions about how the managers and compliance officer expect colleagues to react or behave. For example, it is often a sensible precaution to have evidence that clients have given consent to disclosure of their confidential information or, in the alternative, the steps which have been taken to verify that it is a legal requirement to override a client's consent.

In this regard, there are a number of pieces of legislation which entitle third parties to have access to confidential information relating to clients. These include the disclosure duties in anti-money laundering legislation and the duty to provide information to HMRC when they rely on certain statutory entitlements.

In other circumstances, anyone in the firm could be told something which is subject to the duty of confidentiality but might feel uncomfortable in honouring that duty. Perhaps a client has told a member of support staff that they intend to commit suicide, or leave the country with minors, or that a minor is at risk of abuse, or that they themselves intend to commit a criminal act on a third party. While a knee-jerk reaction may be to put confidentiality immediately to one side, the correct behaviour is to discuss the information with the firm's COLP in order to decide appropriate next steps.

The other SRA indicative behaviours are random in nature and simply state that you should:

- only outsource services when you are satisfied that the provider has taken all appropriate steps to ensure that your client's confidential information is protected (indicative behaviour 4.3);
- not disclose the content of a will on the death of a client unless consent has been provided by the personal representatives for the content to be released (indicative behaviour 4.6);
- not disclose details of bills sent to clients to third parties, such as debt factoring companies in relation to the collection of book debts, unless the client has consented (indicative behaviour 4.7).

Given the nature of twenty-first century law firms, and the regular use of emails and IT generally, it is very likely that there will be risks to achieving this outcome through human error. These are the sorts of mistakes that anyone in the business could make and it is important to remember that the COLP must be made aware that something has gone awry so that he or she can record this, decide what remedial action must be taken, and also consider whether the SRA needs to be told of the event.

6.4.4 Duty of disclosure

The duty of confidentiality runs alongside a sometimes contradictory and conflicting duty of disclosure, which applies in respect of individual fee earners and a personal duty to disclose all relevant information to their current clients. If acting in a fee-earning role, the individual (regardless of whether they are a solicitor or not) must achieve outcome 4.2:

> any individual who is advising a *client* makes that *client* aware of all information material to that retainer of which the individual has personal knowledge.

In other words, when contacted by a prospective client, and in initial meetings with that person, fee earners must assess whether they can act in that person's best interests and that includes reflecting on whether they are able to discuss any material information in their knowledge. Material information is information which will be relevant to the client in terms of the instructions which they give and the decisions that they make, rather than information of a general nature or information which is interesting but not relevant to the matter in hand. It also will be information which is not already known to the client.

The conduct dilemma arises where the material information has been obtained while acting for another client. This is because such information will be confidential to that client and that duty remains for all time. It is essential that the fee earner identifies this conundrum, and the actions which are taken next, because this requires the correct application of further Code outcomes.

Outcome 4.3 is that:

> you ensure that where your duty of confidentiality to one *client* comes into conflict with your duty of disclosure to another *client*, your duty of confidentiality takes precedence.

This outcome, and this very important concept, is further explained through the use of indicative behaviour 4.5:

> not acting for A where B is a *client* for whom you hold confidential information which is material to A unless the confidential information can be protected.

While this answers one important conduct question, another dilemma remains: can you continue to act for the other client and not disclose the material information to them?

6.4.5 Can you continue to act for the other client and not disclose material information to them?

The outcomes do not provide a direct answer for all circumstances but there is a useful clue about SRA thinking in the indicative behaviours. It is useful to include indicative behaviour 4.4 in full:

> Where you are an individual who has responsibility for acting for a *client* or supervising a *client's* matter, you disclose to the *client* all information material to the *client's* matter of which you are personally aware, except when:
>
> (a) the *client* gives specific informed consent to non-disclosure or a different standard of disclosure arises;
>
> (b) there is evidence that serious physical or mental injury will be caused to a person(s) if the information is disclosed to the *client*;
>
> (c) legal restrictions effectively prohibit you from passing the information to the *client*, such as the provisions in the money-laundering and anti-terrorism legislation;
>
> (d) it is obvious that privileged documents have been mistakenly disclosed to you;
>
> (e) you come into possession of information relating to state security or intelligence matters to which the Official Secrets Act 1989 applies.

Creating the environment in which the client gives specific informed consent to what amounts to a change in the professional behaviours which they can expect from a member of a law firm changes the risk diagnosis of the instructions. Is it reasonable to suggest to a client that the firm continues to act for them while withholding material information? After all, the client will not know what the information is. If the client later discovered the nature of the withheld information, would it be an issue for concern?

6.4.6 Managing disclosure risks

Because of this type of dilemma, many firms have developed a way of managing the risks presented by the situation. It is important that everyone in the firm deals with the issue in accordance with any policy and procedure and this protects both them and the firm.

Continuing to act for a current client, while ensuring that confidential information is secure, requires the use of an information barrier. In other words, the means to safeguard and hide the confidential information from the client and the legal team, who cannot have access to it or use it for the benefit of their own client's matter.

The SRA does not speculate on the appearance of an effective information barrier in circumstances where the client to whom confidentiality is owed and the client who has agreed not to have the information do not have adverse interests. However, where there are adverse interests, then an outcome in the SRA Code of Conduct 2011 must be achieved.

Unfortunately, the SRA Handbook does not include a definition for the phrase 'adverse interest'. In common law, it has been held that adversity arises where one party is, or is likely to become, the opposing party on a matter, whether in negotiations or some form of dispute resolution. In recent cases which have examined whether it is appropriate for a solicitor to act in such circumstances, the adverse interests have largely focused on commercial or business adversity with competing businesses engaging the same law firms and the need for information barriers to be erected to protect confidential information from improper disclosure.

The outcome (4.4) which must be achieved is as follows:

> you do not act for A in a matter where A has an interest adverse to B, and B is a *client* for whom you hold confidential information which is material to A in that matter, unless the confidential information can be protected by the use of safeguards, and:
>
> (a) you reasonably believe that A is aware of, and understands, the relevant issues and gives informed consent;
>
> (b) either:
>
> (i) B gives informed consent and you agree with B the safeguards to protect B's information; or
>
> (ii) where this is not possible, you put in place effective safeguards including information barriers which comply with the common law; and
>
> (c) it is reasonable in all the circumstances to act for A with such safeguards in place.

6.5 MANAGEMENT OUTCOMES

The SRA Handbook contains a number of requirements which at first glance appear to be directed at the managers and owners of the law firm. We have already mentioned Principle 8 of the SRA Principles 2011, which states that you must 'run your business or carry out your role in the business effectively and in accordance with proper governance and sound financial and risk management principles'. A careful reading of these words makes it clear that this principle must be achieved by everyone in the law firm regardless of what they do.

The same point can be made about the more detailed outcomes in the SRA Code of Conduct 2011 which relate to the business. Chapter 7 of the Code describes outcomes which must be achieved about the management and supervision of the firm. The introduction to the chapter reinforces the point that management is a team game:

> Everyone has a role to play in the efficient running of a business, although of course that role will depend on the individual's position within the organisation.

The introductory statements also include the following directions:

> However, overarching responsibility for the management of the business in the broadest sense rests with the *manager(s)*. The *manager(s)* should determine what arrangements are appropriate to meet the outcomes. Factors to be taken into account will include the size and complexity of the business; the number, experience and qualifications of the *employees*; the number of offices; and the nature of the work undertaken.

In other words, the managers will be required to take a leading role in determining what management and supervision must look like in their firm but everyone must be satisfied that they understand the managers' systems and can play their part in keeping the firm safe.

For example, some of the outcomes relate to achievements which the managers must put in place. **Table 6.3** shows what these are and how everyone else in the business can demonstrate that they are playing an effective role.

Table 6.3 Demonstrating management outcomes

Required behaviour of managers	The response of employees within the business
You have clear and effective governance structures and reporting lines	Do you know who the managers are? Do you know the identity of people in key compliance roles – the COLP, the COFA, the MLRO – and know when to speak to them? Is it clear who is supervising you and, if applicable, who you are supervising and what that requires you to do?

Required behaviour of managers	The response of employees within the business
You have effective systems and controls in place to achieve and comply with all the principles, rules and outcomes and other requirements of the SRA Handbook, where applicable	Do you understand the SRA Handbook requirements which apply to you? Have you read internal policies which explain how you must behave and why this is so? Have you considered whether the systems will work in practice and have you made suggestions about additions or improvements?
You identify, monitor and manage risks to compliance with all the principles, rules and outcomes and other requirements of the SRA Handbook, if applicable to you, and take steps to address issues identified	Do you know how to report anything that has gone wrong?
You train individuals working in the firm to maintain a level of competence appropriate to their work and level of responsibility	Have you undertaken training as required by the business? Have you requested any training which you think may be helpful to you or your colleagues?
You have a system for supervising clients' matters, to include the regular checking of the quality of work by suitably competent and experienced people	Do you understand the firm's supervision requirements? If you are a supervisor then do you have the time and skills to fulfil this role, do you give constructive feedback and follow up on corrective actions, do you report concerns or training needs to the appropriate people in the firm? If you are being supervised then do you understand your role in preparing for supervisory sessions, do you engage positively in the process etc.?
You do not outsource reserved legal activities to a person who is not authorised to conduct such activities	'Outsourcing' is not a defined term but is generally taken to mean instructing people and businesses outside the law firm to do activities which could be done internally; for example, using a typing service, or a cloud computing company or using another law firm to carry out legal services. Reserved legal activities (those legal activities which can only be performed by qualified people) cannot be outsourced to third parties who are not so qualified. Do you know and follow any policy which the firm has implanted to manage and control outsourcing arrangements?

Required behaviour of managers	The response of employees within the business
Where you outsource legal activities or any operational functions that are critical to the delivery of any legal activities, you ensure such outsourcing: (a) does not adversely affect your ability to comply with, or the SRA's ability to monitor your compliance with, your obligations in the SRA Handbook; (b) is subject to contractual arrangements that enable the SRA or its agent to obtain information from, inspect the records (including electronic records) of, or enter the premises of, the third party, in relation to the outsourced activities or functions; (c) does not alter your obligations towards your clients; and (d) does not cause you to breach the conditions with which you must comply in order to be authorised and to remain so	As above

6.6 RELATIONS WITH THE SRA

As with management requirements, it is dangerous to assume that the relationship with the SRA, and other regulatory and oversight bodies, is simply something which the managers and solicitors must understand. We have already referred to Principle 7 of the SRA Principles 2011 and the compulsory requirement that 'you must comply with your legal and regulatory obligations and deal with your regulators and ombudsmen in an open, timely and co-operative manner' and this applies to everyone working in an SRA-authorised and regulated law firm.

The SRA Code of Conduct 2011 adds some flesh to the bones of this requirement through a series of compulsory outcomes which must be met by everyone. This meat is found in the third section and chapter 10 of the Code entitled 'You and your regulator'. The SRA sets the scene by making the statement that these outcomes focus on the need to co-operate with regulators and ombudsmen. The purpose of such a relationship is to assist with risk-based regulation: what does the regulator need to know about you, about anyone else, or about a regulated business in order to manage risks to clients and the public at large?

With this in mind, it is important to understand that sometimes individuals may be placed in an uncomfortable position where this duty and the need to speak with the regulator may mean that they are putting their head above the parapet. This is an example of the responsibility and burden of working in a regulated industry; sometimes it will be necessary to be brave enough to upset someone, to challenge inappropriate behaviour and to alert the regulator to any concerns that you may have.

6.6.1 Personal relationship with the SRA

These outcomes relate first to your personal position and your individual relationship with the SRA and other third parties (outcomes 10.1–10.10):

- You must comply with all the reporting and notification requirements in the SRA Handbook which apply to you.
- You must provide the SRA with information that enables it to decide upon any application that you are making with a safe, public-interest response. This means, for example, that anyone applying to become the firm's COFA would need to provide the SRA with a full and frank disclosure of their circumstances in order that the SRA has sufficient information with which to make a safe decision.
- You must notify the SRA promptly about any material changes to relevant information about yourself. This will include information about serious financial difficulty, action taken against you by another regulator, and serious failure to comply with SRA Handbook requirements. This would mean, for example, that if legal executives found themselves in the position of being disciplined by their own regulatory body (CILEx Regulation Ltd) while working in an SRA-authorised law firm, they would need to alert the SRA to these circumstances in a timely manner.
- You must co-operate with the SRA and the Legal Ombudsman in respect of any investigations relating to claims for redress.
- You must comply with any written notice served on you by the SRA and assist the regulator in respect of anything which it may have need to investigate.

6.6.2 Personal reporting obligations

Looking at your relationship with your firm, the outcomes also include obligations to report the following:

- You must report to the SRA serious misconduct by any person or firm authorised by the SRA (i.e. any solicitor, REL or RFL and any SRA-authorised law firm), or any employee, managers or owners of these firms in a prompt manner and subject only to any restraints caused by duties of client confidentiality.
- You must ensure that the SRA is in a position to assess whether anyone who requires SRA prior approval to hold roles (such as compliance officers, managers and/or owners) are fit and proper and remain fit and proper.

Different role holders will be able to comply with these obligations in different ways. For example, the managers and compliance officers will have the seniority and experience to see the bigger picture in terms of the safety of the firm as a whole and will be in a better position to address the SRA's expectation to be told about risk-creating situations such as serious financial difficulty and financial weakness in the business. This information is regarded as necessary because of the link which can sometimes be seen between financial viability issues and risks to client money and assets (remembering Principle 10 and the duty to protect client money and assets), providing a proper standard of service to clients (Principle 5), and the need to ensure that nothing is done which would damage the trust in individuals and the profession (Principle 6). The indicative behaviours in the SRA Code of Conduct 2011 give examples of indicators of serious financial difficulty, including the inability to pay the firm's professional indemnity insurance, rent or salaries. The financial viability indicators need to be considered in such circumstances as difficult trading conditions, poor cash flow, increased overheads, loss of managers and employees or loss of sources of income. This is not information which will be known to everyone in the business but where it is in your knowledge then the outcomes would require you to consider your personal duty of disclosure.

6.6.3 Whistle-blowing systems

In practice, many firms have introduced whistle-blowing systems and in fact having a whistle-blowing policy is an indicative behaviour in the Code. The purpose of such a policy is to set the scene for keeping the firm safe, and for the managers and compliance officers to have the assurance that information which may have an impact on an individual within the business, or on the business as a whole, will be brought to their attention rather than brushed under the carpet for fear of personal consequences on the part of the informant. In turn, a correctly drafted whistle-blowing policy provides comfort to those with knowledge that they need to share, that there will be no personal repercussions from sharing and that their role in disclosure will be kept confidential if appropriate.

6.7 UNDERTAKINGS

Alongside our role of being the keeper of our clients' secrets, the ability to give or receive undertakings is another of the hallmarks of the profession. Giving or receiving an undertaking, and not being able to comply with professional conduct duties in connection with the same will have serious consequences for the individuals concerned and also sometimes for their employers, who will be expected to have proper governance and risk management systems in place to manage the consequences of this activity.

Almost everyone in a law firm may be in a position where they could give or receive an undertaking, sometimes without even realising that this is what they have done, through what they may have said or otherwise communicated to a third party.

6.7.1 What is an undertaking?

The SRA Handbook Glossary 2012 includes the following definition of an undertaking:

> a statement, given orally or in writing, whether or not it includes the word 'undertake' or 'undertaking', made by or on behalf of you or your *firm*, in the course of *practice*, or by you outside the course of *practice* but as a *solicitor* or REL, to someone who reasonably places reliance on it, that you or your *firm* will do something or cause something to be done, or refrain from doing something.

It is essential to understand that this definition is deliberately very loosely drafted. Any statement could constitute an undertaking and such a statement does not have to include the words 'undertake' or 'undertaking'. Simply confirming that you will do something, or not do something, can be an undertaking. It does not need to be in writing, so could be given (by mistake or otherwise) in telephone calls or personal meetings.

For solicitors and registered European lawyers, the need to consider their personal conduct obligations in respect of such statements does not end at the close of business each day. For these individuals, any undertaking which they give as a solicitor or an REL outside of practice must be honoured and the relevant outcomes must be achieved. For anyone else employed within an SRA-authorised firm, the conduct obligations arise in terms of what they do in that practice.

6.7.2 Performance of undertakings

The outcome which must be achieved is that you must perform all undertakings given by you within an agreed timescale or within a reasonable amount of time.

Many law firms have come unstuck because of undertakings which have been given by members of the business. Quite often this means a contested court case as well as regulatory consequences, as demonstrated in a very recent example of an undertaking dispute: *Global Marine Drillships Ltd* v. *La Bella* [2014] EWHC 2242 (Ch).

In the *Global Marine* case, it was held that a solicitor who had released funds to third parties had acted in breach of an undertaking and had done this without authorisation. Both she and her firm were found liable and the defence she had raised – that her actions related to client pressure – was not taken into consideration. She was referred to the SDT, which suspended her from practice for three years citing the breach of undertaking in its decision to impose this sanction.

Unlike a few of the other conduct requirements there is no outcome which requires that systems and processes are implemented to monitor the giving or receipt of undertakings. However, it is recommended in indicative behaviour 11.5 that 'maintaining an effective system which records when undertakings have been given and when they have been discharged' is likely to show that the outcomes have been achieved. It is essential to understand the policies which the firm has put in place to ensure that no unnecessary risks are taken.

6.7.3 Recording of undertakings

In some firms, there is a requirement to record an undertaking on the file itself; in others such records are backed-up with diary entries or in a central register. There is no right or wrong method, but the appropriate method will be evaluated on the basis of what system works best for the firm, given the type of work it does and who can give or receive undertakings on behalf of the business. This is an important point to bear in mind too. In some businesses, the risks attached to undertakings are managed by strict control over who has authority to bind the business.

6.7.4 Drafting of undertakings

In terms of the giving of a safe undertaking, many firms rely on previous guidance issued by the Law Society and the SRA which pre-dates the SRA Handbook and has not been reproduced in connection with it, but nevertheless remains best practice. This refers to undertakings being drafted in a 'SMART' format so that they are specific, measurable, agreed, realistic and timed. This requires attention to the following points:

- **Specific:** undertakings should refer to a particular task or action which has been clearly identified and defined. Do not give general or open-ended undertakings and make sure that any undertaking to pay monies out of a fund is qualified by the proviso that the fund comes into your hands, and that it is sufficient.
- **Measurable:** undertakings should include agreed measures or steps which are understood by both parties and can easily be monitored or checked, so that there can be no dispute as to whether an undertaking has been fully discharged. If an undertaking involves the payment of a sum or money, make sure the amount is clear or that it is easy to calculate. Remember, ambiguous undertakings will be construed in favour of the recipient.
- **Agreed:** undertakings should be expressly agreed by both the person giving and the person receiving them and should be confirmed in writing. They may be given orally or in writing and are binding even if they do not include the word 'undertaking' – beware of inadvertent undertakings.
- **Realistic:** undertakings should be achievable. Before giving an undertaking consider carefully whether you will be able to implement it. If any events must happen before you will be able to implement your undertaking, it is good

practice to spell out those events on the face of the undertaking. An undertaking is still binding even if it is to do something outside your control.

- **Timed:** undertakings should indicate when, or on the happening of which event, they will be implemented. In the absence of an express term, there is an implied term that an undertaking will be performed within a reasonable time, having regard to its nature.

The SRA also previously produced some additional guidance to support the SMART message and, again, while this is not part of the current regulatory handbook of resources, it remains useful for managers to take these messages into account and for everyone else to be aware of the following points:

- be clear about who can give undertakings;
- ensure all staff understand they need your client's agreement;
- be clear about how compliance will be monitored;
- maintain a central record to ensure and monitor compliance;
- prescribe the manner in which undertakings may be given;
- prepare standard undertakings, where possible, with clear instructions that any departure be authorised in accordance with supervision and management responsibilities;
- adopt a system that ensures terms are checked by another fee earner;
- confirm oral undertakings (given or received) in writing;
- copy each undertaking and attach it to the relevant file – label the file itself;
- ensure all staff understand the undertakings they give when using the Law Society's formulae for exchange of contracts and its code for completion by post.

6.8 DEALINGS WITH THIRD PARTIES

The undertakings outcome in the SRA Code of Conduct 2011 is grouped together with other outcomes relating to our relations with third parties and they are all designed to assist us in complying with the SRA Principles 2011, i.e. integrity (Principle 2) and the duty to behave in a way that maintains the trust the public places in you and in the provision of legal services (Principle 6).

In this regard, it is important that everyone in the firm understands and can comply with outcome 11.1:

> you do not take unfair advantage of third parties in either your professional or personal capacity.

The following indicative behaviours are used to illustrate how this may be demonstrated:

> **IB(11.1)** providing sufficient time and information to enable the costs in any matter to be agreed;
>
> ...

IB(11.7) [not] taking unfair advantage of an opposing party's lack of legal knowledge where they have not instructed a *lawyer*;

IB(11.8) [not] demanding anything for yourself or on behalf of your *client*, that is not legally recoverable, such as when you are instructed to collect a simple debt, demanding from the debtor the cost of the letter of claim since it cannot be said at that stage that such a cost is legally recoverable;

IB(11.9) [not] using your professional status or qualification to take unfair advantage of another *person* in order to advance your personal interests;

IB(11.10)[not] taking unfair advantage of a public office held by you, or a member of your family, or a member of your *firm* or their family.

CHAPTER 7

Other conduct requirements

7.1 INTRODUCTION

The topics which we have covered in the previous chapter are likely to be the most common scenarios where everyone in the firm will need to understand what the SRA expects to see in terms of the correct regulatory response. After all, everyone has client care responsibilities to some degree or another, many people are involved in the process of conflicts searching and file opening, everyone owes a duty of confidentiality to clients of the law, anyone could place the firm at risk by mistakenly giving an undertaking, and so on.

There are many more requirements in the SRA Code of Conduct 2011 which apply in specific circumstances only. In other words, they are not going to be relevant all the time and to everyone in the firm. Nevertheless, if they do apply to you, it will be necessary to demonstrate that you understand that this is the case and that you are behaving as expected. These are flagged up in the following table with a commentary about what the SRA expects to see.

7.2 DUTIES TO THE COURT

This section of the Code is largely going to be relevant to members of the firm who provide legal services to clients or work in support roles in litigation departments where court processes are undertaken. The conduct duties stem from Principle 1 of the SRA Principles 2011 and the duty to uphold the rule of law and the proper administration of justice.

Table 7.1 SRA Code of Conduct 2011, chapter 5 outcomes

SRA requirement	Observations
You do not attempt to deceive or knowingly or recklessly mislead the court	Do you draw the court's attention to all relevant cases and statutory provisions and any material procedural irregularities?

SRA requirement	Observations
You are not complicit in another person deceiving or misleading the court	Do you understand the ethical dilemmas created by being placed in this position by a third party?
You comply with court orders	Where necessary can you show that this is the case?
You do not place yourself in contempt of court	Do you immediately inform the court, with your client's consent, if during the course of proceedings you become aware that you have inadvertently misled the court, or cease to act if the client does not consent to you informing the court? Do you refrain from constructing facts supporting your client's case or drafting any documents relating to any proceedings containing: • any contention which you do not consider to be properly arguable; or • any allegation of fraud, unless you are instructed to do so and you have material which you reasonably believe shows, on the face of it, a case of fraud?
Where relevant, clients are informed of the circumstances in which your duties to the court outweigh your obligations to the client	Do clients understand your duty to uphold the rule of law and the proper administration of justice? Would you refuse to continue acting for a client if you become aware they have committed perjury or misled the court, or attempted to mislead the court, in any material matter unless the client agrees to disclose the truth to the court?
You comply with your duties to the court	You are required to assist the court in the administration of justice. Are you comfortable that you can demonstrate that this is your default position?
Evidence relating to sensitive issues is not misused	Do you ensure that such evidence is protected from misuse?
You do not make or offer to make payments to witnesses dependent upon their evidence or outcome of the case	Can you demonstrate that you do not attempt to influence a witness, tamper with evidence, coach a witness or seek to persuade them to change their evidence?

7.3 INTRODUCTIONS TO THIRD PARTIES

Sometimes you may need to recommend a third party to your clients, perhaps because they need services you cannot provide yourself. Often the firm will have arrangements with third parties to formalise such introductions. The risk is that such arrangements may not be compatible with Principle 3 (relating to your independence) and Principle 4 (acting in the best interests of each client) of the SRA Principles 2011.

Table 7.2 SRA Code of Conduct 2011, chapter 6 outcomes

SRA requirements	Observations
When you recommend that a client uses a particular person or business, your recommendation is in the best interests of the client and does not compromise your independence	Do you understand the firm's policy on the third parties it will recommend to clients? Do you take time to consider whether a preferred third party is actually a good recommendation for a particular client? Do you make notes to demonstrate how a decision has been made?
Clients are informed about any financial or other interest you have in making the referral	Do you know whether the firm will receive a payment for making the introduction? Is there any other benefit for the firm in making the referral to a particular third party? Has the client been told? Can you provide evidence that this has happened?
Clients are able to make informed decisions about how to progress their matter	Tied up with the above, has the client been given sufficient information so that they can be involved in the decision with the right facts to hand? Have you produced the right records to show that this has happened?
You do not pay a prohibited referral fee	Certain referral fees are prohibited – the SRA currently prohibits payments in respect of the introduction/referral of criminal clients and clients who are eligible for public funding and the Legal Aid, Sentencing and Punishment of Offenders Act 2012 also has statutory prohibitions on the payment of referral fees in certain types of cases. Are you satisfied that you are aware of the restrictions?

7.4 PUBLICITY

The fact that law firms can publicise the services that they offer still surprises some people as this has not always been the case and, in fact there are some restrictions about the extent of what we can do. Knowing the conduct restrictions is essential, particularly for anyone in a marketing role or anyone who instructs a third party to promote the business. This is important, because the restrictions cannot be varied by using someone else to do something which would place a law firm manager or employee in breach of SRA requirements.

Table 7.3 SRA Code of Conduct 2011, chapter 8 outcomes

SRA requirement	**Observation**
Publicity must be accurate and not misleading and must not diminish the trust the public places in you and in the provision of legal services	Publicity is defined to include all promotional material and activity, including the name or description of your firm, stationery, advertisements, brochures, websites, directory entries, media appearances, promotional press releases, and direct approaches to potential clients and other persons, whether conducted in person, in writing, or in electronic form, but does not include press releases prepared on behalf of a client. If you are in a marketing role, are you confident that you understand the restrictions on publicity? If you instruct advertising agencies can you explain to them what the law firm can and can't do? In any other role, are you keeping the firm safe in terms of the representations which you make about yourself and the business?
Your publicity about charges is clearly expressed and identifies whether VAT and disbursements are included	This will include information which anyone in the firm gives to a client so if you are fulfilling client care requirements, or dealing with a client's subsequent questions about costs, are you satisfied that your information is clearly expressed and realistic?

SRA requirement	Observation
You do not make unsolicited approaches in person or by telephone to members of the public in order to publicise your firm	In other words, you do not undertake cold-calling, or allow anyone else to do this. Bear in mind that 'members of the public' for the purposes of this restriction does not include: • a current or former client; • another firm or its manager; • an existing or potential professional or business connection; or • a commercial organisation or public body. Approaching people in the street, at ports of entry, in hospitals or at accident scenes would be improper
Clients and the public have appropriate information about you, the firm and how you are regulated	Do your clients understand who you are and have the right information about the law firm and the relationship with the SRA?
Letterheads, websites and emails contain the correct regulatory information	Is the correct SRA and company information on the stationery and electronic resources?

7.5 FEE SHARING AND REFERRALS

In many ways the outcomes relating to introductions to the law firm have many parallels with the conduct requirements relating to your introductions to third parties. They are designed to support the overarching principles of independence and acting in each client's best interest.

Table 7.4 SRA Code of Conduct 2011, chapter 9 outcomes

SRA requirement	Observations
Your independence and your professional judgment must not be prejudiced because of any arrangement with another person	The client is the person who is introduced and not the introducer. Are you satisfied it is in the client's best interest to be represented by you and your firm?
Your client's interests are protected regardless of the interests of the introducer/fee sharer or your own interest in receiving the introduction	Do you put the client's interests first, even if that is going to create difficulties for you with the introducer?
Clients are able to make informed decisions about how to progress their matter	Do you make sure that the client is told all material facts so that his or she is part of the decision-making process?

SRA requirement	Observations
Clients are told about any financial or other interest which the introducer has in referring the client to you	Have you disclosed any payment arrangement to the client in a clear and transparent way? Is there evidence of this?
Clients are told about any fee sharing arrangement which is relevant to their matter	As above
Payments to introducers in respect of clients who are involved in criminal proceedings or who have the benefit of public funding are prohibited	Are you satisfied that this is not happening?
You must not pay a prohibited referral fee	The Legal Aid, Sentencing and Punishment of Offenders Act 2012 creates a statutory prohibition on making payments in respect of certain types of work. Are you confident that you understand the restrictions and you are not making unlawful payments?

CHAPTER 8

Complying with the SRA Accounts Rules 2011

8.1 INTRODUCTION

The SRA Accounts Rules 2011 (the Accounts Rules) take centre stage in risk-based regulation. Complying with this set of complicated and detailed requirements is no longer something which only the accounts team in a law firm ensures and which the managers oversee. It is now something which requires a firm-wide effort and everyone who handles client money in whatever capacity needs to understand these Rules, the firm's processes and what can go wrong.

8.2 MISUSE OF CLIENT MONEY

There are a number of reasons why this is the case. When talking about risk-based regulation, one of the most disastrous things that a law firm could mismanage is the holding and protection of client money. Getting this wrong undermines the trust and confidence that clients and the public have in the profession. After all, we often ask clients to give us their money on account of costs, or we often receive monies into our accounts on their behalf, and there needs to be assurances and certainty that this money is safe.

When the money is not safe, for whatever reason that may be, the consequences are serious for the client, the law firm and for the SRA, which needs to demonstrate an appropriate response to the wrongdoing. For all of these reasons, the SRA considers misuse of client money and assets as a major risk priority. In a risk document that identified priority risks, which was published on its website in 2015 (**www.sra.org.uk/riskoutlook**), the SRA included misuse of money or assets as a worrying trend saying:

> We are seeing a continuation of the trend we reported in the Risk Outlook 2013 of increased numbers of cases of misuse of money or assets. These are a great concern when client money is involved. Some of these cases are caused by poor systems and controls, whilst other cases involve unethical conduct. We have also seen a number of firms where financial difficulty has been a contributory factor leading to misuse of client money.

The SRA uses a risk-based response to deal with client money issues. Unfortunately there are many examples of individuals – both qualified solicitors and non-solicitors – being stopped from working in the profession because they have defaulted in some way. Two examples are described below.

EXAMPLE 8.1 – Zia Latif

A solicitor, Mr Zia Latif, was struck off the roll of solicitors in 2014. According to an SRA statement, Latif admitted failing to maintain properly written up books of accounts, causing or permitting monies to be withdrawn from client bank accounts in breach of the Solicitors' Accounts Rules 1998, giving false and misleading explanations to the SRA, practising as a solicitor without indemnity insurance cover and failing to deliver an accountant's report. He also admitted dishonesty in relation to giving false and misleading explanations to the SRA. He was ordered to pay £22,500 costs. At the time, the SRA director of legal and enforcement, said:

> Solicitors hold positions of trust and Mr Latif abused that position. He also made misleading statements, which was dishonest, and we don't want dishonesty in the profession.

EXAMPLE 8.2 – Matthew Haines

A former law firm cashier was barred from the legal profession in April 2015, after being found to have misappropriated more than £150,000 in client and office money. Mr Matthew Haines, who worked as a senior cashier at a Lancashire firm, was found to have misappropriated £157,975.67 between 2009 and 2013, according to an SRA notice published on its website. The SRA stated that Haines was convicted of theft in December 2013 at Lancaster Magistrates' Court, and was sentenced to two years' imprisonment by Preston Crown Court in February 2014. Due to his criminal conviction, the SRA took the decision that it is 'undesirable' for Haines to work in the legal profession. He may not be employed in any solicitor's practice or by any solicitor without SRA permission in future.

8.2.1 SRA warning notice, June 2015

With this in mind, it is perhaps not surprising that the SRA issued a warning notice in June 2015 about money missing from client account which included a description of the SRA's view of such an occurrence and the disciplinary issues which would follow. This is available on the SRA website and is also reproduced in **Appendix C1**.

8.2.2 Regulatory tools

The SRA uses a number of regulatory tools in an attempt to minimise the occurrence of risks connected to the holding of client money. Principle 10 of the SRA Principles 2011 is the obvious connection between misuse of money and regulatory behaviour, with its requirement that 'you must protect client money and assets'. This principle is reinforced by the SRA Accounts Rules 2011. Compliance with the Accounts Rules will support the achievement of Principle 10, as it is this section of the SRA Handbook which adds more detail to this high-level requirement.

However, it has to be said that breaches of the Accounts Rules remain the most significant reason for convictions of solicitors by the Solicitors Disciplinary Tribunal. For example, between January and August 2014, 29 per cent of substantiated allegations considered by the SDT related to Accounts Rules breaches, improper utilisation of client money and misappropriation offences. There are a number of reasons why this may be the case, including lack of understanding about what behaviours must be demonstrated in firms where client money is held.

Risk-based regulation therefore means that the managers, and in particular the COFA, must be satisfied that the level of understanding of the Accounts Rules and compliance rates are good. A connection also needs to be made with the requirements of entity-based regulation: everyone in the firm must understand what is required of them in order to ensure that breaches are kept under control. As mentioned at the beginning of the chapter, it would be foolish and worrying if anyone in the firm assumed that the Accounts Rules were relevant only to the accounts team.

In some ways, understanding what is needed to demonstrate compliance with the Accounts Rules is perhaps a more familiar experience than dealing with outcomes and behaviours in the SRA Code of Conduct 2011. This is because, for the time being, the Accounts Rules are in many ways the least outcomes-focused set of regulatory requirements in the SRA Handbook. In fact when they were added to the 2011 Handbook they were very little changed from what had previously been required in the Solicitors' Accounts Rules 1998; and those rules had not changed much from previous sets of requirements either. From this it may be concluded that there is very little excuse for non-compliance.

What we must comply with is a very long and detailed set of requirements with very precise conditions expressed in rule form which must be achieved. This will change in time; the SRA has announced that it will undertake a root and branch review of the purpose of the Accounts Rules and what is needed to keep client money safe. For the time being, however, we have been given a rest from pure outcomes-focused regulation and can enjoy the certainty which comes with such detailed requirements.

Because the Accounts Rules are so precise, it is likely that the COFA will be recording a number of breaches because of book-keeping or housekeeping-type errors, such as missing a time limit or similar. However much of an administration-based mistake this may be, and regardless of whether there is any actual detriment to the client, a breach is a breach and all such breaches must be recorded. With such information, the COFA needs to consider whether patterns of breaches create a problem because the scale of error creates a material breach situation. The COFA will always be considering how systems could improve compliance.

This change, and the role of the COFA in keeping the SRA advised of compliance, has meant that a number of firms have reviewed internal systems and controls to ensure that procedures are adopted to minimise the risk of breach and to create some better housekeeping standards. Everyone in the firm will want to be satisfied that they understand these requirements and can comply with the systems in the work that they do.

It helps to have a good knowledge of the Accounts Rules, an understanding of the language used, and an assessment of some of the common pitfalls.

8.3 THE PURPOSE OF THE ACCOUNTS RULES

The introduction to the SRA Accounts Rules 2011 contains an explanation about what will be achieved by complying with the contents:

- client money is safe;
- clients and the public have confidence that client money held by firms will be safe;
- firms are managed in such a way – and with appropriate systems and procedures in place – as to safeguard client money;
- client accounts are used for appropriate purposes only;
- the SRA is aware of issues in a firm relevant to the protection of client money.

Rule 1 of the Accounts Rules is also a useful guide or scene-setter, as it provides further explanation about what needs to happen when holding client money to ensure that the purpose of the Rules is met. If (or, we should probably say, *when*) the Account Rules are re-styled into an outcomes-focused sets of requirements, then the contents of rule 1 would probably be sufficient to explain what must be achieved. However, for the time being, the statements in rule 1 introduce the more detailed conditions which follow:

(a) keep other people's money separate from money belonging to *you* or *your firm*;
(b) keep other people's money safely in a *bank* or *building society* account identifiable as a *client account* (except when the rules specifically provide otherwise);
(c) use each *client's* money for that *client's* matters only;
(d) use money held as *trustee* of a *trust* for the purposes of that *trust* only;
(e) establish and maintain proper accounting systems, and proper internal controls over those systems, to ensure compliance with the rules;
(f) keep proper accounting records to show accurately the position with regard to the money held for each *client* and *trust*;
(g) account for *interest* on other people's money in accordance with the rules;
(h) co-operate with the *SRA* in checking compliance with the rules; and
(i) deliver annual accountant's reports as required by the rules.

8.4 DEFINED TERMS IN THE ACCOUNTS RULES

The Accounts Rules contain a number of defined terms and phrases which have very precise meanings and it will be hard to understand what is required in terms of compliance without first understanding this language.

The following terms are the most common, and must be understood:

- **Client money** – money held or received for a client or as trustee, and all other money which is not office money, which includes the following:

  12.2 money held or received:

  (a) as *trustee*;
  (b) as agent, bailee, stakeholder, or as the donee of a power of attorney, or as a liquidator, trustee in bankruptcy, *Court of Protection deputy* or trustee of an occupational pension scheme;
  (c) for payment of unpaid *professional disbursements*;
  (d) for payment of stamp duty land tax, Land Registry registration fees, telegraphic transfer fees and court fees …;
  (e) as a payment on account of *costs* generally;
  (f) as a financial benefit paid in respect of a *client*, unless the *client* has given *you* prior authority to retain it …;
  (g) jointly with another person outside the *firm*.

  12.2 Money held to the sender's order …
  12.4 An advance to a client which is paid into a client account …
  12.5 A cheque in respect of damages and costs, made payable to the client but paid into a client account under rule 14.2(e) …
  12.6 Endorsing a cheque or draft over to a *client* or employer in the course of practice amounts to receiving *client money*.

- **Office money** – includes:

  12.7 …

  (a) money held or received in connection with running the *firm*; for example, PAYE, or VAT on the *firm's fees*;
  (b) *interest* on *general client accounts*; the *bank* or *building society* should be instructed to credit such *interest* to the *office account* – but see also rule 14.2(d);
  (c) payments received in respect of:

    (i) *fees* due to the *firm* against a bill or written notification of *costs* incurred, which has been given or sent in accordance with rule 17.2;
    (ii) *disbursements* already paid by the *firm*;
    (iii) *disbursements* incurred but not yet paid by the *firm*, but excluding unpaid *professional disbursements*;
    (iv) money paid for or towards an *agreed fee*;

  (d) money held in a *client account* and earmarked for *costs* under rule 17.3;
  (e) money held or received from the Legal Aid Agency as a *regular payment*.

- **Out of scope money** – money held, or received, by a multi-disciplinary practice (MDP) in relation to activities which are not regulated activities. In truth, this is unlikely to be relevant to many people working in a law firm as an

MDP is an alternative business structure which provides a variety of services only some of which are regulated by the SRA.

- **Client account** – the account in which client money must be held. This must be either a bank account at a branch (or a bank's head office) in England and Wales or a building society account at a branch (or a society's head office) in England and Wales. The title of the account must include the name of the law firm and the word 'client'.
- **Separate designated client account** – an account for money relating to a single client, other person or trust, and which includes in its title, in addition to the name of the business and the word 'client', a reference to the identity of the client, other person or trust.
- **General client account** – any other client account in which several clients' money will be held.
- **Interest** – a sum in lieu of interest payable to the client in certain circumstances when money is held in client account.
- **Fees** – the law firm's own charges or profit.
- **Agreed fee** – a fee that is fixed at the outset. It cannot be varied upwards and it is not dependent on the transaction or matter being completed. There must be written evidence of an agreed fee.
- **Disbursement** – any sum spent or to be spent on behalf of the client or trust, including any VAT element.
- **Professional disbursements** – means in respect of those activities for which the practice is regulated by the SRA, the fees of counsel (barrister) or other lawyer, or of a professional or other agent or expert instructed by the firm, including the fees of interpreters, process servers, surveyors and estate agents, but not travel agents' charges.
- **Earmarking** – funds held in a client account which are used to settle the law firm's fees.
- **Without delay** – relating to the making of payments of client money into client account and means, in normal circumstances, either on the day of receipt or on the next working day.

8.5 COMMON PITFALLS LEADING TO BREACHES OF THE ACCOUNTS RULES

Once these defined terms and phrases are fully understood, it is necessary to be aware of the common pitfalls leading to breaches of the Accounts Rules which must be recorded, and in some cases, reported by the COFA to the SRA. These compliance hotspots are described below.

8.5.1 Operating a client account

All law firms which hold or receive client money must open a client account in which this money must be placed. The only exceptions are where the client money is dealt with in accordance with rules 8, 9, 15 or 16, namely where money is held in a different capacity (such as a trustee in bankruptcy, etc.), where money is held in a joint account, where client money is withheld from a client account on the client's instructions and where other client money is withheld from a client account.

The client account must be opened in accordance with rule 13, which sets out very specific requirements: it must be a bank account or a building society account at a branch (or a bank's or society's head office) in England and Wales and must be in the name of the current principal solicitor/REL or solicitors/RELs. The name of the account must also include the word 'client' in full. It would be a reportable breach of the Rules if this word was not included or even if the word were abbreviated to 'cl'.

There are two types of client account:

1. **Separate designated client account** – an account for money held in respect of a single client, other person or a trust and must include in its title (in addition to all other requirements) a reference to the client's identity.
2. **General client account** – an account where monies belonging to more than one client are kept.

Regardless of the type of client account, it is a requirement of the Accounts Rules that money must be immediately available unless the client gives contrary instructions or the circumstances clearly indicate otherwise. This means that clients are entitled to call for their money at any time during the working day.

8.5.2 Use of the client account

Use of the client account is strictly regulated in accordance with rule 14.

Rule 14.1

Client money must be paid without delay into the client account (except where the Accounts Rules permit otherwise). 'Without delay' is defined in the SRA Handbook Glossary 2012 as meaning 'in normal circumstances, either on the day of receipt or on the next working day'. Difficulties, and an automatic breach, occurs where there is a delay for whatever reason, so care needs to be taken when money is received from a client over the reception counter, in the form of cheques received by post, or during client meetings, that the money is received by the accounts team and paid into the client account in good time.

Rule 14.2

Only client money may be paid into or held in a client account, except in other very specific circumstances as listed in the Accounts Rules such as where an amount of the solicitor's own money is required to open or maintain the account and money is deposited to replace any sum which for any reason has been drawn from the account in breach of the Rules. This makes it very important that everyone understands whether they are handling client money or office money (and sometimes this is not so obvious as it may be imagined) and communicates necessary information to the accounts team.

Rule 14.3

Client money must be returned to the client (or other person on whose behalf the money is held) promptly, as soon as there is no longer any proper reason to retain those funds. Payments received after you have already accounted to the client, for example by way of a refund, must be paid to the client promptly. This means that file closure routines are very sensible. Not only does housekeeping at the end of the matter mean that information about the residual relationship with the client (or to be more precise, the former client) can be explained and original documents can be returned to that client and archiving can be undertaken, it also provides an opportunity for the client balance can be cleared at a time when there is still a relationship and contact with that client.

Rule 14.4

The solicitor must promptly inform a client (or other person on whose behalf the money is held) in writing of the amount of any client money retained at the end of a matter (or the substantial conclusion of a matter), and the reason for that retention. The client (or other person) must be informed in writing at least once every 12 months thereafter of the amount of client money still held and the reason for the retention, for as long as the solicitor continues to hold that money. This requirement is often overlooked. Fee earners should have back-up systems to ensure that these monies and the need to correspond with clients, or third parties on their behalf, is kept under review. They can be assisted in this duty by support staff and accounts colleagues provided that they are made aware of this money and the purpose for which it is being held.

Rule 14.5

The client account must not be used for banking facilities. Payments into, and transfers or withdrawals from, a client account must be in respect of instructions relating to an underlying transaction (and the funds arising therefrom) or to a service forming part of the solicitor's normal regulated activities.

8.5.3 Use of client account for banking purposes

The final part of rule 14 was a significant change from previous versions of the Accounts Rules and makes it clear that solicitors should hold client money only where there is a specific need arising from the legal services. It is not the role of a law firm, or any manager or employee of a law firm, to provide banking facilities and in fact this is one of the most alarming things that could happen in terms of the services provided to clients.

Previously this had been expressed as guidance and the fact that it was one of the few significant changes in the 2011 Rules cannot be underestimated. Its elevation to a mandatory rule reflects many decisions made by the SDT that support the position that banking is not a proper service. Examples of the severity of such a mistake are shown in various cases which have come before the SDT, notably the case of *Wood* v. *Burdett* (SDT 8669/2002). Using a solicitor's client account for services other than those arising from legal activities is also likely to increase the risk of being involved – either knowingly or unwittingly – in money laundering and other fraudulent activities.

Such is the risk of using the client account for banking purposes that the SRA issued a warning notice and case studies in December 2014 to provide some much-needed guidance on the subject. Anyone in the firm could place the business at risk of breaking both the law and regulatory restrictions by their actions and perhaps by not being alert to warning signs or unusual requests from clients and third parties. The notice is produced in full in **Appendix C2**.

The supporting case studies are available on the SRA website (**www.sra.org.uk/solicitors/code-of-conduct/guidance/case-study/improper-use-client-account-banking-facility.page**) and examples are given of activities which may place individuals and the law firm at risk of being seen as providing banking facilities. The examples given are:

- allowing a client's customers to use the law firm client account in terms of the client's business;
- providing execution-only escrow agency services;
- providing services which have little legal service content to private clients (such as the payment of household expenses from money deposited in client account for that purpose when the client is abroad); and
- making payments out of client account to hide such payments from third parties (such as to hold funds to avoid declarations in divorce proceedings).

8.6 PAYMENTS IN RESPECT OF YOUR FEES

Money received in respect of legal fees is office money. Quite often difficulties arise because the firm receives a mixed payment of office and client money and must ensure that the strict requirements of the Accounts Rules are met in terms of where the different types of money are placed.

Therefore, getting this right requires a knowledge of the composition of the sum received and how this should be handled. Compliance with rules 17, 18 and 19 is necessary. These sections of the Accounts Rules give law firms a number of options about receipt of funds:

- Determine the composition of the money and decide what is office money, out of scope money and client account and deal with it in the following way:
  - if it is only office money and/or out of scope money, it must be placed in office account;
  - if it is only client money, it must be placed in client account;
  - if it is a mixture of different types of money it must be treated in accordance with rule 18 which relates to the receipt of mixed payments, or alternatively in the way described below.
- Where rule 18 is not followed, and the sum is a mixed payment then:
  - if the sum is only office money and/or out of scope money and/or client money in the form of professional disbursements which have been incurred but not yet paid then the entire sum can be paid into office account but the unpaid professional disbursement must be paid by the end of the second working day following receipt or a sum in the correct amount must be transferred to client account, or
  - the entire amount must be paid into client account and the office money and/or out of scope money must be transferred out of client account within 14 days.
- Rule 18 allows for two alternatives on receipt of mixed payments:
  - to split the sum between office account and client account as appropriate; or
  - to place the entire sum into client account without delay and then transfer non-client money to office account within 14 days.
- Costs received from the Legal Aid Agency may be paid into office account in accordance with rule 19.
- Cheques in respect of damages and costs, made payable to the client, are paid into the client account pursuant to the Society's Conditional Fee Agreement but the costs element must be transferred out of client account within 14 days of receipt.

We have already made the point that the correct response requires an understanding of a good number of factors including the types of money held. This means that teamwork on the part of fee earners, support staff and bill draftsmen, who need to communicate key information to their accounts team colleagues is essential.

8.7 EARMARKING

Earmarking is another source of Account Rules breaches because it is an often misunderstood right arising in respect of the transfer of costs from client to office account. The process is described in rules 17.2 and 17.3.

Earmarking describes the position where funds are being held in client account on account of costs generally. At the time that this is properly required for the firm's fees, a bill or some other written notification of the amount must be sent to the client. At this point the money becomes earmarked and is treated as office money which must be transferred out of client account within a strict 14-day time period.

The term 'properly' in the rule implies that the work has actually been done, but this may be at the end of the matter or at an interim stage when the firm is entitled to take the money for costs.

Money is 'earmarked' for costs under rule 17.2 and 17.3 when you decide to use funds already held in client account to settle your bill. You do not need client consent to this transfer and sometimes a breach of the Rules occurs because this is sought unnecessarily. In fact, if you wish to obtain the client's prior approval, you will need to agree the amount to be taken with your client before issuing the bill to avoid the possibility of failing to meet the 14-day time limit for making the transfer out of client account. If you wish to retain the funds, for example, as money on account of costs on another matter, you will need to ask the client to send the full amount in settlement of the bill. If, when submitting a bill, you fail to indicate whether you intend to take your costs from client account, or expect the client to make a payment, you will be regarded as having 'earmarked' your costs.

Again, this is another example of the risk of breach being minimised through effective and timely communication between fee earners and support staff and the accounts team.

8.8 WITHDRAWALS FROM CLIENT ACCOUNT

Of equal importance as the use of client account and the appropriate circumstances in which client money should be handled, is compliance with the requirements relating to withdrawals from client account. This is set out in rules 20 and 21 of the Accounts Rules.

Rule 20 sets out very specific and controlled circumstances in which client money may be withdrawn from a client account, including the following scenarios:

- Where the money is properly required for a payment to or on behalf of the client (or other person on whose behalf the money is being held).
- Where the money is properly required for payment of a disbursement on behalf of the client.
- Where the money is properly required in full or partial reimbursement of money the solicitor has spent on behalf of the client.

A number of people in the firm could be involved in a process or service which triggers the need to request the use of funds from client account. In order to avoid a breach of the very strict controls and safeguards, it is important to be satisfied that not only is the payment properly required as specified by rule 20, but also that the correct procedure is used to enable this to happen.

This is in rule 21 which sets out the requirements relating to methods of and authorisation for withdrawals from client account, including the following: a withdrawal from a client account may be made only after a specific authority in respect of that withdrawal has been signed by an appropriate person or persons in accordance with the firm's procedures for signing on client account.

An authority for withdrawals from client account may be signed electronically, subject to appropriate safeguards and control. There must be appropriate systems and procedures governing withdrawals from client account, including who should be permitted to sign on client account.

The SRA allows each firm to decide who will be the authorised signatory. The only advice is in the form of the non-mandatory guidance notes to rule 21:

> A firm should select suitable people to authorise withdrawals from the client account. Firms will wish to consider whether any employee should be able to sign on client account, and whether signing rights should be given to all managers of the practice or limited to those managers directly involved in providing legal services. Someone who has no day-to-day involvement in the business of the practice is unlikely to be regarded as a suitable signatory because of the lack of proximity to client matters. An appropriate understanding of the requirements of the rules is essential.

A signatory must be confident that they can keep themselves compliant and the firm safe when fulfilling this function. A procedure is usually established so that checks can be made as to why the withdrawal is required and that there is in fact client money belonging to the particular client which can be used. Anyone requesting a withdrawal will want to consider similar compliance issues. The firm's systems will specify how a withdrawal should be evidenced and what documentation must be completed and it would be foolhardy to ignore these or attempt shortcuts.

8.9 INTEREST

One of the few changes introduced in the latest version of the Accounts Rules related to the payment of a sum in lieu of interest to clients in appropriate circumstances. Previously, interest payments of this type were subject to very strict specifications imposed by the regulator and which had to be followed by all firms where relevant.

In the 2011 Rules, each firm is required to consider rules 22–25 and note the following regulatory requirements:

- When money is held in client account for a client or a person funding all or part of the firm's legal fees or a trust, the firm must account to that client for interest when it is fair and reasonable to do so.
- Each firm must have a written interest policy which seeks to provide a fair income.
- The policy must be drawn to a client's attention at the beginning of the instructions unless it is inappropriate to do so in the circumstances.

This is a nod to the outcomes-focused approach because the rule is allowing flexibility in approach so that the method of achievement can be the firm's decision. The requirements will be relevant to anyone in a fee-earning or support role in terms of the need to bring details of the interest policy (or not as the case may be) to an individual client's attention. It will also be necessary for the accounts team to ensure that the interest policy is applied when appropriate.

8.10 ACCOUNTING SYSTEMS AND RECORDS

The holding of client money and the operation of a client account triggers the need to have accounting systems and records for the purposes of compliance with Part 4 of the Accounts Rules.

8.10.1 Accounting procedures and systems

Rule 26 of the Accounts Rules sets out guidelines for accounting procedures and systems and states that the SRA may publish guidelines to assist with compliance with Parts 1–4 of the Rules. These guidelines are in Appendix 3 to the Accounts Rules (see **Appendix B3**).

8.10.2 Records

Rule 29 requires that there are properly written up accounting records which show the dealings with client money and any office money, with client money appropriately recorded in a client cash account or in a record of sums transferred from one client ledger account to another; and on the client side of a separate client ledger account for each client. All dealings with office money relating to any client matter, must be appropriately recorded in an office cash account and on the office side of the appropriate client ledger account. The current balance on each client ledger account must always be shown, or be readily ascertainable.

Holding client money (in a general client account or separate designated client account, or any joint account, or any account which is not a client account in which client money is held or any office account maintained in relation to the same) triggers a need for obtaining bank or building society statements as the case may be. Rule 29.11 stipulates that a solicitor holding client money must, at least every five weeks, either obtain hard copy statements (or duplicate statements permitted in lieu of the originals) from banks, building societies or other financial institutions, or obtain and save in the accounting records, in a format which cannot be altered, an electronic version of the bank's, building society's or other financial institution's online record. Each statement or electronic version must begin at the end of the previous statement. Failure to keep such records would be a reportable breach of the Accounts Rules.

Reconciliations must take place at least once every five weeks to compare the balance on the client cash account(s) with the balances shown on the statements and passbooks (after allowing for all unpresented items) of all general client accounts and separate designated client accounts. In addition, you are obliged to carry out a reconciliation of any account which is not a client account but in which you hold client money under rule 15.1(a) or rule 16.1(d), and any client money held by you in cash. At the same date, the reconciliation process must include the preparation of a list of all the balances shown by the client ledger accounts of the liabilities to clients (and other persons, and trusts) and compare the total of those balances with the balance on the client cash account; and also include a preparation of a reconciliation statement. This statement must show the cause of the difference, if any, revealed by each of the above comparisons.

In addition, you must keep readily accessible a central record or file of copies of all bills given or sent by you (other than those relating entirely to activities not regulated by the SRA); and all other written notifications of costs given or sent by you (other than those relating entirely to activities not regulated by the SRA).

The following records must be kept for six years:

- all accounting records in respect of client money;
- reconciliations;
- bank/building society statements;
- bills/notification of costs.

The following records must be kept for two years:

- originals/copies of all authorities other than cheques for the withdrawal of client monies;
- all original paid cheques or digital images of the front and back of cheques, unless there is written agreement with the bank or building society that it will retain these on behalf of the lawyer.

The need to comply with this part of the Accounts Rules is largely the responsibility of the accounts team and they will have the skills needed to apply safe book-keeping practice and record-keeping. However, as with so much else in these Rules, a major element of successful compliance will boil down to good communication between the team and colleagues in other roles, in particular where those colleagues can help by being very specific about timekeeping and reasons for dealings with client money.

8.11 CONCLUSION

While many people, not least solicitors, working in the law firm did not seek such a job with accountancy and book-keeping at the forefront of their minds, working in this environment does require a consideration of the importance of protecting client money. Everyone plays a role in keeping client money safe, not least through an awareness of the personal and firm-based obligations and being aware of what systems to follow and when it is necessary to have a discussion about concerns with the firm's COFA.

CHAPTER 9

Practising certificates, job titles and the risks of holding out

9.1 INTRODUCTION

So far in this book we have provided an overview of the SRA Handbook and examined in more detail those sections of the toolkit which apply to everyone employed in a law firm because they contain the basic behaviours which must be demonstrated.

To recap, therefore, regardless of role, everyone must understand and comply with the following SRA standards and requirements:

- **Authorisation Rules** – because failure to comply may place the firm's continuing authorisation at risk.
- **Principles** – because these are the basic ethical behaviours expected of everyone.
- **Code of Conduct** – because these explain the ethical response which will be expected when faced with different situations.
- **Accounts Rules** – because these explain how client money must be treated.

The rest of the content of the SRA Handbook must be considered and applied on a need-to-know basis and whether or not the sections are relevant will depend on role, what services the firm provides and similar considerations. In many firms, these elements have been assessed by the managers and compliance officers, who will put systems and processes in place to manage requirements. Everyone in the firm will want to be confident that they know what other parts of the SRA Handbook are relevant and what they are expected to do to keep themselves and the firm safe.

9.2 HOLDING OUT AND JOB TITLES

When looking at these other sections, the SRA Practice Framework Rules 2011 are of particular interest to solicitors as they set out the regulatory restrictions on how we can practice and also our need to hold a practising certificate.

Rule 9 of the Practice Framework Rules states that if an individual is practising as a solicitor then (subject to one specific exemption which can be used by a very small percentage of in-house solicitors), they must hold a current practising certificate. This requirement stems from a statutory requirement in the Solicitors Act 1974 so that practising without a certificate will be a criminal offence unless the exemption can be relied on.

In addition the person committing the offence will be in breach of the SRA's requirements and this fact would need to be disclosed to the regulator who would undoubtedly take enforcement action. This could have repercussions for the firm employing the individual and, in particular, the managers and the Compliance Officer for Legal Practice. Bear in mind that one of the COLP's duties in the Authorisation Rules is to 'ensure compliance with any statutory obligations of the body, its managers, employees or interest holders in relation to the body's carrying on of authorised activities'.

For the purposes of this book, it is important to know about this legal and regulatory position for the following reasons:

- anyone who has been admitted to the roll of solicitors must consider their personal position if they are working in a law firm; and
- in this situation anyone working in a law firm must be confident that their role does not trigger the need for a practising certificate.

9.3 PRACTISING CERTIFICATES

Such is the importance of making the right decision, the SRA reissued guidance (**www.sra.org.uk/solicitors/code-of-conduct/guidance/guidance/practising-certificate/working-private-practice-england-wales.page**) on the topic in 2014. The following is an extract from the guidance which must be borne in mind when considering the position of admitted individuals (i.e. individuals on the roll of solicitors) in SRA-authorised law firms:

> you must have a practising certificate if you are:
>
> - a sole practitioner
> - a manager or a member or (subject to the exception referred to below) you have an ownership interest in an authorised body, either directly or through an EU corporate practice which is a manager in the firm
> - an employee, consultant or locum of a recognised sole practitioner or an authorised body if you are on the roll and you are employed in connection with the provision of legal services
>
> and your involvement in the firm must be as a practising solicitor, even if you are not employed in that capacity. ...
>
> For example, you will need a practising certificate if you are employed:
>
> - as a practice manager if your responsibilities include any supervision of fee-earners or dealing with complaints relating to the handling of client matters
> - to provide practice support if you do any of the following:
>   - undertake research in connection with client matters
>   - draft or keep up-dated legal precedents

  - select, adapt or direct fee-earners to precedents
- as a bookkeeper in the firm's accounts department, if your responsibilities include entering information on to the accounts system in compliance with the SRA Accounts Rules 2011
- to carry out conflict checks, since this is part of the legal service provided to the clients of the firm
- as a secretary if you do work for fee-earners, but not, for example, if you only undertake work for the firm's Human Resources Department
- as a paralegal

In each of the above examples, you would be employed in connection with the provision of legal services and must therefore hold a practising certificate, even if you are not held out (or paid) as a solicitor.

Examples

Coming off the roll

Q1. I am on the roll, but am currently unemployed and I do not have a practising certificate. I have been asked by a local firm to provide holiday cover for one of their solicitors for two weeks. The firm is obviously not prepared to pay for a practising certificate for such a short period. Can I do the work without a practising certificate?

Yes, but not as a solicitor on the roll. Whilst you remain on the roll, both rule 11 PFR and section 1A Solicitors Act 1974 means that you must do the work as a solicitor with a practising certificate, even though the work is only temporary.

To avoid this, you can apply to come off the roll via **mySRA**. However:

- you would need to ensure that you are not held out in a way which suggests that you are entitled to practise as a solicitor; this includes no longer being described as a solicitor (although you could be described as a 'former solicitor' or 'retired former solicitor') and avoiding terms which suggest that you are a lawyer (such as 'consultant', 'associate' or 'assistant'), unless you make your status clear by adding words such as 'non-lawyer'
- with regard to the legal work which you can do, please see rule 7.1(b–g) PFR

Employment as a paralegal

Q3. I recently lost my job as an assistant solicitor in private practice. I have now been offered a job as a paralegal and would like to accept. Is there any problem with this?

No, but your participation in the firm must be as a solicitor and you must therefore continue to hold a practicing certificate (rule 11.1(c) PFR and section 1A Solicitors Act 1974).

This does not mean that you cannot be held out, or paid, as a paralegal; the rule allows for this possibility, but there may be circumstances when to be described as a paralegal could be misleading. Both you and your firm therefore need to consider whether you are able to achieve outcome (8.1) of the SRA Code of Conduct 2011 in this respect (misleading publicity).

For example, you may be at risk under Principle 6 (maintaining public trust in the profession and provision of legal services) and outcome (8.1) if, whilst employed in the role of a paralegal, you undertake work relying on your qualification as a solicitor (for example, to appear in court) in the course of the same employment.

Alternatively, you could come off the roll – see Q1 above.

9.3.1 Retirement

The SRA has also produced additional guidance which deals with the not uncommon situation in which a solicitor retires from practice but retains a connection with his or her business by remaining on the firm's notepaper as a consultant. The SRA says:

> If you are completely retired but remain on the roll, you may continue to be on your firm's notepaper as a consultant and will not need a practising certificate provided it is made clear on the notepaper that you are not practising (eg by adding words such as 'non-practising' or 'retired' solicitor).

However, this means that you cannot undertake any legal work, so bear in mind that if you were asked to do the odd bit of work for the firm or supervise fee earners by way of holiday cover, you would be taken to be practising by virtue of the Solicitors Act 1974, s.1A and rules 9 and 11 of the PFR and would have to have a practising certificate or come off the roll.

9.3.2 Delegation of compliance tasks

It is unlikely that managers will do all the routine work necessary to ensure that there is statutory compliance. It will be delegated to other members of the business, so if such delegation is not going to put the firm at risk, it is essential that an admitted person's certification position is correctly established. People who are employed as solicitors, even in the circumstances mentioned above in the SRA guidance, must hold a current practising certificate. This must be checked with the SRA and it is usually sufficient to check an individual's name on the 'Find a Solicitor' website (**http://solicitors.lawsociety.org.uk**).

9.4 ISSUES FOR NON-SOLICITOR MANAGERS AND EMPLOYEES

It is a criminal offence for someone to call themselves a solicitor or act as a solicitor if they are not on the roll of solicitors. The SRA uses the phrase 'bogus solicitors' to describe these people and has the power to prosecute them. Because of the criminal implications, and also for a whole variety of regulatory reasons, it is important that non-solicitors do not hold themselves out as solicitors. Unfortunately, this is not as simple as not calling yourself a solicitor.

A number of job titles and descriptions will be risky in that they may carry an implication or assumption that the person is a solicitor. For example, using any of the following job titles imply a professional qualification as a lawyer which cannot be negated by adding such words as 'non-solicitor' or 'non-practising solicitor', etc: solicitor, lawyer, counsel, attorney or legal practitioner.

The SRA Handbook Glossary 2012 defines a lawyer in the following terms:

> **lawyer** means a member of one of the following professions, entitled to practise as such:

(i) the profession of solicitor, barrister or advocate of the UK;
(ii) a profession whose members are authorised to carry on *legal activities* by an *approved regulator* other than the SRA;
(iii) an *Establishment Directive profession* other than a UK profession;
(iv) a legal profession which has been approved by the SRA for the purpose of *recognised bodies* in England and Wales; and
(v) any other regulated legal profession specified by the SRA for the purpose of this definition.

This will be significant for non-solicitors but otherwise qualified lawyers who will not only need to understand SRA regulation (because they are employed in a SRA-authorised business) but also understand and comply with the requirements of their own regulatory body.

An additional complication arises in respect of the firm's publicity and the need not to mislead clients or the public about an individual manager's or employee's status or qualifications. In chapter 8 of the SRA Code of Conduct 2011 the outcome (8.1) which must be achieved is that:

> your *publicity* in relation to your *firm* . . . is accurate and not misleading, and is not likely to diminish the trust the public places in you and in the provision of legal services.

As the term 'publicity' is italicised, it is a defined term for regulatory purposes and:

> includes all promotional material and activity, including the name or description of your *firm*, stationery, advertisements, brochures, websites, directory entries, media appearances, promotional press releases, and direct approaches to potential *clients* and other *persons*, whether conducted in person, in writing, or in electronic form, but does not include press releases prepared on behalf of a *client*.

The chapter 8 indicative behaviours give clues as to what would tend to show the outcomes had been achieved (or not as the case may be). Indicative behaviour 8.12 shows the importance of making the status of managers and employees clear: 'producing misleading information concerning the professional status of any manager or employee of your firm' tends to indicate that the outcomes had not been achieved. This extends to using misleading job titles, making the firm appear larger by the way that the staff details are represented in publicity, and not making it clear about who is, or is not, a manager in the business.

Turning again to non-solicitor but otherwise qualified lawyers, they need to bear in mind any restrictions imposed by their own regulatory bodies in terms of job titles and descriptions. A case in point is the position of legal executives. Most law firms employ legal executives but care must be taken in terms of how they are described, not only to ensure that there are no repercussions in terms of the relationship with the SRA, but also to take into account the requirements of their own regulatory body, CILEx Regulation (previously known as ILEX Professional Standards).

The following is an extract from guidance originally published in the *CILEX Journal* (October 2012) and is useful advice not only for members of the Chartered

Institute of Legal Executives but also anyone in a law firm involved in communicating with clients, human resources or marketing functions.

What can I call myself?

Only Fellows may refer to themselves as Chartered Legal Executives or lawyers.

The term 'Chartered Legal Executive' is a protected title, so only practising Fellows of The Chartered Institute of Legal Executives may refer to themselves as such. However, the title 'legal executive' is not protected by law, therefore anyone who is not a member of CILEx may use the term.

There is an issue about people misleading the public, but ILEX Professional Standards (IPS) has no remit over non-members and cannot take any action. Some law firms do call their employees 'legal executives' when they are not. If a consumer was misled by this and thought they were receiving advice from a qualified lawyer, and if their complaint to the firm was not resolved to their satisfaction, they could report the firm to the Legal Ombudsman or the Solicitors Regulation Authority (SRA).

Under the Legal Services Act 2007, 'Fellows' fall within the definition of 'authorised person'. Other members do not. A member who is not a Fellow will be in breach of the Code of Conduct for CILEx members if they call themselves a Chartered Legal Executive, and may find themselves subject to disciplinary action by IPS.

It is a criminal offence to hold yourself out as a solicitor and the SRA will take action against people calling themselves a solicitor when they are not. IPS would also take action against a member calling him or herself a solicitor where they are not dual qualified.

What about other job titles?

A lawyer is a person qualified to practise law, so only fully qualified Fellows can call themselves a lawyer. IPS could take action against a member who is not a Fellow but is calling him or herself a lawyer.

The term 'counsel' is not protected by law. However, we would advise members against using it as it is misleading to the public, as in the UK 'counsel' is still much equated with barrister. IPS or the Bar Standards Board might take action against a member calling themselves 'counsel'. This is a term more likely to be used in-house by international firms who equate 'counsel' with 'lawyer'.

Litigation executive is an acceptable title for any member employed to do litigation work. It does not equate to holding out as a Fellow.

With other job titles, so long as they do not breach the rules outlined above and are not misleading to the public, they are acceptable.

Principle 5 of the Code of Conduct for CILEx members states that you have an obligation to act in the best interests of your client. The guidance to this principle states that you must ensure that your client understands your professional status.

This behaviour also has connections with client care conduct requirements and the indicative behaviours in chapter 1 of the SRA code that suggest identifying the name and status of fee earners, and their supervisors, supports compliance.

CHAPTER 10

Key legislation for law firms

10.1 INTRODUCTION

The SRA Code of Conduct 2011 contains a requirement at outcome 7.5, which must be achieved by all solicitors and everyone working in a law firm authorised by the SRA. This is that:

> you must comply with legislation applicable to your business, including anti-money laundering and data protection issues.

This means that law firms (and usually this means the managers and the compliance team) must identify the legislation that is relevant to the business.

Some laws will be relevant because of the type of services which are provided to clients, so that for example conveyancers need to understand the Law of Property Act 1925 and other similar legislation. Not only will such legislation be relevant in the context of achieving outcome 7.5, but they must also be borne in mind in relation to some of the client care outcomes in the Code, including the mandatory requirement that 'the service you provide to clients is competent' or, in other words, you have the necessary knowledge of relevant legislation in order to provide a competent service to your client. Overall, knowledge of legislation will support achievement of Principle 5 (you must provide a proper standard of service to your clients).

Other laws will be relevant because of the type of business which is authorised, so that for example a limited company providing legal services must ensure that there is compliance with the various Companies Acts.

However, in addition to firm-specific requirements, there are also some key pieces of legislation which are relevant to all law firms, and everyone working in them, simply because they are trading and living in the United Kingdom and there must be compliance with the law of the land. These laws must be observed if there is going to be a demonstration that the mandatory outcome in the Code has been achieved. The legislation imposes personal duties on individuals as well as a number of corporate offences.

In this chapter, we provide a commentary on this type of legislation which is likely to be relevant regardless of the specific type of employment. Anyone working in a law firm ignores these laws at their peril; not only would there be legal consequences but there is a strong overlap with regulatory duties.

10.2 MONEY LAUNDERING

Most readers of this book will be familiar with the subject of money laundering or, more accurately, the anti-money laundering procedures which firms must operate in order to avoid the risk of committing various criminal offences. Training on anti-money laundering is one of the regular training exercises in many law firms and the areas where almost everyone in the firm is invited to participate. This is because firms recognise that there is a need to ensure that all managers and employees understand what checks must be made of clients and their instructions in order to keep itself safe and to be able to identify what warning signs would create red risk flags for the business.

It goes without saying that money laundering and terrorist financing are two of the major global concerns of the twenty-first century. UK legislation is designed to be compatible with international safeguards and deterrents and also to provide a network of information about such criminal activity. No one can say with any accuracy how much money is laundered in the United Kingdom, although guestimates put the figure at around £57 billion per year. Unfortunately for us, solicitors and law firms are often attractive and useful targets for criminals wishing to launder their dirty money.

In terms of risk management, and the prioritisation of risk events, money laundering is one of the most worrying issues for the regulator. In SRA risk publications, and its own assessment of the severity of events which may happen in a law firm, money laundering by a law firm is one of the worst risk events. Poor controls, lack of procedure to collect data about money laundering, and inconsistent reporting of knowledge or suspicion of money laundering are of major concern not only to the regulator but also to other third parties which look to the legal profession to assist as an effective deterrent against this type of criminal conduct.

The fact that we are under scrutiny is apparent in a number of ways:

- The National Crime Agency (NCA) issued a warning notice to the legal profession in 2014, flagging up poor reporting practice in terms of the duty to suspicious activity reports to it. The NCA was concerned about both the poor quality content of such reports and the small number of reports which it received from law firms.
- The SRA undertook a thematic review of anti-money laundering practice in SRA-authorised law firms, which ran from September 2014 to May 2015. Five hundred law firms were visited as part of a programme to ascertain what risk management procedures were in operation and to gather information about poor and best practice. The report findings will be released in autumn 2015 but it is clear that examination and scrutiny of this area of practice will continue.

The key pieces of legislation are the Proceeds of Crime Act 2002, the Terrorism Act 2000 and the Money Laundering Regulations 2007.

10.3 PROCEEDS OF CRIME ACT 2002

The Proceeds of Crime Act 2002 (POCA) is designed principally with money laundering in mind. Money laundering can be described in the following way: it is the process by which the proceeds of crime, and the true ownership of those proceeds, are changed so that they have the appearance of coming from legitimate sources.

Everyone in the United Kingdom must comply with POCA, both in their personal lives and in their working environment. Managers and employees in SRA-authorised law firms will need to be vigilant about this in terms of their employment, and with regard to the activities and behaviours of their clients. Being used for money laundering purposes is regarded as a high-risk activity by the SRA but unfortunately solicitors and law firms are often attractive bedfellows for criminals, both because of our client account facilities and the fact that, as a profession, we can do much to help the criminals to use their dirty money.

Money laundering occurs after criminal property has been obtained and before it can be used by the criminal. An example of this would be the situation where a criminal has robbed a bank and has the proceeds of his crime (known as criminal property) in his possession. Not being able to use the money in this form, it is necessary to disguise the fact that the money is the result of a robbery. This is why criminal property needs to be laundered.

The criminal needs the help of other people to launder the money. The stages of money laundering are described as three connected processes: placement, integration and layering:

1. Cash generated from crime is placed in the financial system.
2. When the proceeds of crime are in the financial system, layering obscures their origins by passing the money through complex transactions.
3. When the origin of the funds has been obscured, the criminal is able to make the funds reappear as legitimate funds or assets.

The principal offences are set out in POCA, ss.327–329:

- **Section 327 (Concealing).** An offence is committed if a person conceals, disguises, converts, or transfers criminal property, or removes criminal property from England and Wales, Scotland or Northern Ireland. Concealing or disguising criminal property includes concealing or disguising its nature, source, location, disposition, movement, ownership or any rights connected with it.
- **Section 328 (Arrangements).** An offence is committed if a person enters into, or becomes concerned in an arrangement which they know or suspect facilitates the acquisition, retention, use or control of criminal property by or on behalf of another person.
- **Section 329 (Acquisition, use or possession).** An offence is committed if a person acquires, uses or has possession of criminal property.

The penalties are severe, with a maximum prison sentence of 14 years and/or fining powers.

Solicitors in private practice have traditionally been easy targets for money launderers who are attracted to the endless possibilities which a law firm's client accounts can give them to launder dirty money.

Knowledge, or suspicion, of any of the above offences may result in the individual being implicated in a money laundering offence with the double whammy of repercussions that this will create; first, a criminal offence under the legislation and, secondly, a regulatory offence because of the breach of the SRA Handbook requirements in terms of compliance with this legislation.

We have a number of examples of solicitors both unwittingly and knowingly assisting criminals and facing criminal and regulatory consequences as a result.

These are serious considerations and solicitors found at fault of assisting in money laundering offences have been prosecuted and disciplined. Take for example the Serious Organised Crime Agency (now the National Crime Agency) case of James Thorburn Muirhead (*Gazette* [2011] 20 July), a sole practitioner who was given a 16-month prison sentence after pleading guilty to four counts of theft and false accounting, and one count of failing to disclose:

> Thorburn-Muirhead was the subject of an investigation by the Serious Organised Crime Agency (SOCA) after suspicions about his relationship with a convicted drug trafficker.
>
> A search of his offices and home address in July 2007 resulted in the seizure of several hundred conveyancing files along with accounting records and computers.
>
> The evidence linked Thorburn-Muirhead with the dealer and also pointed to misappropriation of money from clients' accounts.
>
> At Kingston Crown Court, the solicitor's benefit from criminal conduct was agreed at just over £196,000 and a confiscation order was made for that amount, payable within nine months.
>
> A two-year default sentence will apply if he fails to meet that deadline, and he will still be liable to pay the sum. He was also ordered to pay a Compensation Order of £12,666.67 and will pay £25,000 towards prosecution costs.
>
> Regional head of investigation for SOCA, Chris Farrimond, said: 'Muirhead was a professional in a position of trust which he abused for personal benefit. He was derelict in his legal obligations to his clients, regulators and to law enforcement.
>
> 'This case should be a deterrent to anyone in the regulated sector who may be tempted to work with criminals or turn a blind eye to criminality; the short-term gains seem attractive, but the long-term effects for your career and profession are anything but.'
>
> Thorburn & Co was officially closed by the Solicitors Regulation Authority in July 2009.

Mr Muirhead's conduct was referred by the SRA to the SDT (*SRA* v. *Thorburn-Muirhead*, SDT 10409-2009). Mr Muirhead was struck off the roll of solicitors and ordered to pay costs of £35,263.52.

Neither the law nor the SRA distinguishes greatly between dishonesty and naivety as a cause of a breach of the legislation. That this is the case is shown through the circumstances explored in the case of *R* v. *Phillip Griffiths and Leslie Pattinson* [2006] EWCA Crim 2155.

EXAMPLE 10.1 – Phillip Griffiths

Phillip Griffiths was a solicitor practising in Shrewsbury. He received instructions to act for Leslie Pattinson who was buying a house for £43,000. The house was worth £150,000 but had a mortgage on it for £43,000. Griffiths appreciated that the transaction was at an undervalue but accepted an explanation from Pattinson as to why this was the position: he was told that Pattinson had some friends in financial difficulties and he wanted to help them by buying out the mortgage.

In fact, Pattinson was buying the house for drug dealers who had been convicted and were awaiting sentence. The transaction was an attempt to hide assets and to avoid confiscation proceedings. Before the transaction completed, Griffiths was served with a production order and required to hand over information from his files. Pattinson was convicted of entering into a money laundering arrangement by agreeing to buy a house at an undervalue in an attempt to avoid confiscation proceedings. Griffiths was found guilty of failing to report reasonable suspicions of money laundering despite it being held by the court that the transaction showed clear signs of being unusual. He was sentenced to 15 months in prison which was reduced on appeal to six months. In turn, his behaviour was investigated by the regulator and he was referred to the SDT.

10.4 MONEY LAUNDERING REGULATIONS 2007

Everyone must comply with POCA but this is not the case with the Money Laundering Regulations 2007, SI 2007/2157 (MLR) as these are of relevance only to those working in the 'regulated sector' on 'relevant business'. The terms are defined in the following ways. The regulated sector is carrying on business in the UK in credit institutions, financial institutions, as auditors, insolvency practitioners, external accountants and tax advisers, independent legal professionals, trust or company service providers, estate agents, high value dealers and casinos.

In such a position a judgment must be made as to whether the law firm is required to comply with the MLR because of the type of activities that they undertake or, in other words, whether the law firm is carrying on relevant business. Relevant business will be in evidence when solicitors and law firms participate in financial or real property transactions involving the following:

- buying and selling of real property or business entities;
- managing of client money, securities or other assets;
- opening or management of bank, savings or securities accounts;
- organisation of contributions necessary for the creation, operation or management of companies;
- creation, operation or management of trusts, companies or similar structures.

Relevant business does not include giving legal advice, litigation and will-writing services.

In most law firms, with a number of different departments, some teams will be undertaking relevant business and others will not. The firm needs to decide whether it will apply the MLR requirements to the whole firm or just those parts where this must be done. Many firms simply apply the MLR standard throughout the firm on the basis that this manages risks more efficiently and consistently.

It is important to understand what decisions have been made about this, what the managers of the firm expect you to do and what they require you to achieve in terms of compliance obligations.

The purpose of the MLR is to create an intelligence, reporting and auditing network so that national and international agencies can track money launderers and criminal property.

The key requirements of those working in the regulated sector are:

- client due diligence measures – or client identity checks;
- record-keeping;
- training of appropriate staff;
- the appointment of a nominated officer known as the money laundering reporting officer (MLRO).

Any knowledge or suspicion of money laundering must be disclosed to the National Crime Agency (NCA). In a firm which must comply with the MLR, this is done by the MLRO making a suspicious activity report (SAR) to the NCA. Usually, the MLRO will notify the NCA of knowledge or suspicion and request consent to proceed with a transaction. The firm is not allowed to continue with a transaction until such consent has been received, but it would be an offence, known as tipping-off, to disclose to the client that there would be a delay until such consent was received.

This is another reason why the firm needs all managers and employees to be vigilant and watch out for warning signs. It is far easier to raise concerns at an early stage of a transaction than leave an internal report to the last minute when it may be harder to disguise the reason for any delays.

Offences include failure to disclose offences under POCA, ss.330 and 331 and the tipping-off offence under POCA, s.333. Again the penalties are severe, with a maximum five-year prison sentence and/or fining powers.

Dealing with this position, there is an important difference between compliance requirements for the purposes of POCA more generally and the MLR more specifically. Compliance with the MLR means that the business must appoint an MLRO. Under POCA there is no such requirement, although some firms and businesses choose to do so on a voluntary, best practice basis, relating this to their risk strategies. Indeed, considering the appropriateness of such an appointment may well link in with the requirements in chapter 7 of the SRA Code of Conduct 2011 to have effective management systems and the responsibilities of in-house lawyers with managerial duties. However, a warning note comes with POCA, s.332 and the failure to disclose offence which would be committed by anyone in this position regardless of whether this is a voluntary appointment under POCA or one required under the MLR.

This means that any business for which money laundering may be a risk, regardless of whether or not it operates in the regulated sector, must have appropriate risk strategies to minimise the dangers of being implicated.

For anyone working in the law firm, it is essential for their own safety and because of the requirements imposed on their business, that they understand the following matters:

- the name of the MLRO;
- how the MLRO wants to receive information from you about knowledge or suspicions;
- warning signs of criminal activity;
- the firm's requirements in respect of client due diligence including the steps to take if identification checks are not completed;
- the steps which must be taken if clients are not seen face-to-face;
- the considerations if there is a connection with a high-risk territory;
- record-keeping processes;
- the systems and processes which the firm has rolled out to manage this risk.

Undoubtedly, this is an area where the firm will have systems and processes about how the risk will be managed with guidance and template forms on such matters as the client identification and verification process, measures which must be taken at the time of engagement, the ownership of any risk assessment, and internal reporting mechanisms so that concerns can be brought to the MLRO's attention in an efficient manner.

With regard to ownership of risk, this is usually the responsibility of individual fee earners and/or the compliance team and/or the MLRO. It is important that everyone in the firm is aware of the extent of their responsibilities. If support staff are obtaining client due diligence information but not making the decision about whether this is satisfactory, then this division of responsibility must be clear to all concerned.

The fact that the SRA takes the threat of money laundering so seriously can be demonstrated by the fact that they have produced a number of risk publications to alert lawyers and others to the dangers of being targeted by criminals in this way. For examples, two warning notices were published in 2014; one related to suspicious activity reporting and the other was a more general notice to flag up warning signs more generally. Both are available on the SRA website. The more general warning provides a very good analysis of the signs of suspicion which everyone in the firm should understand, and is reproduced in **Appendix C3**.

10.5 TERRORISM ACT 2000

While POCA and the MLR are largely concerned with money laundering, the Terrorism Act 2000 is concerned with terrorist financing; making good money bad to support terrorist activities internationally. So, terrorist financing can be described as monetary support for terrorist purposes.

It is probably a safe assumption that it would be rare for a lawyer or law firm knowingly to support and fund terrorism, but the ways in which individuals and their employers could be implicated in terrorism-related offences might include the following types of behaviour and be related to the following warning signs:

- opening bank accounts where funds arise in respect of suspect territories, behaviour, etc.;
- dealing with clients' unusual requests as to the distribution of funds held in client account;
- dealing with funds or economic resources in a way which is intended to circumvent the financial restrictions on the transfer and use of terrorist funds.

Also, again as with POCA issues, managers and employees need to be vigilant about the knowledge which they may acquire and discuss these concerns and reporting obligations with appropriate colleagues.

10.6 FINANCIAL SERVICES AND MARKETS ACT 2000

Financial services make a significant contribution to the UK economy. Over one million people are employed in the financial services industry and the United Kingdom is the world's leading exporter of financial services.

It is a heavily regulated industry and this is for a number of reasons. The Barlow Clowes, Bank of Credit and Commerce and Robert Maxwell pensions scandals which some readers may recall, occurred in an era of lighter, self-regulation. The more onerous regulatory obligations which are now in place are intended to demonstrate that such events should now be more difficult to repeat and that this is a trusted industry with a good reputation.

The Financial Services and Markets Act 2000 (FSMA) is the key piece of legislation in this area. The Financial Conduct Authority (FCA) and the Prudential Regulation Authority are the statutory regulators of financial services in the United Kingdom and everyone must comply with the general prohibition.

The general prohibition is at FSMA, s.19 and states:

> (1) No person may carry on a regulated activity in the United Kingdom, or purport to do so, unless he is –
>
> (a) an authorised person; or
> (b) an exempt person.

It is an offence to carry on regulated activities in breach of this prohibition. The penalties are in FSMA, s.23; it may be a criminal offence and punishable on indictment by a maximum term of two years imprisonment and/or a fine. Section 26 states that any contract entered into in breach of the general prohibition is unenforceable.

The relevance of this is that many law firms provide regulated activities to their clients when undertaking legal services and must comply with FSMA. Examples include arranging defective title insurance for conveyancing clients and selling shares when dealing with the administration of estates.

Most law firms are not authorised by the FCA but they are not committing a criminal offence. This is because solicitors and other individuals working in law firms which are authorised and regulated by the SRA are able to rely on the Part XX exemption in FSMA (provision of financial services by members of the professions) to avoid breaching the general prohibition. This is because the Law Society is a Designated Professional Body, and because the SRA has made rules to regulate the scope of the regulated activities which law firms may undertake (i.e. the SRA Financial Services (Scope) Rules 2001, which are in the Specialist Services section of the SRA Handbook). In this way the majority of law firms do not need to be authorised by the Financial Conduct Authority and can nevertheless undertake a number of financial services for their clients as part of their professional services.

It is important to understand some of the language of financial services regulation and the extent to which regulated activities can be performed without FCA authorisation.

The meaning of regulated activity is defined in FSMA, s.22:

> (1) An activity is a regulated activity for the purposes of this Act if it is an activity of a specified kind which is carried on by way of business and –
>
> (a) relates to an investment of a specified kind; or
> (b) in the case of an activity of a kind which is also specified for the purposes of this paragraph, is carried on in relation to property of any kind.

Regulated activities and investments are listed in secondary legislation known as the Financial Services and Markets Act (Regulated Activities Order) 2001, SI 2001/544 (the Regulated Activities Order). Common regulated investments and regulated activities are shown below.

10.6.1 Common regulated investments

- deposits;
- electronic money;
- contracts of insurance;
- instruments creating or acknowledging indebtedness;
- shares;
- sukuk (shariah compliant debt instruments);
- government and public securities;
- units in a collective investment scheme;
- rights under a stakeholder pension scheme or a personal pension scheme;
- options;
- futures;
- regulated mortgage contracts;

- Lloyd's syndicate capacity and syndicate membership;
- rights under funeral plan contracts;
- home reversion plans;
- regulated sale and rent back agreements.

10.6.2 Common regulated activities

- accepting deposits;
- issuing e-money;
- effecting or carrying out contracts of insurance as principal;
- dealing in investments (as principal or agent);
- arranging deals in investments;
- managing investments;
- assisting in the administration and performance of a contract of insurance;
- sending dematerialised instructions;
- establishing etc. collective investment schemes;
- advising on investments;
- advising on, arranging, entering into and administering home finance activities;
- Lloyd's market activities.

Identifying investments and activities is relatively straightforward. The more difficult judgment is whether the regulated activity is being carried on by way of business. The FCA gives guidance on this in the FCA Handbook (i.e. its equivalent of the SRA Handbook). Although this guidance arises in respect of a particular regulated activity (specifically home reversion activities), it is a useful indicator of the FCA views as it states that the business test requires the following analysis:

- the degree of continuity;
- the existence of a commercial element;
- the scale of the activity;
- the proportion which the activity bears to other activities carried on by the same person but which are not regulated;
- the nature of the regulated sale and rent back agreements.

Also a very old case, *Smith* v. *Anderson* (1880) 15 Ch D 247, is often quoted in this context. In this case, business for the purpose of the matters under consideration was defined as 'a series of acts which is successful produce gain'.

Using these references it would be very hard to argue that solicitors and law firms were not carrying on regulated activities by way of business. Making an accurate analysis is vital given the offences attached to breaching the general prohibition. If the firm is undertaking a regulated activity by way of business and it is not directly authorised by the FCA, it must either comply with the SRA Handbook or be satisfied that an exclusion can be used.

10.6.3 Exclusions

The Regulated Activities Order contains both regulated activities and regulated investments. It also includes a number of exclusions; broadly, scenarios or conditions in which what would seemingly be a regulated activity is statutorily excluded but in the very strictly controlled environment that all conditions attached to the exclusion can be met.

The practical implication is that reliance on an exclusion means that the business is not carrying on a regulated activity and does not need to comply with the FSMA and either the Part XX Exemption in the case of professional firms or the FSA Handbook in respect of non-exempt firms. The danger is a misinterpretation of the conditions attached to the exclusion is likely to mean that the business breaches the general prohibition and commits an offence under FSMA.

Exclusions which may be of benefit to lawyers are described in **Table 10.1**.[1]

Table 10.1 Regulated activities – exclusions

Exclusion	What you can do	Conditions
Using an authorised person – arts. 22 and 29 of the Regulated Activities Order (RAO)	Deal as agent or arrange a transaction with or through an authorised person where the transaction is entered into on the advice of the authorised person or it is clear that the client has not sought your advice as to the merits of the transaction	(1) Cannot be used where the specified investment is a contract of insurance (2) You account to the client for any commission you receive (see outcome 1.15 of the SRA Code of Conduct 2011
Arrangements not causing a deal – art.26 of the RAO	Excludes from the regulated activity of arranging in respect of securities and regulated mortgage contracts any arrangements which do not bring about the transaction to which it relates	None, but remember the need to achieve outcome 1.15 of the 2011 Code should you receive commission from an authorised person
Introducing – art.33 of the RAO	Introduce a client to an authorised person for independent advice	(1) Cannot be used where the specified investment is a contract of insurance (2) Arrangements must not go beyond introductions

[1] Adapted from a table originally published by the SRA.

Exclusion	What you can do	Conditions
Introducing – art.33A of the RAO	Introduce a client to an authorised person to arrange and/or advise on a regulated mortgage contract	(1) You do not receive any money paid by the client for or in connection with any transaction that the client enters into with the authorised person (2) Before making the introduction you disclose to the client details of any commission, etc. you receive for the introduction (3) Remember the need to achieve outcome 1.15 of the SRA Code of Conduct 2011
Trustees, nominees and personal representatives – art.66 of the RAO	Applicable to lawyers who are acting as trustees, nominees and personal representatives and allows them to arrange, deal, manage investments, safeguard and administer, send dematerialised instructions, and advise	(1) Cannot be used where the specified investment is a contract of insurance (2) The solicitor trustee, nominee or personal representative must not receive remuneration for carrying on the regulated activity in addition to the remuneration obtained for providing the trustee etc. service (3) The advising regulated activity is limited to advice to a fellow trustee (4) For the dealing, managing and safeguarding and administrating regulated activities, the trustee must not hold him/herself out as providing such a service
The necessary exclusion – art.67 of the RAO	Exclusion applies to regulated activities of dealing, arranging, safe custody and assets and applies where the regulated activity may reasonably be regarded as a necessary part of other services provided in the course of that business	(1) Cannot be used where the specified investment is a contract of insurance (2) The regulated activity must not be separately remunerated from the professional services

Exclusion	What you can do	Conditions
Sale/purchase of a company – art.70 of the RAO	Exclusion applies to the regulated activities of dealing as principal or agent, arranging deals and giving advice in connection with the purchase or sale of shares in a company other than an open ended investment company	(1) The shares consist of/include 50%+ of the voting shares in the company OR the shares together with any shares already held by the purchaser consist of 50%+ of the voting shares AND each of the parties to the sale/purchase is either a company, a partnership, a single individual or a group of connected individuals (2) If condition (1) cannot be met, the solicitor can still act where the object of the transaction can reasonably be regarded as the acquisition of day-to-day control of the company's affairs
Provision of information on an incidental basis – art.72C of the RAO	Excludes from the activities of arranging and assisting in the performance of a contract of insurance, the provision of information to a policyholder or potential policyholder	Must be reasonably be regarded as being incidental to the solicitor's business

Where an exclusion cannot be used, it is essential to be able to use the SRA Handbook properly and comply with the SRA Financial Services (Scope) Rules 2001 and the SRA Financial Services (Conduct of Business) Rules 2001. These are in the Specialist Services section of the Handbook.

10.6.4 The SRA Financial Services (Scope) Rules 2001

The Scope Rules set out the conditions of providing regulated activities when not authorised by the FCA but working under the Part XX exemption. The important information in the Rules relates to what cannot be done (rule 3), basic conditions which must be satisfied (rule 4) and other restrictions which apply in certain circumstances (rule 5).

Rule 3 – examples of prohibited activities

- Advising a person to become a member of a particular Lloyd's syndicate.
- Entering into a regulated mortgage contract as a lender.
- Effecting and carrying out contracts of insurance as a principal.

- Establishing, operating or winding up a collective investment scheme.

Rule 4 – examples of basic conditions which must be satisfied

- The activities arise out of, or are complementary to, the provision of a particular professional service to a particular client.
- The manner of the provision by the firm of any service in the course of carrying on the activities is incidental to the provision by the firm of professional services.
- The firm accounts to the client for any pecuniary reward or other advantage which the firm receives from a third party.

Rule 5 – examples of other conditions and restrictions

- Unless a firm is registered in the Financial Services Register it must not carry on any insurance mediation activities.
- Any firm undertaking insurance mediation activities must appoint an insurance mediation officer whose details will be made known to the FCA and who will be responsible for the firm's insurance mediation activities.

Breaching the Scope Rules places the individual outside the Part XX exemption, and they are likely to be committing both a criminal and regulatory offence.

Running alongside the Scope Rules, the individual and the law firm must also comply with the SRA Financial Services (Conduct of Business) Rules 2001. Breach of these is not a criminal offence, but will be a disciplinary issue which may be subject to SRA investigation. The COB Rules contain regulatory requirements about how regulated activities must be performed and it is here that some of the client care or terms of business information about financial services originate.

10.7 THE FINANCIAL SERVICES AND MARKETS ACT 2001 (FINANCIAL PROMOTION) ORDER 2001

Another regulated activity which law firms must be wary of is the making of a financial promotion. FSMA, s.21 contains a restriction on financial promotions in that unauthorised persons cannot, in the course of business, communicate an invitation or inducement to engage in investment activity, unless it has been approved by an authorised person.

This prohibition is enforced by the criminal offence in FSMA, s.25 of making an unauthorised financial promotion. Because of the professional (and personal) consequences of a criminal conviction, an in-house lawyer working in a business which is not itself authorised must take care not to make a financial promotion.

A financial promotion may be made in several ways and it is important to understand terminology such as real time and non-real time, solicited and unsolicited communications and understand the requirements of the secondary legislation which is relevant, namely the Financial Services and Markets Act 2000 (Financial Promotion) Order 2001, SI 2001/1335 (FPO).

A real time communication is described as 'a personal visit, telephone conversation or other interactive dialogue'. Anything else is 'non-real time', e.g. investment information communicated via a letter, fax, email, advertisement, brochure or website (in broad terms, anything in writing).

Real time communications are further subdivided into 'solicited' and 'unsolicited'. If the investment business discussion is initiated by the other person (e.g. the employer or the client) in a meeting with the in-house lawyer, then the communication is 'solicited'. If the issue is raised for the first time by the lawyer, then it is 'unsolicited'.

Because of the risks attached to improper and inappropriate financial promotions, the making of them is heavily regulated so that they must be made by an authorised FCA firm or the law firm must be able to rely on something called an exemption in the FPO.

There are some exemptions in the FPO which allow unauthorised firms to make promotions. Those which are likely to be of use to law firms are listed in Table 10.2,[2] but as with the exclusions from regulated activities described in the preceding paragraphs, great caution should be exercised when using these exemptions.

Table 10.2 Financial promotion – exemptions

Exemption	Permitted financial promotion	Conditions
One-off non-real time communications and solicited real time communications – art.28 of the FPO	Allows individuals to make a one-off financial promotion, e.g. by letter addressed to a specific client or during a meeting with a particular client	(1) The communication must be made to one recipient, or a group of recipients acting together (2) The investment concerned must have been identified having regard to the particular circumstances of the client (3) The communication must not be part of an organised marketing campaign

[2] Adapted from a table originally published by the SRA.

Exemption	Permitted financial promotion	Conditions
One-off unsolicited real time communications – art.28A of the FPO	Allows individuals to make a one-off financial promotion to a client during a meeting or by telephone, etc.	(1) As in art.28, plus (2) The individual believes on reasonable grounds that the client understands the risks of engaging in the investment activity to which the promotion relates (3) The client must have been expecting the individual to contact him/her
Introductions – art.15 of the FPO	Allows an individual to promote the fact that they can make an introduction to an authorised person with a view to the provision of independent financial advice	(1) The individual must account to the client for any commission he/she receives (2) The authorised person cannot be associated with the firm

10.8 EQUALITY ACT 2010

Solicitors have always been under a very strict duty in conduct not to discriminate unlawfully in their dealings with clients and third parties, and handling equality issues correctly is a non-negotiable requirement of being a solicitor or working in any other capacity in an SRA-authorised law firm.

The regulatory objectives in the Legal Services Act 2007 make this clear with such requirements as approved regulators having the duty to improve access to justice, protect and promote the interests of consumers and to encourage an independent, strong, diverse and effective legal profession.

These legal requirements which are imposed on approved regulators run alongside the equalities legislation and are now made clear in Principle 9 ('you must run your business or carry out your role in the business in a way that encourages equality of opportunity and respect for diversity') and by the outcomes which must be achieved in chapter 2 of the SRA Code of Conduct 2011 (both in the SRA Handbook and discussed elsewhere in this book).

Getting any of this wrong can have serious consequences, not only in terms of the disciplinary issues which would follow and but also because of the legal ramifications and consequent reputational issues. There have been a number of high profile court cases involving law firms where the business and individuals within it have misjudged their duties. These cases will carry the same message for all managers and employees working in law about the consequences of breaching the legislation:

- *Bivonas LLP* v. *Bennett* (UKEAT/0254/11/JOJ) – unlawful discrimination against an employee on the grounds of sexual orientation
- *Osborne Clarke Services* v. *Purohit* [2009] IRLR 341 – a failure to consider job applications from non-EEA nationals was indirect racial discrimination
- *Eversheds Legal Services Ltd* v. *De Belin* [2011] ICR 1137 – unlawful sexual discrimination

Getting equality and diversity right promotes a number of benefits by creating the right ethos in the workplace: the ideal environment will be one in which everyone treats colleagues, clients and third parties with respect. Also, a strong culture of equality and diversity is a selling point when tendering for business and in demonstrating adherence to various quality standards and accreditation schemes and the like.

Until 2010, legislative duties were found in countless different statutes (for example, the Sex Discrimination Act 1975 and the Race Relations Act 1968). These have now been consolidated in the Equality Act 2010 and the notes to chapter 2 of the SRA Code of Conduct 2011 make it clear that you must comply with the requirements set out in this legislation.

This legislation identifies nine protected characteristics which are:

1. age;
2. disability;
3. gender reassignment;
4. marriage and civil partnership;
5. pregnancy and maternity;
6. race;
7. religion or belief;
8. sex;
9. sexual orientation.

It is an offence to unlawfully discriminate (either directly or indirectly), victimise or harass someone on the grounds of a protected characteristic.

This legislation means that every individual working within the firm is protected by the legislation but also, of course, must not break the law themselves. Consider the following:

- Are you satisfied that the firm's working practices comply with the legislation?
- Do you understand the equality policies that the firm may have drafted and understand what type of behaviour is expected from you?
- Do you make reasonable adjustments to ensure that clients and employees with disabilities are treated in the same way as their counterparts who are not disabled?
- Are you confident that victimisation and/or harassment is not tolerated and would be challenged as inappropriate behaviour?

10.9 BRIBERY ACT 2010

The Bribery Act 2010 came into force in July 2011. It is intended to be a deterrent to improper behaviour in all types of business, including law firms, and applies to all dealings wherever these may take place in the world.

The Act created some new offences. For example, it is an offence for a UK citizen or resident to pay or receive a bribe, either directly or indirectly. Also, companies and partnerships can commit an offence if a bribe is paid on their behalf by an 'associate' (meaning employees, agents, or anyone else providing services on their behalf). The corporate defence to this offence is to have adequate procedures in place to prevent the action occurring or, in other words, an anti-bribery policy (sometimes known as the anti-bribery and corruption policy or ABC policy).

The penalties for breaking this law are unlimited company fines, up to 10 years' imprisonment for individuals and debarment from tendering for public contracts in the European Union.

As this Act is in its infancy, there are very few examples of prosecutions although the first conviction did arise in a legal environment when a magistrates' court administrative officer admitted taking a £500 bribe to 'get rid' of a speeding charge. The individual in question was sentenced to six years' imprisonment, which was reduced to four years on appeal (*R* v. *Munir Patel* [2012] EWCA Crim 1243).

This Act is of huge relevance to everyone working in a law firm who will want to be satisfied on certain key points: that there is an awareness of the legislation and that the senior managers and compliance team are committed to ensuring that there are no breaches. Risk prevention measures may include adequate training, an adequate whistle-blowing policy and an anti-bribery policy. Much of the risk strategy is likely to be linked to the business's systems and controls to deal with money laundering and other fraudulent activities.

Everyone in the law firm will want to have a good understanding of the anti-bribery policy and what they can and cannot do while working in the business. However, the policy does need not be overly complicated. Guidance issued by the Ministry of Justice (**www.justice.gov.uk/guidance/docs/bribery-act-2010-guidance.pdf**) includes suggestions about the procedures which commercial organisations can put into place to prevent persons associated with them from committing acts of bribery. The guidance makes the following point:

> The objective of the Act is not to bring the full force of the criminal law to bear upon well-run commercial organisations that experience an isolated incident of bribery on their behalf.

With this in mind, the guidance contains six management principles which are:

1. proportionate procedures;
2. top level commitment;
3. risk assessment;
4. due diligence;
5. communication;

6. monitoring and review.

A common law firm dilemma is whether referral fees, hospitality and token gifts are caught by the Act. It is unlikely that legitimate referral fees and reasonable and proportionate hospitality will be subject to the Act. Again, the Ministry of Justice makes this point:

> the government does not intend for the Act to prohibit reasonable and proportionate hospitality and promotional or other similar business expenditure intended for these purposes.

10.10 DATA PROTECTION ACT 1998

No one working in a law firm should underestimate the consequences of breaching the Data Protection Act 1998 (and related legislation), as the connection with conduct duties and the duty of confidentiality, and the risks attached to the information which we hold, make compliance with this legislation essential. The fact that as lawyers we hold great amounts of information about other people, often of a personal and sensitive nature, makes this so. Increasingly, the way in which we use this data, and the threats to the data from cybercriminals, heightens the risks in this area.

In fact the SRA identifies the protection of data, confidentiality and threats from cyber criminals as a current key risk priority. In its 'Risk Outlook 2014/15', it says:

> Keeping the affairs of clients confidential and secure is a key professional duty. Law firms need to be prepared for the increased risk to this duty that is presented by cybercrime. Criminals increasingly use the internet to target their victims. Cybercrime committed against law firms can be used to steal money, to facilitate identity theft or for industrial espionage. Our regulatory remit is primarily concerned with managing the risk that cybercrime presents to consumers. However, it also presents a wider risk to public confidence in the legal sector. For law firms, managing this risk is vital to their reputations and client relations.

Again, and as with money laundering, there is an extra dimension to this risk in that an external body, the Information Commissioner's Office (ICO), has powers to enforce the Data Protection Act alongside the Freedom of Information Act 2000 and a number of other legislative requirements designed to safeguard and uphold information rights.

Lawyers are in the spotlight with the ICO. In August 2014, the Information Commissioner issued a warning notice to lawyers, part of which is reproduced below:

> The Information Commissioner's Office (ICO) is warning barristers and solicitors to keep personal information secure, especially paper files. This follows a number of data breaches reported to the ICO involving the legal profession.
>
> The ICO can serve a monetary penalty of up to £500,000 for a serious breach of the Data Protection Act provided the incident had the potential to cause substantial damage or

> substantial distress to affected individuals. In most cases these penalties are issued to companies or public authorities, but barristers and solicitors are generally classed as data controllers in their own right and are therefore legally responsible for the personal information they process.
>
> In the last three months, 15 incidents involving members of the legal profession have been reported to the ICO. The information handled by barristers and solicitors is often very sensitive. This means that the damage caused by a data breach could meet the statutory threshold for issuing a financial penalty. Legal professionals will also often carry around large quantities of information in folders or files when taking them to or from court, and may store them at home. This can increase the risk of a data breach.
>
> Information Commissioner, Christopher Graham, said:
>
> 'The number of breaches reported by barristers and solicitors may not seem that high, but given the sensitive information they handle, and the fact that it is often held in paper files rather than secured by any sort of encryption, that number is troubling. It is important that we sound the alarm at an early stage to make sure this problem is addressed before a barrister or solicitor is left counting the financial and reputational damage of a serious data breach.'

The warning was accompanied by some ICO tips designed to help barristers and solicitors look after the personal information they handle:

- keep paper records secure;
- do not leave files in a car overnight;
- lock information away when it is not in use;
- consider data minimisation techniques in order to ensure that only information that is essential to the task in hand is carried around;
- where possible, store personal information on an encrypted memory stick or portable device;
- when sending personal information by email consider whether the information needs to be encrypted or password protected;
- avoid the pitfalls of auto-complete by double checking to make sure the email address is correct;
- only keep information for as long as is necessary;
- delete or dispose of information securely if it is no longer needed;
- when disposing of an old computer, or other device, make sure all of the information held on the device is permanently deleted before disposal.

The ICO's role means that it has a number of powers it can use in its toolkit. For example, in connection with the Data Protection Act, it can:

- issue information notices to ensure that it can request information in a timely manner;
- issue undertakings that an organisation will take action to improve compliance;
- serve enforcement notices and 'stop now' orders requiring an organisation to act in a particular way;
- conduct consensual audits of organisations;
- serve assessment notices to conduct compulsory audits of organisations;

- issue monetary penalty notices to organisations with a maximum fining power of £500,000 for very serious breaches of the Data Protection Act occurring on or after 6 April 2010;
- prosecute anyone committing a criminal offence under the Act;
- report any issues of concern to Parliament.

The ICO has taken action against solicitors, law firms, businesses which employ solicitors and employees of law firms. A case in point relates to a paralegal, James Pickles (**www.sra.org.uk/consumers/solicitor-check/431698.article?Decision-1**).

EXAMPLE 10.2 – James Pickles

James Pickles had been employed by a law firm as a paralegal. He was fined £300 by the ICO for illegally taking client information. The individual had taken information about more than 100 clients before leaving a law firm for a rival business in 2013. It was stated that he had hoped to use the information, which included workload lists, file notes and template documents, in his new role.

Stephen Eckersley, head of enforcement at the ICO, said of the matter: 'Employees may think work-related documents that they have produced or worked on belong to them and so they are entitled to take them when they leave. But if they include people's details, then taking them without permission is breaking the law. Don't risk a day in court.' According to Eckersley, the information Pickles took included 'sensitive details relating to individuals involved in ongoing legal proceedings'.

The circumstances were reported to the SRA, which decided to make a ruling that it was undesirable for him to work in the legal profession in future and that he must not be employed in any solicitor's practice or by any solicitor without SRA permission in future.

The business must demonstrate that it complies with the eight principles of data protection contained in the Data Protection Act 1998 which are:

1. Personal information must be fairly and lawfully processed.
2. Personal information must be processed for limited, lawful purposes.
3. Personal information must be adequate, relevant and not excessive.
4. Personal information must be accurate and up to date.
5. Personal information must not be kept for longer than is necessary.
6. Personal information must be processed in line with the data subjects' rights.
7. Personal information must be secure.
8. Personal information must not be transferred to other countries without adequate protection.

This requires an understanding of certain language:

- **Data controller** – the person or company that collects and keeps data about people.

- **Data subject** – the individual who has data stored about him or her somewhere which is outside that individual's direct control.
- **Information Commissioner** – the person who has the powers to enforce the Act.
- **Personal data** – name, address, medical details or banking details.
- **Sensitive personal data** – racial or ethnic origin, political opinions, religion, trade union membership, health, sex life, criminal activity.

Many law firms have a number of internal policies to deal with the risks associated with breaking the law in this area. Data protection measures can sometimes be included in a confidentiality policy, policies about the use of social media, and in respect of the safe use of information technology. In addition, the firm's business continuity plans or disaster recovery strategies will often cover this issue. Everyone will play a role in data protection measures. We will all have access to personal data simply by being a manager or employee in the business. Sometimes there may be additional responsibilities because of the type of work we are employed to do; for example, anyone employed in respect of IT services will need to ensure that they are contributing appropriately to the safe-keeping of data through their review of the firm's technology.

CHAPTER 11

Compliance in a nutshell

11.1 KEY ROLES WITHIN A LAW FIRM

Table 11.1 identifies key roles within a law firm with a commentary on the SRA Handbook and other legal duties which must be understood by the role holders.

Table 11.1 Law firm roles and duties

Role	Key knowledge base
Fee earner/case handler	SRA Authorisation Rules SRA Principles SRA Code of Conduct SRA Accounts Rules Anti-money laundering legislation Bribery Act 2010 Data Protection Act 1998 *et al.* Equality Act 2010 *If working in property selling:* SRA Property Selling Rules *If undertaking financial services for clients:* SRA Scope Rules and SRA Conduct of Business Rules Financial Services and Markets Act 2000 and related legislation The firm's internal systems and procedures including expectations about how SRA Handbook breaches, or high risk decisions, will be made known to the appropriate people in the business Identity of the firm's COLP, COFA, MLRO and anyone else in a risk and compliance role

Role	Key knowledge base
Support staff	All of the above but with particular focus on the following: Behaviours relating to client care, confidentiality, and anything connected to the role in checking for conflicts, identification of clients, suspicious activity reporting
Reception staff	SRA Authorisation Rules SRA Principles SRA Code of Conduct SRA Accounts Rules Anti-money laundering legislation Bribery Act 2010 Data Protection Act 1998 *et al.* Equality Act 2010 Knowledge of client care and confidentiality duties must be strong. Money laundering awareness and SRA Accounts Rules restrictions in respect of client identification must also be understood The firm's internal systems and procedures including expectations about how Handbook breaches, or high risk decisions, will be made known to the appropriate people in the business Identity of the firm's COLP, COFA, MLRO and anyone else in a risk and compliance role
Human resources team	As above. Depending on the extent of the human resources team's role, there is a need to understand statutory obligations in respect of practising certificates for solicitors, job titles for non-solicitors, etc., the need to ensure that the SRA has not imposed restrictions on anyone's ability to be employed within an SRA-authorised law firm

Role	**Key knowledge base**
Marketing/publicity	As above, but with particular emphasis on the outcomes which must be achieved in respect of publicity in the SRA Code of Conduct and the duty of confidentiality (and overlap with Data Protection Act liabilities) This will run into use of social media forums to publicise the firm and its business
Accounts Team	SRA Authorisation Rules SRA Principles SRA Code of Conduct SRA Accounts Rules Anti-money laundering legislation Bribery Act 2010 Data Protection Act 1998 *et al.* Equality Act 2010 It is essential that anyone with information about the firm's accounts has access to the COFA and managers in order to flag up any areas of concern. The internal processes and notification requirements must be understood
IT team	SRA Principles SRA Code of Conduct, chapter 4 outcomes relating to confidentiality plus Data Protection Act responsibilities The IT team can play an invaluable role in ensuring that the firm manages the risk of cybercrime and identity hijack. SRA resources and alerts will be useful to them. They should have reporting lines so that they can feed into risk strategies Details of any internal systems and policies which are relevant (for example any policy relating to the use of social media, etc.), the identity of the compliance officers, and information about what they need to know and how they need to be notified

Role	Key knowledge base
Post room/clerking services	SRA Authorisation Rules SRA Principles SRA Code of Conduct SRA Accounts Rules Anti-money laundering legislation Bribery Act 2010 Data Protection Act 1998 *et al.* Equality Act 2010 For anyone fulfilling a position which is not client-facing but nevertheless a key role in the way in which the business needs are met, it is vital to ensure that behaviours such as confidentiality are understood Also, because of the need to tell the compliance officers about any cause for concern, information about internal systems and processes, the identity of the compliance officers, and means of flagging up issues, is necessary
Cleaners	SRA Code of Conduct, chapter 4 outcomes relating to confidentiality plus Data Protection Act responsibilities Details of any internal systems and policies which are relevant (for example any policy relating to the use of social media, etc.), the identity of the compliance officers, and information about what they need to know and how they need to be notified

CHAPTER 12

Conclusion

12.1 THE CHALLENGES OF COMPLIANCE AND ETHICS

The SRA has the power to scrutinise the behaviour of anyone who works in an SRA-authorised firm and to make decisions about whether it is appropriate for them to be employed in these entities. The justification for using such powers is the need to ensure that law firms are safe businesses and deliver services to clients of an acceptable standard.

This means that there are challenges in working in a law firm. It is not for the faint-hearted, nor is it the right type of employment for anyone who is not happy to work within a business where the framework is set by an external regulator and includes some non-negotiable requirements.

This means that everyone must accept that they need to ensure that client information is secure, that client money is safe, that marketing complies with restrictions that are not found in other businesses, that employment matters may create a regulatory issue which may not be the case in other industries and so on. In fact we are talking about knowledge of, and compliance with, all the Principles, outcomes, rules and regulations which have been discussed in this book and which set the scene for SRA regulation of you and your firm. In other words, it is important to understand and agree to the need to act ethically and to acknowledge that the regulator decides the form of ethical behaviour for you.

In most law firms in the past few years, there has been a renewed interest in ethics and the connected topics of compliance and risk. The bottom line is that every individual must play their part in creating the right environment in the firm, and that the firm is only as safe as its weakest link in terms of ensuring it has a good relationship with the regulator and demonstrates the right behaviours. Overall this is a team activity. Individuals should not be left to work out ethics for themselves. The lead should come from the managers and compliance officers in the business with systems and processes and support networks for everyone to use and follow.

12.2 KEY MESSAGES

The key messages for everyone working in the law firm are these:

- The law firm can continue to provide services only while it is authorised and regulated.
- Authorisation is dependent on the existence of a culture of compliance.
- Compliance requires a knowledge of professional ethics and a commitment from everyone to act ethically.
- Compliance systems must also include the management of the risks which are present and it is important to understand what these are in your business.
- The firm will have internal systems and processes; these are created to promote consistency in approach. Everyone must be familiar with the systems which are relevant to them and be prepared to act in accordance with an internal requirement.
- Compliance is a firm-wide effort. Be prepared to make suggestions about how compliance could be improved.
- While everyone should strive to get compliance right, no one is perfect and mistakes will happen.
- It is important to be open and accountable; if something has gone wrong, and it will from time to time, then it is essential that the right people within the business are told as soon as possible.
- Know the identity of the compliance officers and other risk managers and know how they would like you to raise issues and concerns with them.
- It is important to discuss concerns. There is no such thing as a stupid question.
- Remember that no one in the firm should be able to assert that they are not bound to comply with the internal systems or the SRA's requirements. This type of behaviour must be challenged.
- Above all else, be ethical.

APPENDIX A

Statute law

APPENDIX A1

Legal Services Act 2007 (extracts)[1]

PART 1 THE REGULATORY OBJECTIVES

1 The regulatory objectives

(1) In this Act a reference to 'the regulatory objectives' is a reference to the objectives of –

(a) protecting and promoting the public interest;
(b) supporting the constitutional principle of the rule of law;
(c) improving access to justice;
(d) protecting and promoting the interests of consumers;
(e) promoting competition in the provision of services within subsection (2);
(f) encouraging an independent, strong, diverse and effective legal profession;
(g) increasing public understanding of the citizen's legal rights and duties;
(h) promoting and maintaining adherence to the professional principles.

(2) The services within this subsection are services such as are provided by authorised persons (including services which do not involve the carrying on of activities which are reserved legal activities).

(3) The 'professional principles' are—

(a) that authorised persons should act with independence and integrity,
(b) that authorised persons should maintain proper standards of work,
(c) that authorised persons should act in the best interests of their clients,
(d) that persons who exercise before any court a right of audience, or conduct litigation in relation to proceedings in any court, by virtue of being authorised persons should comply with their duty to the court to act with independence in the interests of justice, and
(e) that the affairs of clients should be kept confidential.

(4) In this section 'authorised persons' means authorised persons in relation to activities which are reserved legal activities.

. . .

[1] Sections 1(1)–(3), 12.

PART 3 RESERVED LEGAL ACTIVITIES

Reserved legal activities

12 Meaning of 'reserved legal activity' and 'legal activity'

(1) In this Act 'reserved legal activity' means –

(a) the exercise of a right of audience;
(b) the conduct of litigation;
(c) reserved instrument activities;
(d) probate activities;
(e) notarial activities;
(f) the administration of oaths.

(2) Schedule 2 makes provision about what constitutes each of those activities.
(3) In this Act 'legal activity' means –

(a) an activity which is a reserved legal activity within the meaning of this Act as originally enacted, and
(b) any other activity which consists of one or both of the following –

(i) the provision of legal advice or assistance in connection with the application of the law or with any form of resolution of legal disputes;
(ii) the provision of representation in connection with any matter concerning the application of the law or any form of resolution of legal disputes.

(4) But 'legal activity' does not include any activity of a judicial or quasi-judicial nature (including acting as a mediator).
(5) For the purposes of subsection (3) 'legal dispute' includes a dispute as to any matter of fact the resolution of which is relevant to determining the nature of any person's legal rights or liabilities.
(6) Section 24 makes provision for adding legal activities to the reserved legal activities.

APPENDIX B

SRA Handbook

APPENDIX B1

SRA Principles 2011[1]

PREAMBLE

The SRA Principles dated 17 June 2011 commencing 6 October 2011 made by the Solicitors Regulation Authority Board under sections 31, 79 and 80 of the Solicitors Act 1974, sections 9 and 9A of the Administration of Justice Act 1985 and section 83 of the Legal Services Act 2007, with the approval of the Legal Services Board under paragraph 19 of Schedule 4 to the Legal Services Act 2007, regulating the conduct of solicitors and their employees, registered European lawyers, recognised bodies and their managers and employees, and licensed bodies and their managers and employees.

PART 1: SRA PRINCIPLES

1: SRA PRINCIPLES

These are mandatory *Principles* which apply to all.

You must:

1. uphold the rule of law and the proper administration of justice;
2. act with integrity;
3. not allow your independence to be compromised;
4. act in the best interests of each *client*;
5. provide a proper standard of service to your *clients*;
6. behave in a way that maintains the trust the public places in you and in the provision of legal services;
7. comply with your legal and regulatory obligations and deal with your regulators and ombudsmen in an open, timely and co-operative manner;
8. run your business or carry out your role in the business effectively and in accordance with proper governance and sound financial and risk management principles;
9. run your business or carry out your role in the business in a way that encourages equality of opportunity and respect for diversity; and
10. protect *client* money and *assets*.

2: SRA PRINCIPLES – NOTES

2.1 The Principles embody the key ethical requirements on firms and individuals who

[1] See version 14 of the SRA Handbook, published on 30 April 2015, updated regularly at **www.sra.org.uk**.

are involved in the provision of legal services. You should always have regard to the Principles and use them as your starting point when faced with an ethical dilemma.

2.2 Where two or more Principles come into conflict, the Principle which takes precedence is the one which best serves the public interest in the particular circumstances, especially the public interest in the proper administration of justice.

2.3 These Principles:

(a) apply to individuals and firms we regulate, whether traditional firms of solicitors or ABSs, in private practice or in-house. Where a firm or individual is *practising overseas*, the Overseas Principles apply;
(b) will be breached by you if you permit another person to do anything on your behalf which if done by you would breach the Principles; and
(c) apply to you to the fullest extent if a sole practitioner or manager in a firm, but still apply to you if you work within a firm or in-house and have no management responsibility (for example, even if you are not a manager you may have an opportunity to influence, adopt and implement measures to comply with Principles 8 and 9).

2.4 Compliance with the Principles is also subject to any overriding legal obligations.

Principle 1: You must uphold the rule of law and the proper administration of justice.

2.5 You have obligations not only to clients but also to the court and to third parties with whom you have dealings on your clients' behalf – see, e.g., Chapter 5 (Your client and the court) and Chapter 11 (Relations with third parties) of the Code.

Principle 2: You must act with integrity.

2.6 Personal integrity is central to your role as the client's trusted adviser and should characterise all your professional dealings with clients, the court, other lawyers and the public.

Principle 3: You must not allow your independence to be compromised.

2.7 'Independence' means your own and your firm's independence, and not merely your ability to give independent advice to a client. You should avoid situations which might put your independence at risk – e.g. giving control of your practice to a third party which is beyond the regulatory reach of the SRA or other approved regulator.

Principle 4: You must act in the best interests of each client.

2.8 You should always act in good faith and do your best for each of your clients. Most importantly, you should observe:

(a) your duty of confidentiality to the client – see Chapter 4 (Confidentiality and disclosure) of the Code; and
(b) your obligations with regard to conflicts of interests – see Chapter 3 (Conflicts of interests) of the Code.

Principle 5: You must provide a proper standard of service to your clients.

2.9 You should, e.g., provide a proper standard of client care and of work. This would include exercising competence, skill and diligence, and taking into account the individual needs and circumstances of each client.

2.10 For a *solicitor*, meeting the competencies set out in the Competence Statement forms an integral part of the requirement to provide a proper standard of service.

Principle 6: You must behave in a way that maintains the trust the public places in you and in the provision of legal services.

2.11 Members of the public should be able to place their trust in you. Any behaviour either within or outside your professional practice which undermines this trust damages not only you, but also the ability of the legal profession as a whole to serve society.

Principle 7: You must comply with your legal and regulatory obligations and deal with your regulators and ombudsmen in an open, timely and co-operative manner.

2.12 You should, e.g., ensure that you comply with all the reporting and notification requirements – see Chapter 10 (You and your regulator) of the Code – and respond promptly and substantively to communications.

Principle 8: You must run your business or carry out your role in the business effectively and in accordance with proper governance and sound financial and risk management principles.

2.13 Whether you are a manager or an employee, you have a part to play in helping to ensure that your business is well run for the benefit of your clients and, e.g. in meeting the outcomes in Chapter 7 (Management of your business) of the Code.

Principle 9: You must run your business or carry out your role in the business in a way that encourages equality of opportunity and respect for diversity.

2.14 Whether you are a manager or an employee, you have a role to play in achieving the outcomes in Chapter 2 (Equality and diversity) of the Code. Note that a finding of unlawful discrimination outside practice could also amount to a breach of Principles 1 and 6.

Principle 10: You must protect client money and assets.

2.15 This Principle goes to the heart of the duty to act in the best interests of your clients. You should play your part in e.g. protecting money, documents or other property belonging to your clients which has been entrusted to you or your firm.

Breach of the Principles

2.16 Our approach to enforcement is proportionate, outcomes-focused and risk-based. Therefore, how we deal with failure to comply with the Principles will depend on all the particular circumstances of each case. Our primary aim is to achieve the right outcomes for clients.

PART 2: SRA PRINCIPLES – APPLICATION PROVISIONS

The *Principles* apply to you in the following circumstances (and 'you' must be construed accordingly).

3: APPLICATION OF THE SRA PRINCIPLES IN ENGLAND AND WALES

3.1 Subject to paragraphs 3.2 to 6.1 below and any other provisions in the *SRA Code of Conduct*, the *Principles* apply to you, in relation to your activities carried out from an office in England and Wales, if you are:

(a) a *solicitor*, *REL* or *RFL* who is *practising* as such, whether or not the entity through which you *practise* is subject to these *Principles*;
(b) a *solicitor*, *REL* or *RFL* who is:

(i) a *manager*, *employee* or *owner* of a body which should be a *recognised body*, but has not been recognised by the *SRA*;
(ii) a *manager*, *employee* or *owner* of a body that is a *manager* or *owner* of a body that should be a *recognised body*, but has not been recognised by the *SRA*;
(iii) an *employee* of a *sole practitioner* which should be a *recognised sole practitioner*, but has not been recognised by the *SRA*;
(iv) an *owner* of an *authorised body* or of a body which should be a *recognised body* but has not been recognised by the *SRA*, even if you undertake no work for the body's *clients*;
(v) a *manager* or *employee* of an *authorised non-SRA firm*, or a *manager* of a body which is a *manager* of an *authorised non-SRA firm*, when doing work of a sort authorised by the *SRA*, for that firm;

(c) an *authorised body*, or a body which should be a *recognised body* but has not been recognised by the *SRA*;
(d) any other person who is a *manager*, or *employee* of an *authorised body*, or of a body which should be a *recognised body* but has not been recognised by the *SRA*;
(e) any other person who is an *employee* of a *recognised sole practitioner*, or of a *sole practitioner* who should be a *recognised sole practitioner* but has not been recognised by the *SRA*;

and 'you' includes 'your' as appropriate.

3.2 The *Principles* apply to you if you are a *solicitor*, *REL* or *RFL*, and you are:

(a) *practising* as a *manager* or *employee* of an *authorised non-SRA firm* when doing work of a sort authorised by the *authorised non-SRA firm's approved regulator* or carrying on any other activity that is not precluded by the terms of your authorisation from the firm's *approved regulator*; or
(b) an *owner* of an *authorised non-SRA firm* even if you undertake no work for the body's *clients*.

3.3 The *Principles* apply to you if you are an *REL practising* as a *manager*, *employee*, *member* or *interest holder*, of an *Exempt European Practice*.

4: APPLICATION OF THE SRA PRINCIPLES IN RELATION TO PRACTICE FROM AN OFFICE OUTSIDE ENGLAND AND WALES

4.1 The *Principles* apply to you if you are:

(a) a body practising from an office outside England and Wales only if you are required to be an *authorised body* as a result of the nature of your practice and you have been authorised by the *SRA* accordingly; or

(b) a *manager* of such a body.

Guidance note

(i) In most circumstances, overseas offices of authorised bodies based in England and Wales will not require authorisation with the SRA and will be governed by the SRA Overseas Rules. However, in some circumstances, because of the work that is being carried out from the overseas office, it will need to be authorised (see Rule 2.1(e) and have regard to Rule 2.1(g) of the SRA Overseas Rules). In those circumstances, the SRA Principles and Code of Conduct apply.

4.2 The *Principles* apply to you if you are an individual engaged in *temporary practice overseas*.

5: APPLICATION OF THE SRA PRINCIPLES OUTSIDE PRACTICE

5.1 In relation to activities which fall outside *practice*, whether undertaken as a *lawyer* or in some other business or private capacity, *Principles* 1, 2 and 6 apply to you if you are a *solicitor*, *REL* or *RFL*.

6: GENERAL PROVISIONS

6.1 You must comply with the *Principles* at all times, but the extent to which you are expected to implement the requirements of the *Principles* will depend on your role in the *firm*, or your way of *practising*. For example, those who are managing a business will be expected to have more influence on how the *firm* or business is run than those *practising* in-house but not managing a legal department, or those *practising* as *employees* of a *firm*.

PART 3: TRANSITIONAL PROVISIONS

7: TRANSITIONAL PROVISIONS

7.1 For the avoidance of doubt, where a breach of any provision of the Solicitors' Code of Conduct 2007 comes to the attention of the *SRA* after 6 October 2011, this shall be subject to action by the *SRA* notwithstanding any repeal of the relevant provision.

7.2 [Deleted]

7.3 The *Principles* shall not apply to *licensed bodies* until such time as the *Society* is designated as a *licensing authority* under Part 1 of Schedule 10 to the *LSA* and all definitions shall be construed accordingly.

7.4 References in the preamble to:

(a) the *Principles* being made under section 83 of the Legal Services Act 2007, and
(b) *licensed bodies* and their *managers* and *employees*,

shall have no effect until such time as the *Society* is designated as a *licensing authority* under Part 1 of Schedule 10 to the *LSA*.

PART 4: INTERPRETATION

8: INTERPRETATION

8.1 The SRA Handbook Glossary 2012 shall apply to these rules and, unless the context otherwise requires:

(a) all italicised terms within these rules shall be defined; and
(b) terms within these rules shall be interpreted,

in accordance with the *Glossary*.

APPENDIX B2

SRA Code of Conduct 2011 (extracts)[1]

INTRODUCTION TO THE SRA CODE OF CONDUCT

OVERVIEW

Outcomes-focused regulation concentrates on providing positive outcomes which when achieved will benefit and protect *clients* and the public. The SRA Code of Conduct (the Code) sets out our outcomes-focused conduct requirements so that you can consider how best to achieve the right outcomes for your *clients* taking into account the way that your *firm* works and its *client* base. The Code is underpinned by effective, risk-based supervision and enforcement.

Those involved in providing legal advice and representation have long held the role of trusted adviser. There are fiduciary duties arising from this role and obligations owed to others, especially the *court*. No code can foresee or address every issue or ethical dilemma which may arise. You must strive to uphold the intention of the Code as well as its letter.

THE PRINCIPLES

The Code forms part of the Handbook, in which the 10 mandatory *Principles* are all-pervasive. They apply to all those we regulate and underpin all aspects of *practice*. They define the fundamental ethical and professional standards that we expect of all *firms* and individuals (including owners who may not be *lawyers*) when providing legal services. You should always have regard to the *Principles* and use them as your starting point when faced with an ethical dilemma.

Where two or more *Principles* come into conflict the one which takes precedence is the one which best serves the public interest in the particular circumstances, especially the public interest in the proper administration of justice. Compliance with the *Principles* is also subject to any overriding legal obligations.

You must:

1. uphold the rule of law and the proper administration of justice;
2. act with integrity;
3. not allow your independence to be compromised;
4. act in the best interests of each *client*;
5. provide a proper standard of service to your *clients*;
6. behave in a way that maintains the trust the public places in you and in the provision of legal services;

[1] Chapters 1–4, 7 and 10. See version 14 of the SRA Handbook, published on 30 April 2015, updated regularly at **www.sra.org.uk**.

7. comply with your legal and regulatory obligations and deal with your regulators and ombudsmen in an open, timely and co-operative manner;
8. run your business or carry out your role in the business effectively and in accordance with proper governance and sound financial and risk management principles;
9. run your business or carry out your role in the business in a way that encourages equality of opportunity and respect for diversity; and
10. protect *client* money and *assets*.

STRUCTURE OF THE CODE

The Code is divided into 5 sections:

- You and your client
- You and your business
- You and your regulator
- You and others
- Application, waivers and interpretation

Each section is divided into chapters dealing with particular regulatory issues, for example, client care, *conflicts of interests*, and *publicity*.

These chapters show how the *Principles* apply in certain contexts through mandatory and non-mandatory provisions.

MANDATORY PROVISIONS

The following provisions are mandatory:

- the outcomes;
- the application and waivers provisions in Chapters 13 and 13A;
- the interpretations; and
- the transitional provisions in Chapter 15.

The outcomes describe what *firms* and individuals are expected to achieve in order to comply with the relevant *Principles* in the context of the relevant chapter. In the case of *in-house practice*, we have set out at the end of each chapter which outcomes apply and in some cases have specified different outcomes.

In respect of *in-house practice*, different outcomes may apply depending on whether you are acting for your employer or for a *client* other than your employer as permitted by rules 4.1 to 4.10 of the *SRA Practice Framework Rules*.

The outcomes contained in each chapter are not an exhaustive list of the application of all the *Principles*. We have tried to make them as helpful as possible.

NON-MANDATORY PROVISIONS

The following provisions are non-mandatory:

- indicative behaviours;
- notes.

The outcomes are supplemented by indicative behaviours. The indicative behaviours specify, but do not constitute an exhaustive list of, the kind of behaviour which may establish compliance with, or contravention of the *Principles*. These are not mandatory but they may help us to decide whether an outcome has been achieved in compliance with the *Principles*.

We recognise that there may be other ways of achieving the outcomes. Where you have chosen a different method from those we have described as indicative behaviours, we might require you to demonstrate how you have nevertheless achieved the outcome. We encourage *firms* to consider how they can best achieve the outcomes, taking into account the nature of the *firm*, the particular circumstances of the matter and, crucially, the needs of their particular *clients*.

WAIVERS

Due to the flexibility of approach this structure allows, we do not anticipate receiving many applications for waivers from the mandatory outcomes. The *SRA*, nonetheless, reserves power to waive a provision in exceptional circumstances.

INTERPRETATION

Words shown in italics are defined in the *Glossary*.

SOURCES OF HELP

You can access the Code and other elements of the Handbook and find information on particular issues on the *SRA* website. You can also seek guidance on professional conduct from our Professional Ethics Guidance Team.

LIST OF CONTENTS OF THE CODE

PREAMBLE

The SRA Code of Conduct dated 17 June 2011 commencing 6 October 2011 made by the Solicitors Regulation Authority Board under sections 31, 79 and 80 of the Solicitors Act 1974, sections 9 and 9A of the Administration of Justice Act 1985 and section 83 of the Legal Services Act 2007, with the approval of the Legal Services Board under paragraph 19 of Schedule 4 to the Legal Services Act 2007, regulating the conduct of solicitors and their employees, registered European lawyers and their employees, registered foreign lawyers, recognised bodies and their managers and employees and licensed bodies and their managers and employees.

1ST SECTION: YOU AND YOUR CLIENT

CHAPTER 1: CLIENT CARE

This chapter is about providing a proper standard of service, which takes into account the individual needs and circumstances of each *client*. This includes providing *clients* with the information they need to make informed decisions about the services they need, how these will be delivered and how much they will cost. This will enable you and your *client* to understand each other's expectations and responsibilities. This chapter is also about ensuring that if *clients* are not happy with the service they have received they know how to make a *complaint* and that all *complaints* are dealt with promptly and fairly.

Your relationship with your *client* is a contractual one which carries with it legal, as well as conduct, obligations. This chapter focuses on your obligations in conduct.

You are generally free to decide whether or not to accept instructions in any matter, provided you do not discriminate unlawfully (see Chapter 2).

The outcomes in this chapter show how the *Principles* apply in the context of client care.

Outcomes

You must achieve these outcomes:

O(1.1) you treat your *clients* fairly;
O(1.2) you provide services to your *clients* in a manner which protects their interests in their matter, subject to the proper administration of justice;
O(1.3) when deciding whether to act, or terminate your instructions, you comply with the law and the Code;
O(1.4) you have the resources, skills and procedures to carry out your *clients'* instructions;
O(1.5) the service you provide to *clients* is competent, delivered in a timely manner and takes account of your *clients'* needs and circumstances;
O(1.6) you only enter into fee agreements with your *clients* that are legal, and which you consider are suitable for the *client's* needs and take account of the *client's* best interests;
O(1.7) you inform *clients* whether and how the services you provide are regulated and how this affects the protections available to the *client*;
O(1.8) *clients* have the benefit of your *compulsory professional indemnity insurance* and you do not exclude or attempt to exclude liability below the minimum level of cover required by the *SRA Indemnity Insurance Rules*;

O(1.9) *clients* are informed in writing at the outset of their matter of their right to complain and how *complaints* can be made;
O(1.10) *clients* are informed in writing, both at the time of engagement and at the conclusion of your *complaints* procedure, of their right to complain to the *Legal Ombudsman*, the time frame for doing so and full details of how to contact the *Legal Ombudsman*;
O(1.11) *clients' complaints* are dealt with promptly, fairly, openly and effectively;
O(1.12) *clients* are in a position to make informed decisions about the services they need, how their matter will be handled and the options available to them;
O(1.13) *clients* receive the best possible information, both at the time of engagement and when appropriate as their matter progresses, about the likely overall cost of their matter;
O(1.14) *clients* are informed of their right to challenge or complain about your bill and the circumstances in which they may be liable to pay interest on an unpaid bill;
O(1.15) you properly account to *clients* for any *financial benefit* you receive as a result of your instructions;
O(1.16) you inform current *clients* if you discover any act or omission which could give rise to a claim by them against you.

Indicative behaviours

Acting in the following way(s) may tend to show that you have achieved these outcomes and therefore complied with the *Principles*:

Dealing with the client's matter

IB(1.1) agreeing an appropriate level of service with your *client*, for example the type and frequency of communications;
IB(1.2) explaining your responsibilities and those of the *client*;
IB(1.3) ensuring that the *client* is told, in writing, the name and status of the person(s) dealing with the matter and the name and status of the person responsible for its overall supervision;
IB(1.4) explaining any arrangements, such as fee sharing or *referral arrangements*, which are relevant to the *client's* instructions;
IB(1.5) explaining any limitations or conditions on what you can do for the *client*, for example, because of the way the *client's* matter is funded;
IB(1.6) in taking instructions and during the course of the retainer, having proper regard to your *client's* mental capacity or other vulnerability, such as incapacity or duress;
IB(1.7) considering whether you should decline to act or cease to act because you cannot act in the *client's* best interests;
IB(1.8) if you seek to limit your liability to your *client* to a level above the minimum required by the *SRA Indemnity Insurance Rules*, ensuring that this limitation is in writing and is brought to the *client's* attention;
IB(1.9) refusing to act where your *client* proposes to make a gift of significant value to you or a member of your family, or a member of your *firm* or their family, unless the *client* takes independent legal advice;
IB(1.10) if you have to cease acting for a *client*, explaining to the *client* their possible options for pursuing their matter;
IB(1.11) you inform *clients* if they are not entitled to the protections of the SRA Compensation Fund;
IB(1.12) considering whether a *conflict of interests* has arisen or whether the *client* should be advised to obtain independent advice where the *client* notifies you of their intention to make a claim or if you discover an act or omission which might give rise to a claim;

Fee arrangements with your client

IB(1.13) discussing whether the potential outcomes of the *client's* matter are likely to justify the expense or risk involved, including any risk of having to pay someone else's legal fees;
IB(1.14) clearly explaining your fees and if and when they are likely to change;
IB(1.15) warning about any other payments for which the *client* may be responsible;
IB(1.16) discussing how the *client* will pay, including whether public funding may be available, whether the *client* has insurance that might cover the fees, and whether the fees may be paid by someone else such as a trade union;
IB(1.17) where you are acting for a *client* under a fee arrangement governed by statute, such as a conditional fee agreement, giving the *client* all relevant information relating to that arrangement;
IB(1.18) where you are acting for a publicly funded *client*, explaining how their publicly funded status affects the costs;
IB(1.19) providing the information in a clear and accessible form which is appropriate to the needs and circumstances of the *client*;
IB(1.20) where you receive a *financial benefit* as a result of acting for a *client*, either:

(a) paying it to the *client*;
(b) offsetting it against your fees; or
(c) keeping it only where you can justify keeping it, you have told the *client* the amount of the benefit (or an approximation if you do not know the exact amount) and the *client* has agreed that you can keep it;

IB(1.21) ensuring that *disbursements* included in your bill reflect the actual amount spent or to be spent on behalf of the *client*;

Complaints handling

IB(1.22) having a written *complaints* procedure which:

(a) is brought to *clients'* attention at the outset of the matter;
(b) is easy for *clients* to use and understand, allowing for *complaints* to be made by any reasonable means;
(c) is responsive to the needs of individual *clients*, especially those who are vulnerable;
(d) enables *complaints* to be dealt with promptly and fairly, with decisions based on a sufficient investigation of the circumstances;
(e) provides for appropriate remedies; and
(f) does not involve any charges to *clients* for handling their *complaints*;

IB(1.23) providing the *client* with a copy of the *firm's complaints* procedure on request;
IB(1.24) in the event that a *client* makes a *complaint*, providing them with all necessary information concerning the handling of the *complaint*.

Acting in the following way(s) may tend to show that you have not achieved these outcomes and therefore not complied with the *Principles*:

Accepting and refusing instructions

IB(1.25) acting for a *client* when instructions are given by someone else, or by only one *client* when you act jointly for others unless you are satisfied that the *person* providing the instructions has the authority to do so on behalf of all of the *clients*;
IB(1.26) ceasing to act for a *client* without good reason and without providing reasonable notice;
IB(1.27) entering into unlawful fee arrangements such as an unlawful contingency fee;

IB(1.28) acting for a *client* when there are reasonable grounds for believing that the instructions are affected by duress or undue influence without satisfying yourself that they represent the *client's* wishes.

In-house practice

Outcomes 1.1 to 1.5, 1.7, 1.15 and 1.16 apply to your *in-house practice*.

Outcomes 1.6 and 1.9 to 1.14 apply to your *in-house practice* where you act for someone other than your employer unless it is clear that the outcome is not relevant to your particular circumstances.

IHP(1.1) Instead of Outcome 1.8 you comply with the *SRA Practice Framework Rules* in relation to professional indemnity insurance.

Notes

(i) The information you give to *clients* will vary according to the needs and circumstances of the individual *client* and the type of work you are doing for them, for example an individual instructing you on a conveyancing matter is unlikely to need the same information as a sophisticated commercial *client* who instructs you on a regular basis.

(ii) Information about the *Legal Ombudsman*, including the scheme rules, contact details and time limits, can be found at **www.legalombudsman.org.uk**.

CHAPTER 2: EQUALITY AND DIVERSITY

This chapter is about encouraging equality of opportunity and respect for diversity, and preventing unlawful discrimination, in your relationship with your *clients* and others. The requirements apply in relation to age, disability, gender reassignment, marriage and civil partnership, pregnancy and maternity, race, religion or belief, sex and sexual orientation.

Everyone needs to contribute to compliance with these requirements, for example by treating each other, and *clients*, fairly and with respect, by embedding such values in the workplace and by challenging inappropriate behaviour and processes. Your role in embedding these values will vary depending on your role.

As a matter of general law you must comply with requirements set out in legislation – including the Equality Act 2010 – as well as the conduct duties contained in this chapter.

The outcomes in this chapter show how the *Principles* apply in the context of equality and diversity.

Outcomes

You must achieve these outcomes:

O(2.1) you do not discriminate unlawfully, or victimise or harass anyone, in the course of your professional dealings;

O(2.2) you provide services to *clients* in a way that respects diversity;

O(2.3) you make reasonable adjustments to ensure that disabled *clients*, *employees* or *managers* are not placed at a substantial disadvantage compared to those who are not disabled, and you do not pass on the costs of these adjustments to these disabled *clients*, *employees* or *managers*;

O(2.4) your approach to recruitment and employment encourages equality of opportunity and respect for diversity;
O(2.5) *complaints* of discrimination are dealt with promptly, fairly, openly, and effectively.

Indicative behaviours

Acting in the following way(s) may tend to show that you have achieved these outcomes and therefore complied with the *Principles*:

IB(2.1) having a written equality and diversity policy which is appropriate to the size and nature of the *firm* and includes the following features:

- (a) a commitment to the principles of equality and diversity and legislative requirements;
- (b) a requirement that all *employees* and *managers* comply with the outcomes;
- (c) provisions to encompass your recruitment and interview processes;
- (d) details of how the *firm* will implement, monitor, evaluate and update the policy;
- (e) details of how the *firm* will ensure equality in relation to the treatment of *employees*, *managers*, *clients* and third parties instructed in connection with *client* matters;
- (f) details of how *complaints* and disciplinary issues are to be dealt with;
- (g) details of the *firm's* arrangements for workforce diversity monitoring; and
- (h) details of how the *firm* will communicate the policy to *employees*, *managers* and *clients*;

IB(2.2) providing *employees* and *managers* with training and information about complying with equality and diversity requirements;
IB(2.3) monitoring and responding to issues identified by your policy and reviewing and updating your policy.

Acting in the following way(s) may tend to show that you have not achieved these outcomes and therefore not complied with the *Principles*:

IB(2.4) being subject to any decision of a court or tribunal of the *UK*, that you have committed, or are to be treated as having committed, an unlawful act of discrimination;
IB(2.5) discriminating unlawfully when accepting or refusing instructions to act for a *client*.

In-house practice

Outcomes 2.1 and 2.2 apply to all *in-house practice*.
Instead of Outcomes 2.3 to 2.5 you must achieve the following outcome:

IHP(2.1) if you have management responsibilities you take all reasonable steps to encourage equality of opportunity and respect for diversity in your workplace.

Notes

- (i) The obligations in this chapter closely mirror your legal obligations. You can obtain further information from the Equality and Human Rights Commission, **www.equalityhumanrights.com**.
- (ii) See also Chapter 1 (Client care) for the handling of *client complaints*.

(iii) See also Chapter 7 (Management of your business) for your obligation to have in place appropriate systems and controls for complying with the outcomes in this chapter.

CHAPTER 3: CONFLICTS OF INTERESTS

This chapter deals with the proper handling of *conflicts of interests*, which is a critical public protection. It is important to have in place systems that enable you to identify and deal with potential conflicts.

Conflicts of interests can arise between:

1. you and current *clients* ('*own interest conflict*'); and
2. two or more current *clients* ('*client conflict*').

You can never act where there is a conflict, or a significant risk of conflict, between you and your *client*.

If there is a conflict, or a significant risk of a conflict, between two or more current *clients*, you must not act for all or both of them unless the matter falls within the scope of the limited exceptions set out at Outcomes 3.6 or 3.7. In deciding whether to act in these limited circumstances, the overriding consideration will be the best interests of each of the *clients* concerned and, in particular, whether the benefits to the *clients* of you acting for all or both of the *clients* outweigh the risks.

You should also bear in mind that *conflicts of interests* may affect your duties of confidentiality and disclosure which are dealt with in Chapter 4.

The outcomes in this chapter show how the *Principles* apply in the context of *conflicts of interests*.

Outcomes

You must achieve these outcomes:

Systems

O(3.1) you have effective systems and controls in place to enable you to identify and assess potential *conflicts of interests*;

O(3.2) your systems and controls for identifying *own interest conflicts* are appropriate to the size and complexity of the *firm* and the nature of the work undertaken, and enable you to assess all the relevant circumstances, including whether your ability as an individual, or that of anyone within your *firm*, to act in the best interests of the *client(s)*, is impaired by:

(a) any financial interest;
(b) a personal relationship;
(c) the appointment of you, or a member of your *firm* or family, to public office;
(d) commercial relationships; or
(e) your employment;

O(3.3) your systems and controls for identifying *client conflicts* are appropriate to the size and complexity of the *firm* and the nature of the work undertaken, and enable you to assess all relevant circumstances, including whether:

(a) the *clients'* interests are different;
(b) your ability to give independent advice to the *clients* may be fettered;
(c) there is a need to negotiate between the *clients*;
(d) there is an imbalance in bargaining power between the *clients*; or

(e) any *client* is vulnerable;

Prohibition on acting in conflict situations

O(3.4) you do not act if there is an *own interest conflict* or a significant risk of an *own interest conflict*;

O(3.5) you do not act if there is a *client conflict*, or a significant risk of a *client conflict*, unless the circumstances set out in Outcomes 3.6 or 3.7 apply;

Exceptions where you may act, with appropriate safeguards, where there is a client conflict

O(3.6) where there is a *client conflict* and the *clients* have a *substantially common interest* in relation to a matter or a particular aspect of it, you only act if:

(a) you have explained the relevant issues and risks to the *clients* and you have a reasonable belief that they understand those issues and risks;
(b) all the *clients* have given informed consent in writing to you acting;
(c) you are satisfied that it is reasonable for you to act for all the *clients* and that it is in their best interests; and
(d) you are satisfied that the benefits to the *clients* of you doing so outweigh the risks;

O(3.7) where there is a *client conflict* and the *clients* are *competing for the same objective*, you only act if:

(a) you have explained the relevant issues and risks to the *clients* and you have a reasonable belief that they understand those issues and risks;
(b) the *clients* have confirmed in writing that they want you to act, in the knowledge that you act, or may act, for one or more other *clients* who are *competing for the same objective*;
(c) there is no other *client conflict* in relation to that matter;
(d) unless the *clients* specifically agree, no individual acts for, or is responsible for the supervision of work done for, more than one of the *clients* in that matter; and
(e) you are satisfied that it is reasonable for you to act for all the *clients* and that the benefits to the *clients* of you doing so outweigh the risks.

Indicative behaviours

Acting in the following way(s) may tend to show that you have achieved these outcomes and therefore complied with the *Principles*:

IB(3.1) training *employees* and *managers* to identify and assess potential *conflicts of interests*;

IB(3.2) declining to act for *clients* whose interests are in direct conflict, for example claimant and defendant in litigation;

IB(3.3) declining to act for *clients* where you may need to negotiate on matters of substance on their behalf, for example negotiating on price between a buyer and seller of a property;

IB(3.4) declining to act where there is unequal bargaining power between the *clients*, for example acting for a seller and buyer where a builder is selling to a non-commercial *client*;

IB(3.5) declining to act for *clients* under Outcome 3.6 (*substantially common interest*) or Outcome 3.7 (*competing for the same objective*) where the *clients* cannot be represented even-handedly, or will be prejudiced by lack of separate representation;

IB(3.6) acting for *clients* under Outcome 3.7 (*competing for the same objective*) only where the *clients* are sophisticated users of legal services;

IB(3.7) acting for *clients* who are the lender and borrower on the grant of a mortgage of land only where:

(a) the mortgage is a standard mortgage (i.e. one provided in the normal course of the lender's activities, where a significant part of the lender's activities consists of lending and the mortgage is on standard terms) of property to be used as the borrower's private residence;

(b) you are satisfied that it is reasonable and in the *clients'* best interests for you to act; and

(c) the certificate of title required by the lender is in the form approved by the *Society* and the Council of Mortgage Lenders.

Acting in the following way(s) may tend to show that you have not achieved these outcomes and therefore not complied with the *Principles*:

IB(3.8) in a personal capacity, selling to or buying from, lending to or borrowing from a *client*, unless the *client* has obtained independent legal advice;

IB(3.9) advising a *client* to invest in a business, in which you have an interest which affects your ability to provide impartial advice;

IB(3.10) where you hold a power of attorney for a *client*, using that power to gain a benefit for yourself which in your professional capacity you would not have been prepared to allow to a third party;

IB(3.11) acting for two or more *clients* in a *conflict of interests* under Outcome 3.6 (*substantially common interest*) where the *clients'* interests in the end result are not the same, for example one partner buying out the interest of the other partner in their joint business or a seller transferring a property to a buyer;

IB(3.12) acting for two or more *clients* in a *conflict of interests* under Outcome 3.6 (*substantially common interest*) where it is unreasonable to act because there is unequal bargaining power;

IB(3.13) acting for two buyers where there is a *conflict of interests* under Outcome 3.7 (*competing for the same objective*), for example where two buyers are competing for a residential property;

IB(3.14) acting for a buyer (including a lessee) and seller (including a lessor) in a transaction relating to the transfer of land for value, the grant or assignment of a lease or some other interest in land for value.

In-house practice

Outcomes 3.4 to 3.7 apply to your *in-house practice*.

Outcomes 3.1 to 3.3 apply if you have management responsibilities.

CHAPTER 4: CONFIDENTIALITY AND DISCLOSURE

This chapter is about the protection of *clients'* confidential information and the disclosure of material information to *clients*.

Protection of confidential information is a fundamental feature of your relationship with *clients*. It exists as a concept both as a matter of law and as a matter of conduct. This duty continues despite the end of the retainer and even after the death of the *client*.

It is important to distinguish the conduct duties from the concept of law known as legal professional privilege.

Bear in mind that all members of the *firm* or *in-house practice*, including support staff, consultants and locums, owe a duty of confidentiality to your *clients*.

The duty of confidentiality to all *clients* must be reconciled with the duty of disclosure to *clients*. This duty of disclosure is limited to information of which you are aware which is material to your *client's* matter. Where you cannot reconcile these two duties, then the protection of confidential information is paramount. You should not continue to act for a *client* for whom you cannot disclose material information, except in very limited circumstances, where safeguards are in place. Such situations often also give rise to a *conflict of interests* which is discussed in Chapter 3.

The outcomes in this chapter show how the *Principles* apply in the context of confidentiality and disclosure.

Outcomes

You must achieve these outcomes:

O(4.1) you keep the affairs of *clients* confidential unless disclosure is required or permitted by law or the *client* consents;

O(4.2) any individual who is advising a *client* makes that *client* aware of all information material to that retainer of which the individual has personal knowledge;

O(4.3) you ensure that where your duty of confidentiality to one *client* comes into conflict with your duty of disclosure to another *client*, your duty of confidentiality takes precedence;

O(4.4) you do not act for A in a matter where A has an interest adverse to B, and B is a *client* for whom you hold confidential information which is material to A in that matter, unless the confidential information can be protected by the use of safeguards, and:

- (a) you reasonably believe that A is aware of, and understands, the relevant issues and gives informed consent;
- (b) either:
  - (i) B gives informed consent and you agree with B the safeguards to protect B's information; or
  - (ii) where this is not possible, you put in place effective safeguards including information barriers which comply with the common law; and
- (c) it is reasonable in all the circumstances to act for A with such safeguards in place;

O(4.5) you have effective systems and controls in place to enable you to identify risks to *client* confidentiality and to mitigate those risks.

Indicative behaviours

Acting in the following way(s) may tend to show that you have achieved these outcomes and therefore complied with the *Principles*:

IB(4.1) your systems and controls for identifying risks to *client* confidentiality are appropriate to the size and complexity of the *firm* or *in-house practice* and the nature of the work undertaken, and enable you to assess all the relevant circumstances;

IB(4.2) you comply with the law in respect of your fiduciary duties in relation to confidentiality and disclosure;

IB(4.3) you only outsource services when you are satisfied that the provider has taken all appropriate steps to ensure that your *clients'* confidential information will be protected;

IB(4.4) where you are an individual who has responsibility for acting for a *client* or supervising a *client's* matter, you disclose to the *client* all information material to the *client's* matter of which you are personally aware, except when:

(a) the *client* gives specific informed consent to non-disclosure or a different standard of disclosure arises;
(b) there is evidence that serious physical or mental injury will be caused to a person(s) if the information is disclosed to the *client*;
(c) legal restrictions effectively prohibit you from passing the information to the *client*, such as the provisions in the money-laundering and anti-terrorism legislation;
(d) it is obvious that privileged documents have been mistakenly disclosed to you;
(e) you come into possession of information relating to state security or intelligence matters to which the Official Secrets Act 1989 applies;

IB(4.5) not acting for A where B is a *client* for whom you hold confidential information which is material to A unless the confidential information can be protected.

Acting in the following way(s) may tend to show that you have not achieved these outcomes and therefore not complied with the *Principles*:

IB(4.6) disclosing the content of a will on the death of a *client* unless consent has been provided by the personal representatives for the content to be released;
IB(4.7) disclosing details of bills sent to *clients* to third parties, such as debt factoring companies in relation to the collection of book debts, unless the *client* has consented.

In-house practice

The outcomes listed above apply to your *in-house practice*.

Notes

(i) The protection of confidential information may be at particular risk where:

(a) two or more *firms* merge;
(b) when you leave one *firm* and join another, such as if you join a *firm* acting against one of your former *clients*.

(ii) The following circumstances may make it difficult to implement effective safeguards and information barriers:

(a) you are a small *firm*;
(b) the physical structure or layout of the *firm* means that it will be difficult to preserve confidentiality; or
(c) the *clients* are not sophisticated users of legal services.

...

2ND SECTION: YOU AND YOUR BUSINESS

CHAPTER 7: MANAGEMENT OF YOUR BUSINESS

This chapter is about the management and supervision of your *firm* or *in-house practice*.

Everyone has a role to play in the efficient running of a business, although of course that role will depend on the individual's position within the organisation. However, over-arching responsibility for the management of the business in the broadest sense rests with the *manager(s)*. The *manager(s)* should determine what arrangements are appropriate to meet the outcomes. Factors to be taken into account will include the size and complexity of the business; the number, experience and qualifications of the *employees*; the number of offices; and the nature of the work undertaken.

Where you are using a third party to provide services that you could provide, (often described as 'outsourcing'), this chapter sets out the outcomes you need to achieve.

The outcomes in this chapter show how the *Principles* apply in the context of the management of your business.

Outcomes

You must achieve these outcomes:

O(7.1) you have a clear and effective governance structure and reporting lines;
O(7.2) you have effective systems and controls in place to achieve and comply with all the *Principles*, rules and outcomes and other requirements of the Handbook, where applicable;
O(7.3) you identify, monitor and manage risks to compliance with all the *Principles*, rules and outcomes and other requirements of the Handbook, if applicable to you, and take steps to address issues identified;
O(7.4) you maintain systems and controls for monitoring the financial stability of your *firm* and risks to money and *assets* entrusted to you by *clients* and others, and you take steps to address issues identified;
O(7.5) you comply with legislation applicable to your business, including anti-money laundering and data protection legislation;
O(7.6) you train individuals working in the *firm* to maintain a level of competence appropriate to their work and level of responsibility;
O(7.7) you comply with the statutory requirements for the direction and supervision of *reserved legal activities* and *immigration work*;
O(7.8) you have a system for supervising *clients'* matters, to include the regular checking of the quality of work by suitably competent and experienced people;
O(7.9) you do not outsource *reserved legal activities* to a *person* who is not authorised to conduct such activities;
O(7.10) subject to Outcome 7.9, where you outsource *legal activities* or any operational functions that are critical to the delivery of any *legal activities*, you ensure such outsourcing:

(a) does not adversely affect your ability to comply with, or the *SRA's* ability to monitor your compliance with, your obligations in the Handbook;
(b) is subject to contractual arrangements that enable the *SRA* or its agent to obtain information from, inspect the records (including electronic records) of, or enter the premises of, the third party, in relation to the outsourced activities or functions;
(c) does not alter your obligations towards your *clients*; and
(d) does not cause you to breach the conditions with which you must comply in order to be authorised and to remain so;

O(7.11) you identify, monitor and manage the compliance of your *overseas practices* with the SRA Overseas Rules;
O(7.12) you identify, monitor and manage all risks to your business which may arise from your *connected practices*;
O(7.13) you assess and purchase the level of professional indemnity insurance cover that is appropriate for your current and past practice, taking into account potential levels of claim by your *clients* and others and any alternative arrangements you or your *client* may make.

Indicative behaviours

Acting in the following way(s) may tend to show that you have achieved these outcomes and therefore complied with the *Principles*:

IB(7.1) safekeeping of documents and *assets* entrusted to the *firm*;
IB(7.2) controlling budgets, expenditure and cash flow;
IB(7.3) identifying and monitoring financial, operational and business continuity risks including *complaints*, credit risks and exposure, claims under legislation relating to matters such as data protection, IT failures and abuses, and damage to offices;
IB(7.4) making arrangements for the continuation of your *firm* in the event of absences and emergencies, for example holiday or sick leave, with the minimum interruption to *clients'* business;
IB(7.5) you maintain systems and controls for managing the risks posed by any financial inter-dependence which exists with your *connected practices*;
IB(7.6) you take appropriate action to control the use of your brand by any body or individual outside of England and Wales which is not an *overseas practice*.

In-house practice

Outcomes 7.5 and 7.7 apply to your *in-house practice*.

Outcomes 7.1 to 7.3, and 7.6 and 7.8 to 7.10 apply to you if you have management responsibilities.

Notes

(i) All of the chapters in the Code will be relevant to the management of your business, in particular those which require you to have systems and controls in place.
(ii) This chapter should also be read with the *SRA Authorisation Rules*, the SRA Financial Services (Conduct of Business) Rules 2001 and the *SRA Indemnity Insurance Rules*.

...

3RD SECTION: YOU AND YOUR REGULATOR

CHAPTER 10: YOU AND YOUR REGULATOR

This chapter is about co-operation with your regulators and ombudsmen, primarily the *SRA* and the *Legal Ombudsman*.

The information which we request from you will help us understand any risks to *clients*, and the public interest more generally.

The outcomes in this chapter show how the *Principles* apply in the context of you and your regulator.

Outcomes

You must achieve these outcomes:

O(10.1) you ensure that you comply with all the reporting and notification requirements in the Handbook that apply to you;
O(10.2) you provide the *SRA* with information to enable the *SRA* to decide upon any application you make, such as for a practising certificate, registration, recognition or a licence and whether any conditions should apply;
O(10.3) you notify the *SRA* promptly of any material changes to relevant information about you including serious financial difficulty, action taken against you by another regulator and serious failure to comply with or achieve the *Principles*, rules, outcomes and other requirements of the Handbook;
O(10.4) you report to the *SRA* promptly, serious misconduct by any person or *firm* authorised by the *SRA*, or any *employee*, *manager* or *owner* of any such *firm* (taking into account, where necessary, your duty of confidentiality to your *client*);
O(10.5) you ensure that the *SRA* is in a position to assess whether any persons requiring prior approval are fit and proper at the point of approval and remain so;
O(10.6) you co-operate fully with the *SRA* and the *Legal Ombudsman* at all times including in relation to any investigation about a *claim for redress* against you;
O(10.7) you do not attempt to prevent anyone from providing information to the *SRA* or the *Legal Ombudsman*;
O(10.8) you comply promptly with any written notice from the *SRA*;
O(10.9) pursuant to a notice under Outcome 10.8, you:

(a) produce for inspection by the *SRA documents* held by you, or held under your control;
(b) provide all information and explanations requested; and
(c) comply with all requests from the *SRA* as to the form in which you produce any *documents* you hold electronically, and for photocopies of any *documents* to take away;

in connection with your *practice* or in connection with any trust of which you are, or formerly were, a trustee;
O(10.10) you provide any necessary permissions for information to be given, so as to enable the *SRA* to:

(a) prepare a report on any *documents* produced; and
(b) seek verification from *clients*, staff and the banks, building societies or other financial institutions used by you;

O(10.11) when required by the *SRA* in relation to a matter specified by the *SRA*, you:

(a) act promptly to investigate whether any *person* may have a *claim for redress* against you;
(b) provide the *SRA* with a report on the outcome of such an investigation, identifying *persons* who may have such a claim;
(c) notify *persons* that they may have a right of redress against you, providing them with information as to the nature of the possible claim, about the *firm's complaints* procedure and about the *Legal Ombudsman*; and
(d) ensure, where you have identified a *person* who may have a *claim for redress*, that the matter is dealt with under the *firm's complaints* procedure as if that *person* had made a *complaint*;

O(10.12) you do not attempt to abrogate to any third party your regulatory responsibilities in the Handbook, including the role of Compliance Officer for Legal Practice (*COLP*) or Compliance Officer for Finance and Administration (*COFA*);
O(10.13) once you are aware that your *firm* will cease to *practise*, you effect the orderly and transparent wind-down of activities, including informing the *SRA* before the *firm* closes.

Indicative behaviours

Acting in the following way(s) may tend to show that you have achieved these outcomes and therefore complied with the *Principles*:

IB(10.1) actively monitoring your achievement of the outcomes in order to improve standards and identify non-achievement of the outcomes;
IB(10.2) actively monitoring your financial stability and viability in order to identify and mitigate any risks to the public;
IB(10.3) notifying the *SRA* promptly of any indicators of serious financial difficulty, such as inability to pay your professional indemnity insurance premium, or rent or salaries, or breach of bank covenants;
IB(10.4) notifying the *SRA* promptly when you become aware that your business may not be financially viable to continue trading as a going concern, for example because of difficult trading conditions, poor cash flow, increasing overheads, loss of *managers* or *employees* and/or loss of sources of revenue;
IB(10.5) notifying the *SRA* of any serious issues identified as a result of monitoring referred to in IB10.1 and IB10.2 above, and producing a plan for remedying issues that have been identified;
IB(10.6) responding appropriately to any serious issues identified concerning competence and fitness and propriety of your *employees*, *managers* and *owners*;
IB(10.7) reporting disciplinary action taken against you by another regulator;
IB(10.8) informing the *SRA* promptly when you become aware of a significant change to your *firm*, for example:

(a) key personnel, such as a *manager*, *COLP* or *COFA*, joining or leaving the *firm*;
(b) a merger with, or an acquisition by or of, another *firm*;

IB(10.9) having appropriate arrangements for the orderly transfer of *clients'* property to another *authorised body* if your *firm* closes;
IB(10.10) having a 'whistle-blowing' policy.

Acting in the following way(s) may tend to show that you have not achieved these outcomes and therefore not complied with the *Principles*:

IB(10.11) entering into an agreement which would attempt to preclude the *SRA* or the *Legal Ombudsman* from investigating any actual or potential *complaint* or allegation of professional misconduct;
IB(10.12) unless you can properly allege malice, issuing defamation proceedings in respect of a *complaint* to the *SRA*.

In-house practice

The outcomes in this chapter apply to your *in-house practice*.

Notes

(i) A notice under this chapter is deemed to be duly served:

(a) on the date on which it is delivered to or left at your last notified *practising* address;
(b) on the date on which it is sent electronically to your e-mail or fax address; or
(c) seven days after it has been sent by post or document exchange to your last notified *practising* address.

(ii) The outcomes in this chapter should be considered in conjunction with the following:

(a) Chapter 7 (Management of your business) – requirements for risk management procedures; and
(b) note (xv) to Rule 8 of the *SRA Authorisation Rules*.

…

APPENDIX B3

SRA Accounts Rules 2011 (extracts)[1]

RULE 12: CATEGORIES OF MONEY

12.1 These rules do not apply to *out-of-scope money*, save to the limited extent specified in the rules. All other money held or received in the course of practice falls into one or other of the following categories:

(a) 'client money' – money held or received for a *client* or as *trustee*, and all other money which is not *office money*; or
(b) 'office money' – money which belongs to *you* or *your firm*.

12.2 'Client money' includes money held or received:

(a) as *trustee*;
(b) as agent, bailee, stakeholder, or as the donee of a power of attorney, or as a liquidator, trustee in bankruptcy, *Court of Protection deputy* or trustee of an occupational pension scheme;
(c) for payment of unpaid *professional disbursements*;
(d) for payment of stamp duty land tax, Land Registry registration fees, telegraphic transfer fees and court fees (but see also guidance note (i));
(e) as a payment on account of *costs* generally;
(f) as a financial benefit paid in respect of a *client*, unless the *client* has given *you* prior authority to retain it (see Chapter 1, outcome 1.15 and indicative behaviour 1.20 of the *SRA Code of Conduct*);
(g) jointly with another person outside the *firm*.

12.3 Money held to the sender's order is *client money*.

(a) If money is accepted on such terms, it must be held in a *client account*.
(b) However, a cheque or draft sent to *you* on terms that the cheque or draft (as opposed to the money) is held to the sender's order must not be presented for payment without the sender's consent.
(c) The recipient is always subject to a professional obligation to return the money, or the cheque or draft, to the sender on demand.

12.4 An advance to a *client* which is paid into a *client account* under rule 14.2(b) becomes *client money*.

12.5 A cheque in respect of damages and *costs*, made payable to the *client* but paid into a *client account* under rule 14.2(e), becomes *client money*.

12.6 Endorsing a cheque or draft over to a *client* or employer in the course of practice amounts to receiving *client money*. Even if no other *client money* is held or received, *you* must comply with some provisions of the rules, e.g.:

(a) rule 7 (duty to remedy breaches);

[1] Rules 12–25 and Appendix 3. See version 14 of the SRA Handbook, published on 30 April 2015, updated regularly at **www.sra.org.uk**.

(b) rule 29 (accounting records for client accounts, etc.);
(c) rule 31 (production of documents, information and explanations);
(d) rule 32 (delivery of accountants' reports).

12.7 'Office money' includes:

(a) money held or received in connection with running the *firm*; for example, PAYE, or VAT on the *firm's fees*;
(b) *interest* on *general client accounts*; the *bank* or *building society* should be instructed to credit such *interest* to the *office account* – but see also rule 14.2(d);
(c) payments received in respect of:

(i) *fees* due to the *firm* against a bill or written notification of *costs* incurred, which has been given or sent in accordance with rule 17.2;
(ii) *disbursements* already paid by the *firm*;
(iii) *disbursements* incurred but not yet paid by the *firm*, but excluding unpaid *professional disbursements*;
(iv) money paid for or towards an *agreed fee*;

(d) money held in a *client account* and earmarked for *costs* under rule 17.3;
(e) money held or received from the Legal Aid Agency as a *regular payment* (see rule 19.2).

12.8 If a *firm* conducts a personal or office transaction – for instance, conveyancing – for a *principal* (or for a number of *principals*), money held or received on behalf of the *principal(s)* is *office money*. However, other circumstances may mean that the money is *client money*, for example:

(a) If the *firm* also acts for a lender, money held or received on behalf of the lender is *client money*.
(b) If the *firm* acts for a *principal* and, for example, his or her spouse jointly (assuming the spouse is not a *partner* in the practice), money received on their joint behalf is *client money*.
(c) If the *firm* acts for an assistant *solicitor*, consultant or non-solicitor employee, or (if it is a *company*) a *director*, or (if it is an *LLP*) a member, he or she is regarded as a *client* of the *firm*, and money received for him or her is *client money* – even if he or she conducts the matter personally.

Guidance notes

(i) Money held or received for payment of stamp duty land tax, Land Registry registration fees, telegraphic transfer fees and court fees is not office money because you have not incurred an obligation to HMRC, the Land Registry, the bank or the court to pay the duty or fee; (on the other hand, if you have already paid the duty or fee out of your own resources, or have received the service on credit, or the bank's charge for a telegraphic transfer forms part of your profit costs, payment subsequently received from the client will be office money);
(ii) Money held:

(a) by liquidators, trustees in bankruptcy, Court of Protection deputies and trustees of occupational pension schemes;
(b) jointly with another person outside the practice (for example, with a lay trustee, or with another firm);

is client money, subject to a limited application of the rules – see rules 8 and 9. The donee of a power of attorney, who operates the donor's own account, is also subject to a limited application of the rules (see rule 10), although money kept in the donor's own account is not 'client money' because it is not 'held or received' by the donee.

(iii) If the SRA intervenes in a practice, money from the practice is held or received by the SRA's intervention agent subject to a trust under Schedule 1 paragraph 7(1) of the Solicitors Act 1974, and is therefore client money. The same provision requires the agent to pay the money into a client account.

(iv) Money held or received in the course of employment when practising in one of the capacities listed in rule 5 (persons exempt from the rules) is not 'client money' for the purpose of the rules, because the rules do not apply at all.

(v) The receipt of out-of-scope money of an MDP which is mixed with other types of money is dealt with in rules 17 and 18.

(vi) See Appendices 1 and 2 (which do not form part of the rules) for a summary of the effect of the rules and the treatment of different types of money.

PART 2: CLIENT MONEY AND OPERATION OF A CLIENT ACCOUNT

RULE 13: CLIENT ACCOUNTS

13.1 If *you* hold or receive *client money*, *you* must keep one or more *client accounts* (unless all the *client money* is always dealt with outside any *client account* in accordance with rule 8, rule 9, rule 15 or rule 16).

13.2 A 'client account' is an account of a practice kept at a *bank* or *building society* for holding *client money*, in accordance with the requirements of this part of the rules.

13.3 The *client account(s)* of:

(a) a *sole practitioner* must be in the name under which the *sole practitioner* is recognised by the *SRA*, whether that is the *sole practitioner's* own name or the *firm* name;

(b) a *partnership* must be in the name under which the *partnership* is recognised by the *SRA*;

(c) an incorporated practice must be in the company name, or the name of the *LLP*, as registered at Companies House;

(d) in-house *solicitors* or *RELs* must be in the name of the current *principal solicitor/REL* or *solicitors/RELs*;

(e) *trustees*, where all the *trustees* of a *trust* are *managers* and/or employees of the same *recognised body* or *licensed body*, must be either in the name of the *recognised body/licensed body* or in the name of the *trustee(s)*;

(f) *trustees*, where all the *trustees* of a *trust* are the *sole practitioner* and/or his or her employees, must be either in the name under which the *sole practitioner* is recognised by the *SRA* or in the name of the *trustee(s)*;

and the name of the account must also include the word 'client' in full (an abbreviation is not acceptable).

13.4 A *client account* must be:

(a) a *bank* account at a branch (or a *bank's* head office) in England and Wales; or

(b) a *building society* account at a branch (or a society's head office) in England and Wales.

13.5 There are two types of *client account*:

(a) a 'separate designated client account', which is an account for money relating to a single *client*, other person or *trust*, and which includes in its title, in addition to the requirements of rule 13.3 above, a reference to the identity of the *client*, other person or *trust*; and

(b) a 'general client account', which is any other *client account*.

13.6 [Deleted]

13.7 The *clients* of a *licensed body* must be informed at the outset of the retainer, or during the course of the retainer as appropriate, if the *licensed body* is (or becomes) owned by a *bank* or *building society* and its *client account* is held at that *bank* or *building society* (or another *bank* or *building society* in the same group).

13.8 Money held in a *client account* must be immediately available, even at the sacrifice of *interest*, unless the *client* otherwise instructs, or the circumstances clearly indicate otherwise.

Guidance notes

(i) In the case of in-house practice, any client account should include the names of all solicitors or registered European lawyers held out on the notepaper as principals. The names of other employees who are solicitors or registered European lawyers may also be included if so desired. Any person whose name is included will have to be included on the accountant's report.

(ii) A firm may have any number of separate designated client accounts and general client accounts.

(iii) Compliance with rule 13.1 to 13.4 ensures that clients, as well as the bank or building society, have the protection afforded by section 85 of the Solicitors Act 1974 or article 4 of the Legal Services Act 2007 (Designation as a Licensing Authority) (No. 2) Order 2011 as appropriate.

RULE 14: USE OF A CLIENT ACCOUNT

14.1 *Client money* must *without delay* be paid into a *client account*, and must be held in a *client account*, except when the rules provide to the contrary (see rules 8, 9, 15, 16, 17 and 19).

14.2 Only *client money* may be paid into or held in a *client account*, except:

(a) an amount of the *firm's* own money required to open or maintain the account;

(b) an advance from the *firm* to fund a payment on behalf of a *client* or *trust* in excess of funds held for that *client* or *trust*; the sum becomes *client money* on payment into the account (for *interest* on *client money*, see rule 22.2(c));

(c) money to replace any sum which for any reason has been drawn from the account in breach of rule 20; the replacement money becomes *client money* on payment into the account;

(d) *interest* which is paid into a *client account* to enable payment from the *client account* of all money owed to the *client*; and

(e) a cheque in respect of damages and *costs*, made payable to the *client*, which is paid into the *client account* pursuant to the *Society's* Conditional Fee Agreement; the sum becomes *client money* on payment into the account (but see rule 17.1(e) for the transfer of the *costs* element from *client account*);

and except when the rules provide to the contrary (see guidance note (ii) below).

14.3 *Client money* must be returned to the *client* (or other person on whose behalf the money is held) promptly, as soon as there is no longer any proper reason to retain those funds. Payments received after *you* have already accounted to the *client*, for example by way of a refund, must be paid to the *client* promptly.

14.4 *You* must promptly inform a *client* (or other person on whose behalf the money is held) in writing of the amount of any *client money* retained at the end of a matter (or the substantial conclusion of a matter), and the reason for that retention. *You* must inform the *client* (or other person) in writing at least once every twelve months thereafter of the amount of *client money* still held and the reason for the retention, for as long as *you* continue to hold that money.

14.5 *You* must not provide banking facilities through a *client account*. Payments into, and transfers or withdrawals from, a *client account* must be in respect of instructions relating to an underlying transaction (and the funds arising therefrom) or to a service forming part of *your* normal regulated activities.

Guidance notes

(i) Exceptions to rule 14.1 (client money must be paid into a client account) can be found in:

- (a) rule 8 – liquidators, trustees in bankruptcy, Court of Protection deputies and trustees of occupational pension schemes;
- (b) rule 9 – joint accounts;
- (c) rule 15 – client's instructions;
- (d) rule 16 – cash paid straight to client, beneficiary or third party;
  - (A) cheque endorsed to client, beneficiary or third party;
  - (B) money withheld from client account on the SRA's authority;
  - (C) money withheld from client account in accordance with a trustee's powers;
- (e) rule 17.1(b) – receipt and transfer of costs;
- (f) rule 19.1 – payments by the Legal Aid Agency.

(ii) Rule 14.2(a) to (e) provides for exceptions to the principle that only client money may be paid into a client account. Additional exceptions can be found in:

- (a) rule 17.1(c) – receipt and transfer of costs;
- (b) rule 18.2(b) – receipt of mixed payments;
- (c) rule 19.2(c)(ii) – transfer to client account of a sum for unpaid professional disbursements, where regular payments are received from the Legal Aid Agency.

(iii) Only a nominal sum will be required to open or maintain an account. In practice, banks will usually open (and, if instructed, keep open) accounts with nil balances.

(iv) If client money is invested in the purchase of assets other than money – such as stocks or shares – it ceases to be client money, because it is no longer money held by the firm. If the investment is subsequently sold, the money received is, again, client money. The records kept under rule 29 will need to include entries to show the purchase or sale of investments.

(v) Rule 14.5 reflects decisions of the Solicitors Disciplinary Tribunal that it is not a proper part of a solicitor's everyday business or practice to operate a banking facility for third parties, whether they are clients of the firm or not. It should be noted that any exemption under the Financial Services and Markets Act 2000 is likely to be lost if a deposit is taken in circumstances which do not form part of your practice. It should also be borne in mind that there are criminal sanctions against assisting money launderers.

(vi) As with rule 7 (Duty to remedy breaches), 'promptly' in rule 14.3 and 14.4 is not defined but should be given its natural meaning in the particular circumstances. Accounting to a client for any surplus funds will often fall naturally at the end of a matter. Other retainers may be more protracted and, even when the principal work has been completed, funds may still be needed, for example, to cover outstanding work in a conveyancing transaction or to meet a tax liability. (See also paragraphs 4.8 and 4.9 of the Guidelines for accounting procedures and systems at Appendix 3.)

(vii) There may be some instances when, during the course of a retainer, the specific purpose for which particular funds were paid no longer exists, for example, the need to instruct counsel or a medical expert. Rule 14.3 is concerned with returning funds to clients at the end of a matter (or the substantial conclusion of a matter) and is not intended to apply to ongoing retainers. However, in order to act in the best interests of your client, you may need to take instructions in such circumstances to ascertain, for instance, whether the money should be returned to the client or retained to cover the general funding or other aspects of the case.

(viii) See rule 20.1(j)–(k) for withdrawals from a client account when the rightful owner of funds cannot be traced. The obligation to report regularly under rule 14.4 ceases to apply if you are no longer able to trace the client, at which point rule 20.1(j) or (k) would apply.

RULE 15: CLIENT MONEY WITHHELD FROM CLIENT ACCOUNT ON CLIENT'S INSTRUCTIONS

15.1 *Client money* may be:

(a) held by *you* outside a *client account* by, for example, retaining it in the *firm's* safe in the form of cash, or placing it in an account in the *firm's* name which is not a *client account*, such as an account outside England and Wales; or

(b) paid into an account at a *bank*, *building society* or other financial institution opened in the name of the *client* or of a person designated by the *client*;

but only if the *client* instructs *you* to that effect for the *client's* own convenience, and only if the instructions are given in writing, or are given by other means and confirmed by *you* to the *client* in writing.

15.2 It is improper to seek blanket agreements, through standard terms of business or otherwise, to hold *client money* outside a *client account*.

15.3 If a *client* instructs *you* to hold part only of a payment in accordance with rule 15.1(a) or (b), the entire payment must first be placed in a *client account*, before transferring the relevant part out and dealing with it in accordance with the *client's* instructions.

15.4 A payment on account of *costs* received from a person who is funding all or part of *your fees* may be withheld from a *client account* on the instructions of that person given in accordance with rule 15.1.

Guidance notes

(i) Money withheld from a client account under rule 15.1(a) remains client money, and all the record-keeping provisions of rule 29 will apply.

(ii) Once money has been paid into an account set up under rule 15.1(b), it ceases to be client money. Until that time, the money is client money and, under rule 29, a record is required of your receipt of the money, and its payment into the account in the name of the client or designated person. If you can operate the account, rule 10 (operating a client's own account) and rule 30 (accounting records for clients' own accounts) will apply. In the absence of instructions to the contrary, rule 14.1 requires any money withdrawn to be paid into a client account.

(iii) Rule 29.17(d) requires clients' instructions under rule 15.1 to be kept for at least six years.

RULE 16: OTHER CLIENT MONEY WITHHELD FROM A CLIENT ACCOUNT

16.1 The following categories of *client money* may be withheld from a *client account*:

(a) cash received and *without delay* paid in cash in the ordinary course of business to the *client* or, on the *client's* behalf, to a third party, or paid in cash in the execution of a *trust* to a beneficiary or third party;

(b) a cheque or draft received and endorsed over in the ordinary course of business to the *client* or, on the *client's* behalf, to a third party, or *without delay* endorsed over in the execution of a *trust* to a beneficiary or third party;

(c) money withheld from a *client account* on instructions under rule 15;

(d) money which, in accordance with a *trustee's* powers, is paid into or retained in an account of the *trustee* which is not a *client account* (for example, an account outside England and Wales), or properly retained in cash in the performance of the *trustee's* duties;

(e) unpaid *professional disbursements* included in a payment of *costs* dealt with under rule 17.1(b);

(f) in respect of payments from the Legal Aid Agency:

(i) advance payments from the Legal Aid Agency withheld from *client account* (see rule 19.1(a)); and

(ii) unpaid *professional disbursements* included in a payment of *costs* from the Legal Aid Agency (see rule 19.1(b)); and

(g) money withheld from a *client account* on the written authorisation of the *SRA*. The *SRA* may impose a condition that the money is paid to a charity which gives an indemnity against any legitimate claim subsequently made for the sum received.

Guidance notes

(i) If money is withheld from a client account under rule 16.1(a) or (b), rule 29 requires records to be kept of the receipt of the money and the payment out.

(ii) If money is withheld from a client account under rule 16.1(d), rule 29 requires a record to be kept of the receipt of the money, and requires the inclusion of the money in the monthly reconciliations. (Money held by a trustee jointly with another party is subject only to the limited requirements of rule 9.)

(iii) It makes no difference, for the purpose of the rules, whether an endorsement is effected by signature in the normal way or by some other arrangement with the bank.

(iv) The circumstances in which authorisation would be given under rule 16.1(g) must be extremely rare. Applications for authorisation should be made to the Professional Ethics Guidance Team.

RULE 17: RECEIPT AND TRANSFER OF COSTS

17.1 When *you* receive money paid in full or part settlement of *your* bill (or other notification of *costs*) *you* **must follow one of the following five options:**

(a) determine the composition of the payment without delay, and deal with the money accordingly:

(i) if the sum comprises *office money* and/or *out-of-scope money* only, it must be placed in an *office account*;

(ii) if the sum comprises only *client money*, the entire sum must be placed in a *client account*;

(iii) if the sum includes both *office money* and *client money*, or *client money* and *out-of-scope money*, or *client money*, *out-of-scope money* and *office money*, *you* must follow rule 18 (receipt of mixed payments); or

(b) ascertain that the payment comprises only *office money* and/or *out-of-scope money*, and/or *client money* in the form of *professional disbursements* incurred but not yet paid, and deal with the payment as follows:

(i) place the entire sum in an *office account* at a *bank* or *building society* branch (or head office) in England and Wales; and

(ii) by the end of the second working day following receipt, either pay any unpaid *professional disbursement*, or transfer a sum for its settlement to a *client account*; **or**

(c) pay the entire sum into a *client account* (regardless of its composition), and transfer any *office money* and/or *out-of-scope money* out of the *client account* within 14 days of receipt; or

(d) on receipt of *costs* from the Legal Aid Agency, follow the option in rule 19.1(b); or

(e) in relation to a cheque paid into a *client account* under rule 14.2(e), transfer the *costs* element out of the *client account* within 14 days of receipt.

17.2 If *you* properly require payment of *your fees* from money held for a *client* or *trust* in a *client account*, *you* must first give or send a bill of *costs*, or other written notification of the *costs* incurred, to the *client* or the paying party.

17.3 Once *you* have complied with rule 17.2 above, the money earmarked for *costs* becomes *office money* and must be transferred out of the *client account* within 14 days.

17.4 A payment on account of *costs* generally in respect of those activities for which the practice is regulated by the *SRA* is *client money*, and must be held in a *client account* until *you* have complied with rule 17.2 above. (For an exception in the case of legal aid payments, see rule 19.1(a). See also rule 18 on dealing with mixed payments of *client money* and/or *out-of-scope money* when part of a payment on account of *costs* relates to activities not regulated by the *SRA*.)

17.5 A payment for an *agreed fee* must be paid into an *office account*. An 'agreed fee' is one that is fixed – not a *fee* that can be varied upwards, nor a *fee* that is dependent on the transaction being completed. An *agreed fee* must be evidenced in writing.

17.6 *You* will not be in breach of rule 17 as a result of a misdirected electronic payment or other direct transfer from a *client* or paying third party, provided:

(a) appropriate systems are in place to ensure compliance;
(b) appropriate instructions were given to the *client* or paying third party;
(c) the *client's* or paying third party's mistake is remedied promptly upon discovery; and
(d) appropriate steps are taken to avoid future errors by the *client* or paying third party.

17.7 *Costs* transferred out of a *client account* in accordance with rule 17.2 and 17.3 must be specific sums relating to the bill or other written notification of *costs*, and covered by the amount held for the particular *client* or *trust*. Round sum withdrawals on account of *costs* are a breach of the rules.

17.8 In the case of a *trust* of which the only *trustee(s)* are within the *firm*, the paying party will be the *trustee(s)* themselves. *You* must keep the original bill or notification of *costs* on the file, in addition to complying with rule 29.15 (central record or file of copy bills, etc.).

17.9 Undrawn *costs* must not remain in a *client account* as a 'cushion' against any future errors which could result in a shortage on that account, and cannot be regarded as available to set off against any general shortage on *client account*.

Guidance notes

(i) This note lists types of disbursement and how they are categorised:

(a) Money received for paid disbursements is office money.
(b) Money received for unpaid professional disbursements is client money.
(c) Money received for other unpaid disbursements for which you have incurred a liability to the payee (for example, travel agents' charges, taxi fares, courier charges or Land Registry search fees, payable on credit) is office money.
(d) Money received for disbursements anticipated but not yet incurred is a payment on account, and is therefore client money.

(ii) The option in rule 17.1(a) allows you to place all payments in the correct account in the first instance. The option in rule 17.1(b) allows the prompt banking into an office account of an invoice payment when the only uncertainty is whether or not the payment includes some client money in the form of unpaid professional disbursements. The option in rule 17.1(c) allows the prompt banking into a client account of any invoice payment in advance of determining whether the payment is a mixture of office and client money (of whatever description), or client money and out-of-scope money, or client money, out-of-scope money and office money, or is only office money and/or out-of-scope money.

(iii) If you are not in a position to comply with the requirements of rule 17.1(b), you cannot take advantage of that option.

(iv) The option in rule 17.1(b) cannot be used if the money received includes a payment on account – for example, a payment for a professional disbursement anticipated but not yet incurred.

(v) In order to be able to use the option in rule 17.1(b) for electronic payments or other direct transfers from clients, you may choose to establish a system whereby clients are given an office account number for payment of costs. The system must be capable of ensuring that, when invoices are sent to the client, no request is made for any client money, with the sole exception of money for professional disbursements already incurred but not yet paid.

(vi) Rule 17.1(c) allows clients to be given a single account number for making direct payments by electronic or other means – under this option, it has to be a client account.

(vii) 'Properly' in rule 17.2 implies that the work has actually been done, whether at the end of the matter or at an interim stage, and that you are entitled to appropriate the money for costs. For example, the costs set out in a completion statement in a conveyancing transaction will become due on completion and should be transferred out of the client account within 14 days of completion in accordance with rule 17.3. The requirement to transfer costs out of the client account within a set time is intended to prevent costs being left on client account to conceal a shortage.

(viii) Money is 'earmarked' for costs under rule 17.2 and 17.3 when you decide to use funds already held in client account to settle your bill. If you wish to obtain the client's prior approval, you will need to agree the amount to be taken with your client before issuing the bill to avoid the possibility of failing to meet the 14 day time limit for making the transfer out of client account. If you wish to retain the funds, for example, as money on account of costs on another matter, you will need to ask the client to send the full amount in settlement of the bill. If, when submitting a bill, you fail to indicate whether you intend to take your costs from client account, or expect the client to make a payment, you will be regarded as having 'earmarked' your costs.

(ix) An amendment to section 69 of the Solicitors Act 1974 by the Legal Services Act 2007 permits a solicitor or recognised body to sue on a bill which has been signed electronically and which the client has agreed can be delivered electronically.

(x) The rules do not require a bill of costs for an agreed fee, although your VAT position may mean that in practice a bill is needed. If there is no bill, the written evidence of the agreement must be filed as a written notification of costs under rule 29.15(b).

(xi) The bill of an MDP may be in respect of costs for work of the SRA-regulated part of the practice, and also for work that falls outside the scope of SRA regulation. Money received in respect of the non-SRA regulated work, including money for disbursements, is out-of-scope money and must be dealt with in accordance with rule 17.

(xii) See Chapter 1, indicative behaviour 1.21 of the SRA Code of Conduct in relation to ensuring that disbursements included in a bill reflect the actual amount spent or to be spent.

RULE 18: RECEIPT OF MIXED PAYMENTS

18.1 A 'mixed payment' is one which includes *client money* as well as *office money* and/or *out-of-scope money*.

18.2 A *mixed payment* must either:

(a) be split between a *client account* and *office account* as appropriate; or

(b) be placed *without delay* in a *client account*.

18.3 If the entire payment is placed in a *client account*, all *office money* and/or *out-of-scope money* must be transferred out of the *client account* within 14 days of receipt.

Guidance notes

(i) See rule 17.1(b) and (c) for additional ways of dealing with (among other things) mixed payments received in response to a bill or other notification of costs.
(ii) See rule 19.1(b) for (among other things) mixed payments received from the Legal Aid Agency.
(iii) Some out-of-scope money may be subject to the rules of other regulators which may require an earlier withdrawal from the client account operated under these rules.

RULE 19: TREATMENT OF PAYMENTS TO LEGAL AID PRACTITIONERS

Payments from the Legal Aid Agency

19.1 Two special dispensations apply to payments (other than *regular payments*) from the Legal Aid Agency:

(a) An advance payment, which may include *client money*, may be placed in an *office account*, provided the Legal Aid Agency instructs in writing that this may be done.
(b) A payment for *costs* (interim and/or final) may be paid into an *office account* at a *bank* or *building society* branch (or head office) in England and Wales, regardless of whether it consists wholly of *office money*, or is mixed with *client money* in the form of:

(i) advance payments for *fees* or *disbursements*; or
(ii) money for unpaid *professional disbursements*;

provided all money for payment of *disbursements* is transferred to a *client account* (or the *disbursements* paid) within 14 days of receipt.

19.2 The following provisions apply to *regular payments* from the Legal Aid Agency:

(a) 'Regular payments' (which are *office money*) are:

(i) standard monthly payments paid by the Legal Aid Agency under the civil legal aid contracting arrangements;
(ii) standard monthly payments paid by the Legal Aid Agency under the criminal legal aid contracting arrangements; and
(iii) any other payments for work done or to be done received from the Legal Aid Agency under an arrangement for payments on a regular basis.

(b) *Regular payments* must be paid into an *office account* at a *bank* or *building society* branch (or head office) in England and Wales.
(c) *You* must within 28 days of submitting a report to the Legal Aid Agency, notifying completion of a matter, either:

(i) pay any unpaid *professional disbursement(s)*, or
(ii) transfer to a *client account* a sum equivalent to the amount of any unpaid *professional disbursement(s)*,

relating to that matter.

(d) In cases where the Legal Aid Agency permits *you* to submit reports at various stages during a matter rather than only at the end of a matter, the requirement in rule 19.2(c) above applies to any unpaid *professional disbursement(s)* included in each report so submitted.

Payments from a third party

19.3 If the Legal Aid Agency has paid any *costs* to *you* or a previously nominated *firm* in a matter (advice and assistance or legal help *costs*, advance payments or interim *costs*), or has paid *professional disbursements* direct, and *costs* are subsequently settled by a third party:

(a) The entire third party payment must be paid into a *client account*.
(b) A sum representing the payments made by the Legal Aid Agency must be retained in the *client account*.
(c) Any balance belonging to *you* must be transferred to an *office account* within 14 days of *your* sending a report to the Legal Aid Agency containing details of the third party payment.
(d) The sum retained in the *client account* as representing payments made by the Legal Aid Agency must be:

(i) **either** recorded in the individual *client's* ledger account, and identified as the Legal Aid Agency's money;
(ii) **or** recorded in a ledger account in the Legal Aid Agency's name, and identified by reference to the *client* or matter;

and kept in the *client account* until notification from the Legal Aid Agency that it has recouped an equivalent sum from subsequent payments due to *you*. The retained sum must be transferred to an *office account* within 14 days of notification.

19.4 Any part of a third party payment relating to unpaid *professional disbursements* or outstanding *costs* of the *client's* previous *firm* is *client money*, and must be kept in a *client account* until *you* pay the *professional disbursement* or outstanding *costs*.

Guidance notes

(i) This rule deals with matters which specifically affect legal aid practitioners. It should not be read in isolation from the remainder of the rules which apply to everyone, including legal aid practitioners.
(ii) In cases carried out under public funding certificates, firms can apply for advance payments ('Payments on Account' under the Standard Civil Contract). The Legal Aid Agency has agreed that these payments may be placed in office account.
(iii) Rule 19.1(b) deals with the specific problems of legal aid practitioners by allowing a mixed or indeterminate payment of costs (or even a payment consisting entirely of unpaid professional disbursements) to be paid into an office account, which for the purpose of rule 19.1(b) must be an account at a bank or building society. However, it is always open to you to comply with rule 17.1(a) to (c), which are the options for everyone for the receipt of costs. For regular payments, see guidance notes (v)–(vii) below.
(iv) Firms are required by the Legal Aid Agency to report promptly to the Legal Aid Agency on receipt of costs from a third party. It is advisable to keep a copy of the

report on the file as proof of compliance with the Legal Aid Agency's requirements, as well as to demonstrate compliance with the rule.

(v) Rule 19.2(c) permits a firm, which is required to transfer an amount to cover unpaid professional disbursements into a client account, to make the transfer from its own resources if the regular payments are insufficient.

(vi) The 28 day time limit for paying, or transferring an amount to a client account for, unpaid professional disbursements is for the purposes of these rules only. An earlier deadline may be imposed by contract with the Legal Aid Agency or with counsel, agents or experts. On the other hand, you may have agreed to pay later than 28 days from the submission of the report notifying completion of a matter, in which case rule 19.2(c) will require a transfer of the appropriate amount to a client account (but not payment) within 28 days.

(vii) For the appropriate accounting records for regular payments, see rule 29.7.

RULE 20: WITHDRAWALS FROM A CLIENT ACCOUNT

20.1 *Client money* may only be withdrawn from a *client account* when it is:

(a) properly required for a payment to or on behalf of the *client* (or other person on whose behalf the money is being held);
(b) properly required for a payment in the execution of a particular *trust*, including the purchase of an investment (other than money) in accordance with the *trustee's* powers;
(c) properly required for payment of a *disbursement* on behalf of the *client* or *trust*;
(d) properly required in full or partial reimbursement of money spent by *you* on behalf of the *client* or *trust*;
(e) transferred to another *client account*;
(f) withdrawn on the *client's* instructions, provided the instructions are for the *client's* convenience and are given in writing, or are given by other means and confirmed by *you* to the *client* in writing;
(g) transferred to an account other than a *client account* (such as an account outside England and Wales), or retained in cash, by a *trustee* in the proper performance of his or her duties;
(h) a refund to *you* of an advance no longer required to fund a payment on behalf of a *client* or *trust* (see rule 14.2(b));
(i) money which has been paid into the account in breach of the rules (for example, money paid into the wrong *separate designated client account*) – see rule 20.5 below;
(j) money not covered by (a) to (i) above, where *you* comply with the conditions set out in rule 20.2; or
(k) money not covered by (a) to (i) above, withdrawn from the account on the written authorisation of the *SRA*. The *SRA* may impose a condition that *you* pay the money to a charity which gives an indemnity against any legitimate claim subsequently made for the sum received.

20.2 A withdrawal of *client money* under rule 20.1(j) above may be made only where the amount held does not exceed £500 in relation to any one individual *client* or *trust* matter and *you*:

(a) establish the identity of the owner of the money, or make reasonable attempts to do so;
(b) make adequate attempts to ascertain the proper destination of the money, and

to return it to the rightful owner, unless the reasonable costs of doing so are likely to be excessive in relation to the amount held;

(c) pay the funds to a charity;

(d) record the steps taken in accordance with rule 20.2(a)–(c) above and retain those records, together with all relevant documentation (including receipts from the charity), in accordance with rule 29.16 and 29.17(a); and

(e) keep a central register in accordance with rule 29.22.

20.3 *Office money* may only be withdrawn from a *client account* when it is:

(a) money properly paid into the account to open or maintain it under rule 14.2(a);

(b) properly required for payment of *your costs* under rule 17.2 and 17.3;

(c) the whole or part of a payment into a *client account* under rule 17.1(c);

(d) part of a *mixed payment* placed in a *client account* under rule 18.2(b); or

(e) money which has been paid into a *client account* in breach of the rules (for example, *interest* wrongly credited to a *general client account*) – see rule 20.5 below.

20.4 *Out-of-scope money* must be withdrawn from a *client account* in accordance with rules 17.1(a), 17.1(c) and 18 as appropriate.

20.5 Money which has been paid into a *client account* in breach of the rules must be withdrawn from the *client account* promptly upon discovery.

20.6 Money withdrawn in relation to a particular *client* or *trust* from a *general client account* must not exceed the money held on behalf of that *client* or *trust* in all *your general client accounts* (except as provided in rule 20.7 below).

20.7 *You* may make a payment in respect of a particular *client* or *trust* out of a *general client account*, even if no money (or insufficient money) is held for that *client* or *trust* in *your general client account(s)*, provided:

(a) sufficient money is held for that *client* or *trust* in a *separate designated client account*; and

(b) the appropriate transfer from the *separate designated client account* to a *general client account* is made immediately.

20.8 Money held for a *client* or *trust* in a *separate designated client account* must not be used for payments for another *client* or *trust*.

20.9 A *client account* must not be overdrawn, except in the following circumstances:

(a) A *separate designated client account* operated in *your* capacity as *trustee* can be overdrawn if *you* make payments on behalf of the *trust* (for example, inheritance tax) before realising sufficient assets to cover the payments.

(b) If a *sole practitioner* dies and his or her *client accounts* are frozen, overdrawn *client accounts* can be operated in accordance with the rules to the extent of the money held in the frozen accounts.

Guidance notes

(i) Withdrawals in favour of firm, and for payment of disbursements

(a) Disbursements to be paid direct from a client account, or already paid out of your own money, can be withdrawn under rule 20.1(c) or (d) in advance of preparing a bill of costs. Money to be withdrawn from a client account for the payment of costs (fees and disbursements) under rule 17.2 and 17.3 becomes office money and is dealt with under rule 20.3(b).

(b) Money is 'spent' under rule 20.1(d) at the time when you despatch a cheque, unless the cheque is to be held to your order. Money is also regarded as 'spent' by the use of a credit account, so that, for example, search fees, taxi fares and courier charges incurred in this way may be transferred to your office account.

(c) See rule 21.4 for the way in which a withdrawal from a client account in your favour must be effected.

(ii) Cheques payable to banks, building societies, etc.

(a) In order to protect client money against misappropriation when cheques are made payable to banks, building societies or other large institutions, it is strongly recommended that you add the name and number of the account after the payee's name.

(iii) Drawing against uncleared cheques

(a) You should use discretion in drawing against a cheque received from or on behalf of a client before it has been cleared. If the cheque is not met, other clients' money will have been used to make the payment in breach of the rules (see rule 7 (duty to remedy breaches)). You may be able to avoid a breach of the rules by instructing the bank or building society to charge all unpaid credits to your office or personal account.

(iv) Non-receipt of electronic payments

(a) If you withdraw money from a general client account on the strength of information that an electronic payment is on its way, but the electronic payment does not arrive, you will have used other clients' money in breach of the rules. See also rule 7 (duty to remedy breaches).

(v) Withdrawals on instructions

(a) One of the reasons why a client might authorise a withdrawal under rule 20.1(f) might be to have the money transferred to a type of account other than a client account. If so, the requirements of rule 15 must be complied with.

(vi) Withdrawals where the rightful owner cannot be traced, on the SRA's authorisation and without SRA authorisation

(a) Applications for authorisation under rule 20.1(k) should be made to the Professional Ethics Guidance Team, who can advise on the criteria which must normally be met for authorisation to be given. You may under rule 20.1(j) pay to a charity sums of £500 or less per client or trust matter without the SRA's authorisation, provided the safeguards set out in rule 20.2 are followed.

(b) You will need to apply to the SRA, whatever the amount involved, if the money to be withdrawn is not to be paid to a charity. This situation might arise, for example, if you have been unable to deliver a bill of costs because the client has become untraceable and so cannot make a transfer from client account to office account in accordance with rule 17.2–17.3.

(c) After a practice has been wound up, surplus balances are sometimes discovered in an old client account. This money remains subject to rule 20 and rule 21. An application can be made to the SRA under rule 20.1(k).

RULE 21: METHOD OF AND AUTHORITY FOR WITHDRAWALS FROM CLIENT ACCOUNT

21.1 A withdrawal from a *client account* may be made only after a specific authority in respect of that withdrawal has been signed by an appropriate person or persons in accordance with the *firm's* procedures for signing on *client account*. An authority for withdrawals from *client account* may be signed electronically, subject to appropriate safeguards and controls.

21.2 *Firms* must put in place appropriate systems and procedures governing withdrawals from *client account*, including who should be permitted by the *firm* to sign on *client account*. A non-*manager* owner or a non-employee owner of a *licensed body* is not an appropriate person to be a signatory on *client account* and must not be permitted by the *firm* to act in this way.

21.3 There is no need to comply with rule 21.1 above when transferring money from one *general client account* to another *general client account* at the same *bank* or *building society*.

21.4 A withdrawal from a *client account* in *your* favour must be either by way of a cheque, or by way of a transfer to the *office account* or to *your* personal account. The withdrawal must not be made in cash.

Guidance notes

(i) A firm should select suitable people to authorise withdrawals from the client account. Firms will wish to consider whether any employee should be able to sign on client account, and whether signing rights should be given to all managers of the practice or limited to those managers directly involved in providing legal services. Someone who has no day-to-day involvement in the business of the practice is unlikely to be regarded as a suitable signatory because of the lack of proximity to client matters. An appropriate understanding of the requirements of the rules is essential – see paragraph 4.2 of the Guidelines for accounting procedures and systems at Appendix 3.

(ii) Instructions to the bank or building society to withdraw money from a client account (rule 21.1) may be given over the telephone, provided a specific authority has been signed in accordance with this rule before the instructions are given. It is of paramount importance that there are appropriate in-built safeguards, such as passwords, to give the greatest protection possible for client money. Suitable safeguards will also be needed for practices which operate a CHAPS terminal or other form of electronic instruction for payment.

(iii) In the case of a withdrawal by cheque, the specific authority (rule 21.1) is usually a signature on the cheque itself. Signing a blank cheque is not a specific authority.

(iv) A withdrawal from a client account by way of a private loan from one client to another can only be made if the provisions of rule 27.2 are complied with.

(v) If, in your capacity as trustee, you instruct an outside administrator to run, or continue to run, on a day-to-day basis, the business or property portfolio of an estate or trust, you will not need to comply with rule 21.1, provided all cheques are retained in accordance with rule 29.18. (See also rule 29, guidance note (ii)(d).)

(vi) You may set up a 'direct debit' system of payment for Land Registry application fees on either the office account or a client account. If a direct debit payment is to be taken from a client account for the payment of Land Registry application fees, a signature, which complies with the firm's systems and procedures set up under rule 21, on the application for registration will constitute the specific authority required by rule 21.1. As with any other payment method, care must be taken to ensure that sufficient uncommitted funds are held in the client account for the particular client before signing the authority. You should also bear in mind that should the Land Registry take an incorrect amount in error from a firm's client account (for example, a duplicate payment), the firm will be in breach of the rules if other clients' money has been used as a result.

(vii) If you fail to specify the correct Land Registry fee on the application for registration (either by specifying a lesser amount than that actually due, or failing to specify any fee at all), you will be in breach of rule 21.1 if the Land Registry takes a sum from your client account greater than that specified on the application, without a specific authority for the revised sum being in place as required by rule 21. In order that you can comply with the rules, the Land Registry will need to contact you before taking the revised amount, so that the necessary authority may be signed prior to the revised amount being taken.

(viii) Where the Land Registry contacts you by telephone, and you wish to authorise an immediate payment by direct debit over the telephone, you will first need to check that there is sufficient money held in client account for the client and, if there is, that it is not committed to some other purpose.

(ix) The specific authority required by rule 21.1 can be signed after the telephone call has ended but must be signed before the additional payment (or correct full payment) is taken by the Land Registry. It is advisable to sign the authority promptly and, in any event, on the same day as the telephone instruction is given to the Land Registry to take the additional (or correct full) amount. If you decide to fund any extra amount from the office account, the transfer of office money to the client account would need to be made, preferably on the same day but, in any event, before the direct debit is taken. Your internal procedures would need to make it clear how to deal with such situations; for example, who should be consulted before a direct debit for an amount other than that specified on the application can be authorised, and the mechanism for ensuring the new authority is signed by a person permitted by the firm to sign on client account.

(x) You may decide to set up a direct debit system of payment on the office account because, for example, you do not wish to allow the Land Registry to have access to the firm's client account. Provided you are in funds, a transfer from the client account to the office account may be made under rule 20.1(d) to reimburse you as soon as the direct debit has been taken.

(xi) Variable 'direct debit' payments to the Land Registry, as described in guidance notes (vi)–(x) above, are not direct debits in the usual sense as each payment is authorised and confirmed individually. A traditional direct debit or standing order should not be set up on a client account because of the need for a specific authority for each withdrawal.

PART 3: INTEREST

RULE 22: WHEN INTEREST MUST BE PAID

22.1 When *you* hold money in a *client account* for a *client*, or for a person funding all or part of *your fees*, or for a *trust*, *you* must account to the *client* or that person or *trust* for *interest* when it is fair and reasonable to do so in all the circumstances. (This also applies if money should have been held in a *client account* but was not. It also applies to money held in an account in accordance with rule 15.1(a) (or which should have been held in such an account), or rule 16.1(d).)

22.2 *You* are not required to pay *interest*:

(a) on money held for the payment of a *professional disbursement*, once counsel etc. has requested a delay in settlement;
(b) on money held for the Legal Aid Agency;
(c) on an advance from *you* under rule 14.2(b) to fund a payment on behalf of the *client* or *trust* in excess of funds held for that *client* or *trust*; or
(d) if there is an agreement to contract out of the provisions of this rule under rule 25.

22.3 *You* must have a written policy on the payment of *interest*, which seeks to provide a fair outcome. The terms of the policy must be drawn to the attention of the *client* at the outset of a retainer, unless it is inappropriate to do so in the circumstances.

Guidance notes

(i) Requirement to pay interest

(a) Money is normally held for a client as a necessary, but incidental, part of the retainer, to facilitate the carrying out of the client's instructions. The main purpose of the rules is to keep that money safe and available for the purpose for which it was provided. The rules also seek to provide for the payment of a fair sum of interest, when appropriate, which is unlikely to be as high as that obtainable by the client depositing those funds.
(b) An outcomes-focused approach has been adopted in this area, allowing firms the flexibility to set their own interest policies in order to achieve a fair outcome for both the client and the firm.
(c) In addition to your obligation under rule 22.3, it is good practice to explain your interest arrangements to clients. These will usually be based on client money being held in an instant access account to facilitate a transaction. Clients are unlikely to receive as much interest as might have been obtained had they held and invested the money themselves. A failure to explain the firm's policy on interest may lead to unrealistic expectations and, possibly, a complaint to the Legal Ombudsman.
(d) The Legal Services Act 2007 has abolished the distinction in the Solicitors Act 1974 between interest earned on client money held in a general client account or a separate designated client account, meaning that interest earned on the latter type of account is, in theory, to be accounted for like interest on any other client money on a 'fair and reasonable' basis. In practice, however, a firm which wishes to retain any part of the interest earned on client money will need to hold that money in a general client account and continue to have interest paid to the office account (see rule 12.7(b)). The tax regime still treats interest arising on money held in a separate designated client account as belonging to the client, and requires banks to deduct tax at source from that interest (subject to the tax status of the individual client) and credit the interest to the separate designated client account. This makes it impracticable for firms to retain any part of the interest earned on a separate designated client account.
(e) Some firms may wish to apply a de minimis by reference to the amount held and period for which it was held, for example, providing that no interest is

payable if the amount calculated on the balance held is £20 or less. Any de minimis will need to be set at a reasonable level and regularly reviewed in the light of current interest rates.

(f) It is likely to be appropriate for firms to account for all interest earned in some circumstances, for example, where substantial sums of money are held for lengthy periods of time.

(g) If sums of money are held in relation to separate matters for the same client, it is normally appropriate to treat the money relating to the different matters separately but there may be cases when the matters are so closely related that they ought to be considered together, for example, when you are acting for a client in connection with numerous debt collection matters. Similarly, it may be fair and reasonable in the circumstances to aggregate sums of money held intermittently during the course of acting for a client.

(h) There is no requirement to pay interest on money held on instructions under rule 15.1(a) in a manner which attracts no interest.

(i) Accounts opened in the client's name under rule 15.1(b) (whether operated by you or not) are not subject to rule 22, as the money is not held by you. All interest earned belongs to the client. The same applies to any account in the client's own name operated by you as signatory under rule 10.

(ii) Interest policy (rule 22.3)

(a) It is important that your clients should be aware of the terms of your interest policy. This should normally be covered at the outset of a retainer, although it may be unnecessary where you have acted for the client previously. It is open to you and your client to agree that interest will be dealt with in a different way (see rule 25).

(iii) Unpresented cheques

(a) A client may fail to present a cheque to his or her bank for payment. Whether or not it is reasonable to recalculate the amount due will depend on all the circumstances of the case. A reasonable charge may be made for any extra work carried out if you are legally entitled to make such a charge.

(iv) Liquidators, trustees in bankruptcy, Court of Protection deputies and trustees of occupational pension schemes

(a) Under rule 8, Part 3 of the rules does not normally apply to liquidators, etc. You must comply with the appropriate statutory rules and regulations, and rule 8.3 and 8.4 as appropriate.

(v) Joint accounts

(a) Under rule 9, Part 3 of the rules does not apply to joint accounts. If you hold money jointly with a client, interest earned on the account will be for the benefit of the client unless otherwise agreed. If money is held jointly with another practice, the allocation of interest earned will depend on the agreement reached.

(vi) Failure to pay interest

(a) A client, including one of joint clients, or a person funding all or part of your fees, may complain to the Legal Ombudsman if he or she believes that interest was due and has not been paid, or that the amount paid was insufficient. It is advisable for the client (or other person) to try to resolve the matter with you before approaching the Legal Ombudsman.

(vii) Role of the reporting accountant

(a) Paragraph 2.8 of the Guidelines for accounting procedures and systems at Appendix 3 states the need for policies and systems in relation to the payment of interest.

(b) The reporting accountant does not check for compliance with the interest provisions but has a duty under rule 40 to report any substantial departures from the Guidelines discovered whilst carrying out work in preparation of the accountant's report. The accountant is not, however, required to determine the adequacy of a firm's interest policy (see rule 41.1(d)).

RULE 23: AMOUNT OF INTEREST

23.1 The *interest* paid must be a fair and reasonable sum calculated over the whole period for which the money is held.

Guidance notes

(i) You will usually account to the client for interest at the conclusion of the client's matter, but might in some cases consider it appropriate to account to the client at intervals throughout.

(ii) The sum paid by way of interest need not necessarily reflect the highest rate of interest obtainable but it is unlikely to be appropriate to look only at the lowest rate of interest obtainable. A firm's policy on the calculation of interest will need to take into account factors such as:

(a) the amount held;
(b) the length of time for which cleared funds were held;
(c) the need for instant access to the funds;
(d) the rate of interest payable on the amount held in an instant access account at the bank or building society where the client account is kept;
(e) the practice of the bank or building society where the client account is kept in relation to how often interest is compounded.

(iii) A firm needs to have regard to the effect of the overall banking arrangements negotiated between it and the bank, on interest rates payable on individual balances. A fair sum of interest is unlikely to be achieved by applying interest rates which are set at an artificially low level to reflect, for example, more favourable terms in relation to the firm's office account.

(iv) A firm might decide to apply a fixed rate of interest by reference, for example, to the base rate. In setting that rate, the firm would need to consider (and regularly review) the level of interest it actually receives on its client accounts, but also take into account its overall banking arrangements so far as they affect the rates received.

(v) When looking at the period over which interest must be calculated, it will usually be unnecessary to check on actual clearance dates. When money is received by cheque and paid out by cheque, the normal clearance periods will usually cancel each other out, so that it will be satisfactory to look at the period between the dates when the incoming cheque is banked and the outgoing cheque is drawn.

(vi) Different considerations apply when payments in and out are not both made by cheque. So, for example, the relevant periods would normally be:

(a) from the date when you receive incoming money in cash until the date when the outgoing cheque is sent;
(b) from the date when an incoming telegraphic transfer begins to earn interest until the date when the outgoing cheque is sent;
(c) from the date when an incoming cheque or banker's draft is or would normally be cleared until the date when the outgoing telegraphic transfer is made or banker's draft is obtained.

(vii) Rule 13.8 requires that money held in a client account must be immediately available, even at the sacrifice of interest, unless the client otherwise instructs, or the circumstances clearly indicate otherwise. The need for access can be taken into account in assessing the appropriate rate for calculating interest to be paid.
(viii) For failure to pay a sufficient sum by way of interest, see guidance note (vi)(a) to rule 22.

RULE 24: INTEREST ON STAKEHOLDER MONEY

24.1 When *you* hold money as stakeholder, *you* must pay *interest* on the basis set out in rule 22 to the person to whom the stake is paid, unless the parties have contracted out of this provision (see rule 25.3).

RULE 25: CONTRACTING OUT

25.1 In appropriate circumstances *you* and *your client* may by a written agreement come to a different arrangement as to the matters dealt with in rule 22 (payment of interest).
25.2 *You* must act fairly towards *your clients* when entering into an agreement to depart from the *interest* provisions, including providing sufficient information at the outset to enable them to give informed consent.
25.3 When acting as stakeholder *you* may, by a written agreement with *your* own *client* and the other party to the transaction, come to a different arrangement as to the matters dealt with in rule 22.

Guidance notes

(i) Whether it is appropriate to contract out depends on all the circumstances, for example, the size of the sum involved or the nature, status or bargaining position of the client. It might, for instance, be appropriate to contract out by standard terms of business if the client is a substantial commercial entity and the interest involved is modest in relation to the size of the transaction. The larger the sum of interest involved, the more there would be an onus on you to show that a client who had accepted a contracting out provision was properly informed and had been treated fairly.
(ii) Contracting out which on the face of it appears to be against the client's interests is permissible where the client has given informed consent. For example, some clients may wish to contract out for reasons related to their tax position or to comply with their religious beliefs.
(iii) A firm which decides not to receive or pay interest, due to the religious beliefs of

its principals, will need to ensure that clients are informed at the outset, so that they can choose to instruct another firm if the lack of interest is an issue for them.

(iv) Another example of contracting out is when the client stipulates, and the firm agrees, that all interest earned should be paid to the client despite the terms of the firm's interest policy.

(v) In principle, you are entitled to make a reasonable charge to the client for acting as stakeholder in the client's matter.

(vi) Alternatively, it may be appropriate to include a special provision in the contract that you retain the interest on the deposit to cover your charges for acting as stakeholder. This is only acceptable if it will provide a fair and reasonable payment for the work and risk involved in holding a stake. The contract could stipulate a maximum charge, with any interest earned above that figure being paid to the recipient of the stake.

(vii) Any right to charge the client, or to stipulate for a charge which may fall on the client, would be excluded by, for instance, a prior agreement with the client for a fixed fee for the client's matter, or for an estimated fee which cannot be varied upwards in the absence of special circumstances. It is therefore not normal practice for a stakeholder in conveyancing transactions to receive a separate payment for holding the stake.

(viii) A stakeholder who seeks an agreement to exclude the operation of rule 24 should be particularly careful not to take unfair advantage either of the client, or of the other party if unrepresented.

APPENDIX 3: SRA GUIDELINES – ACCOUNTING PROCEDURES AND SYSTEMS

1. INTRODUCTION

1.1 These guidelines, published under rule 26 of the SRA Accounts Rules 2011, are intended to be a benchmark or broad statement of good practice requirements which should be present in an effective regime for the proper control of client money. They should therefore be of positive assistance to firms in establishing or reviewing appropriate procedures and systems. They do not override, or detract from the need to comply fully with, the Accounts Rules.

1.2 References to managers or firms in the guidelines are intended to include sole practitioners, recognised bodies and licensed bodies, and the managers of those bodies.

2. GENERAL

2.1 Compliance with the Accounts Rules is the equal responsibility of all managers in a firm. This responsibility also extends to the Compliance Officer for Finance and Administration, whether or not a manager (see rule 6). They should establish policies and systems to ensure that the firm complies fully with the rules, including procedures for verifying that the controls are operating effectively. Responsibility for day to day supervision may be delegated to one or more managers to enable effective control to be exercised. Delegation of total responsibility to a cashier or book-keeper is not acceptable.

2.2 The firm should hold a copy of the current version of the Accounts Rules and/or have ready access to the current on-line version. The person who maintains the books of account must have a full knowledge of the requirements of the rules and the accounting requirements of firms.

2.3 Proper books of account should be maintained on the double-entry principle. They should be legible, up to date and contain narratives with the entries which identify and/or provide adequate information about the transaction. Entries should be made in chronological order and the current balance should be shown on client ledger accounts, or be readily ascertainable, in accordance with rule 29.9.

2.4 Ledger accounts for clients, other persons or trusts should include the name of the client or other person or trust and contain a heading which provides a description of the matter or transaction.

2.5 Manual systems for recording client money are capable of complying with these guidelines. A computer system, with suitable support procedures will, however, provide an efficient means of producing the accounts and associated control information.

2.6 When introducing new systems, care must be taken to ensure:

(1) that balances transferred from the books of account of the old system are reconciled with the opening balances held on the new system before day to day operation commences;

(2) that the new system operates correctly before the old system is abandoned. This may require a period of parallel running of the old and new systems and the satisfactory reconciliation of the two sets of records before the old system ceases.

2.7 The firm should ensure that office account entries in relation to each client or trust matter are maintained up to date as well as the client account entries. Credit balances on office account in respect of client or trust matters should be fully investigated.

2.8 The firm should establish policies and operate systems for the payment of fair and reasonable interest to clients in accordance with rules 22 and 23.

3. RECEIPT OF CLIENT MONEY

3.1 The firm should have procedures for identifying client money, including cash, when received in the firm, and for promptly recording the receipt of the money either in the books of account or a register for later posting to the client cash book and ledger accounts. The procedures should cover money received through the post, electronically or direct by fee earners or other personnel. They should also cover the safekeeping of money prior to payment to bank.

3.2 The firm should have a system which ensures that client money is paid promptly into a client account.

3.3 The firm should have a system for identifying money which should not be in a client account and for transferring it without delay.

3.4 The firm should determine a policy and operate a system for dealing with money which is a mixture of office money and client money, or client money and out-of-scope money, or client money, out-of-scope money and office money, in compliance with rules 17–19.

4. PAYMENTS FROM CLIENT ACCOUNT

4.1 The firm should have clear procedures for ensuring that all withdrawals from client accounts are properly authorised. In particular, suitable persons should be named for the following purposes:

(1) authorisation of internal payment vouchers;
(2) signing client account cheques;
(3) authorising telegraphic or electronic transfers.

No other personnel should be allowed to authorise or sign the documents.

4.2 The firm should establish clear procedures and systems for ensuring that persons permitted to authorise the withdrawal of client money from a client account have an appropriate understanding of the requirements of the rules, including rules 20 and 21 which set out when and how a withdrawal from client account may properly be made.

4.3 Persons nominated for the purpose of authorising internal payment vouchers should, for each payment, ensure there is supporting evidence showing clearly the reason for the payment, and the date of it. Similarly, persons signing cheques and authorising transfers should ensure there is a suitable voucher or other supporting evidence to support the payment.

4.4 The firm should have clear systems and procedures for authorising withdrawals from client accounts by electronic means, with appropriate safeguards and controls to ensure that all such withdrawals are properly authorised.

4.5 The firm should have a system for checking the balances on client ledger accounts to ensure no debit balances occur. Where payments are to be made other than out of cleared funds, clear policies and procedures must be in place to ensure that adequate risk assessment is applied.

N.B. If incoming payments are ultimately dishonoured, a debit balance will arise, in breach of the rules, and full replacement of the shortfall will be required under rule 7. See also rule 20, guidance notes (iii)(a) and (iv)(a).

4.6 The firm should establish systems for the transfer of costs from client account to office account in accordance with rule 17.2 and 17.3. Normally transfers should be made only on the basis of rendering a bill or written notification. The payment from the client account should be by way of a cheque or transfer in favour of the firm or sole principal – see rule 21.4.

4.7 The firm should establish policies and operate systems to control and record accurately any transfers between clients of the firm. Where these arise as a result of loans between clients, the written authority of both the lender and borrower must be obtained in accordance with rule 27.2.

4.8 The firm should establish policies and operate systems for the timely closure of files, and the prompt accounting for surplus balances in accordance with rule 14.3.

4.9 The firm should establish systems in accordance with rule 14.4 to keep clients (or other people on whose behalf money is held) regularly informed when funds are retained for a specified reason at the end of a matter or the substantial conclusion of a matter.

5. OVERALL CONTROL OF CLIENT ACCOUNTS

5.1 The firm should maintain control of all its bank and building society accounts opened for the purpose of holding client money. In the case of a joint account, a suitable degree of control should be exercised.

5.2 Central records or central registers must be kept in respect of:

(1) accounts held for client money, which are not client accounts (rules 15.1(a), 16.1(d) and 29.19);

(2) practice as a liquidator, trustee in bankruptcy, Court of Protection deputy or trustee of an occupational pension scheme (rules 8 and 29.20);
(3) joint accounts (rules 9 and 29.21);
(4) dividend payments received by an executor, trustee or nominee company as nominee (rules 28.2 and 29.23); and
(5) clients' own accounts (rules 10, 15.1(b) and 30.3).

5.3 In addition, there should be a master list of all:

- general client accounts;
- separate designated client accounts;
- accounts held in respect of 5.2 above; and
- office accounts.

The master list should show the current status of each account; e.g. currently in operation or closed with date of closure.

5.4 The firm should operate a system to ensure that accurate reconciliations of the client accounts are carried out at least every five weeks. In particular it should ensure that:

(1) a full list of client ledger balances is produced. Any debit balances should be listed, fully investigated and rectified immediately. The total of any debit balances cannot be 'netted off' against the total of credit balances;
(2) a full list of unpresented cheques is produced;
(3) a list of outstanding lodgements is produced;
(4) formal statements are produced reconciling the client account cash book balances, aggregate client ledger balances and the client bank accounts. All unresolved differences must be investigated and, where appropriate, corrective action taken;
(5) a manager or the Compliance Officer for Finance and Administration checks the reconciliation statement and any corrective action, and ensures that enquiries are made into any unusual or apparently unsatisfactory items or still unresolved matters.

5.5 The firm should have clear policies, systems and procedures to control access to computerised client accounts by determining the personnel who should have 'write to' and 'read only' access. Passwords should be held confidentially by designated personnel and changed regularly to maintain security. Access to the system should not unreasonably be restricted to a single person nor should more people than necessary be given access.

5.6 The firm should establish policies and systems for the retention of the accounting records to ensure:

- books of account, reconciliations, bills, bank statements and passbooks are kept for at least six years;
- paid cheques, digital images of paid cheques and other authorities for the withdrawal of money from a client account are kept for at least two years;
- other vouchers and internal expenditure authorisation documents relating directly to entries in the client account books are kept for at least two years.

5.7 The firm should ensure that unused client account cheques are stored securely to prevent unauthorised access. Blank cheques should not be pre-signed. Any cancelled cheques should be retained.

APPENDIX C

Warning notices

APPENDIX C1

Money missing from client account

WARNING NOTICE

Issued on 12 June 2015

Status

Whilst this document does not form part of the SRA Handbook, we may have regard to it when exercising our regulatory functions.

Who is this notice relevant to?

This warning notice is aimed at all those we regulate but is particularly relevant to you if you are a manager of a firm or a firm's COFA or COLP.

Any deficiency on client account exposes clients and others to a risk of financial loss and damage to public confidence. Missing money must be replaced with extreme urgency.

The Solicitors Regulation Authority's Principles

You have a duty to ensure that client money is safe. Operating a deficient client account may cause you to breach one or more of the SRA Principles, including:

- Principle 2 – acting with integrity
- Principle 5 – acting in the best interests of each client;
- Principle 6 – behaving in a way that maintains the trust the public places in you and in the provision of legal services;
- Principle 10 – protecting client money and assets.

The Solicitors Regulation Authority's mandatory outcomes

You should also have regard to the following mandatory Outcomes:

O(1.1) You treat your clients fairly;
O(1.2) You provide services to your clients in a manner which protects their interests in their matter, subject to the proper administration of justice;
O(1.12) Clients are in a position to make informed decisions about the services they need, how their matter will be handled and the options available to them;
O(1.16) You inform current clients if you discover any act or omission which could give rise to a claim by them against you.
O(4.2) Any individual who is advising a client makes that client aware of all information material to that retainer of which the individual has personal knowledge.

SRA Accounts Rules 2011

It is your duty to remedy breaches of the SRA Accounts Rules 2011. Specifically, Rule 7 states:

> 7.1 Any breach of the rules must be remedied promptly upon discovery. This includes the replacement of any money improperly withheld or withdrawn from a client account.
>
> 7.2 In a private practice, the duty to remedy breaches rests not only on the person causing the breach, but also on all the principals in the firm. This duty extends to replacing missing client money from the principals' own resources, even if the money has been misappropriated by an employee or another principal, and whether or not a claim is subsequently made on the firm's insurance or the Compensation Fund.

The implications of missing money

It is important that all managers and employees of a firm fully understand the implications of money being missing from client account, including:

- There is a clear duty in the SRA Accounts Rules to replace a deficiency in a client account.
- In the general law, trustees in breach of trust also have a duty to replace a deficiency.
- In any event, operating a deficient client account is very likely to involve immediate and continuing breaches of trust – by paying some clients their full entitlement, the amount left for other clients reduces.
- Ultimately, a deficient trust account is likely to be distributed pro rata.
- You may well breach your duty to act in the best interests of clients if you pay client money into an already deficient account without fully informed consent – no properly advised client would pay funds into a deficient account with the risk of only receiving a proportion back. Failing to inform clients exposes them to a risk of loss (see O 4.2).
- Until missing money is replaced, you should not take costs from the client account – you cannot 'properly' require payment of your fees from money held in a client account in such circumstances and so Rules 17.2 and 17.3 of the SRA Accounts Rules 2011 will not apply. Nor is it in the best interests of clients for you to take costs from client account when there is insufficient in the account for you to pay them in full.
- If you or your insurers do not replace the money promptly, you are at serious risk of intervention by the SRA. Intervention may be necessary in any event if there is reason to suspect dishonesty or other grounds for intervention arise.
- Since it is unlikely that a deficient client account can be operated without further breach of trust, you may well need to apply to the court for directions as to how to distribute the remaining funds.
- Offences under the Fraud Act 2006 may be committed once you are on notice that money is missing if you do not act properly and honestly.

Complying with the Principles

It is critical that to protect your clients, you do not operate a deficient client account and that you keep client money safe.

If you are the firm's COFA, you must take all reasonable steps to ensure compliance with the SRA Accounts Rules 2011 and record any failure to comply. You also have an obligation to report material breaches to the SRA as soon as reasonably practicable.

If you are a manager, the COFA is not a substitute for you and your firm's responsibilities and obligations. Systems and actions that should aid compliance include:

- having appropriate accounting procedures for your business;

- having clear reporting lines to encourage appropriate reporting by all members of staff;
- ensuring that your systems only allow appropriate individuals to authorise payments from client account;
- immediately investigating and taking action against any member of staff who may have acted dishonestly or committed any financial impropriety whether in relation to client account or not;
- taking regular steps to monitor, review and manage risks.

Behaviours of concern that you should be alert to in your firm include:

- failure to deliver bills or provide written notification of costs;
- any suggestions of overcharging;
- borrowing from clients in the capacity of trustee or attorney, which is unsecured;
- borrowing that remains outstanding, in breach of any agreement to pay;
- delay or failure to account for monies due;
- any accumulation or pattern of one or more of the above.

If you identify that money is missing

If you identify that money is missing, you have a duty to take steps to ensure it is replaced, in full, immediately.

If you are a manager of the firm, you have a duty to replace missing client money from your own resources. It may be necessary for you to obtain a loan to do this. It is irrelevant that fault may not lie with you personally.

You may be able to make a claim on your professional indemnity insurance. The obligation to remedy a breach of the SRA Accounts Rules 2011 is treated as civil liability for the purposes of clause 1 of the Minimum Terms and Conditions.

Operating the client account when it is deficient may make you liable for breach of trust and failure to act in the best interests of your clients. If you cannot replace the missing money and your insurers do not do so very promptly, you may be unable lawfully to operate the account. You will have to consider the position as a matter of trust law including whether you need to apply to court for directions as trustee.

Enforcement action

Whilst we are committed to working constructively with you, we will take enforcement action if missing money is not replaced. Failure to replace missing money will usually lead to an intervention. It should not be assumed that replacing the money means that an intervention is not necessary since the conduct giving rise to the shortage may evidence dishonesty or other breaches giving rise to a need to intervene to protect clients and the public.

Further assistance

If you require further assistance with understanding your obligations in relation to anything please contact the Professional Ethics Guidance Team.

APPENDIX C2

Improper use of a client account as a banking facility

WARNING NOTICE

Issued on 18 December 2014

This notice is relevant to all regulated persons holding client monies, and must be read in conjunction with our four case studies on improper use of client account as a banking facility also published on 18 December 2014.

The Solicitors Disciplinary Tribunal and the courts have sanctioned solicitors for many years for processing funds through client account for purposes unconnected with legal advice.

Since 1998, guidance note (ix) to Rule 15 of the Solicitors Accounts Rules 1998 has warned solicitors of the need to exercise caution if asked to provide banking facilities through a client account and in 2004 the note was amended to state expressly that solicitors 'should not provide banking facilities through a client account'. In 2011, the guidance note was elevated to an Accounts Rule (Rule 14.5 of the SRA Accounts Rules 2011).

We have seen an increase in reports to us that client bank accounts are being used improperly as a banking facility, with its attendant risks of involvement in financial crime and the evasion of insolvency processes.

This guidance sets out a summary of the current position and some key issues that you should be aware of. We have also set out some case studies to assist you in complying with your obligations.

Whilst this guidance does not form part of the SRA Handbook, we may have regard to it when exercising its regulatory functions.

Our rules/principles/outcomes

Rule 14.5 of the SRA Accounts Rules 2011 provides:

> You must not provide banking facilities through a client account. Payments into, and transfers or withdrawals from, a client account must be in respect of instructions relating to an underlying transaction (and the funds arising therefrom) or to a service forming part of your normal regulated activities.

Guidance note (v) to Rule 14.5 states that:

> Rule 14.5 reflects decisions of the Solicitors Disciplinary Tribunal that it is not a proper part of a solicitor's everyday business or practice to operate a banking facility for third parties, whether they are clients of the firm or not. It should be noted that any exemption under the Financial Services and Markets Act 2000 is likely to be lost if a deposit is taken in circumstances which do not form part of your practice. It should also be borne in mind that there are criminal sanctions against assisting money launderers.

The Principles

A breach of Rule 14.5 is a serious matter. In addition, allowing your firm's bank account to be used improperly may also involve a breach of the SRA Principles including:

- Principle 1: upholding the rule of law and the proper administration of justice;
- Principle 3: not allowing your independence to be compromised;
- Principle 6: behaving in a way that maintains the trust the public places in you and the provision of legal services; and
- Principle 8: running your business or carrying out your role in the business effectively and in accordance with proper governance and sound financial and risk management principles.

Outcome 7.5 of the SRA Code of Conduct 2011 also states that you must 'comply with legislation applicable to your business, including anti-money laundering . . .'

Where clients ask you to process funds through your client account, you need to balance the client's best interests against the other Principles and your legal obligations. You should bear in mind note 2.2 to the Principles, which states that, where two or more Principles come into conflict, the Principle which takes precedence is the one which best serves the public interest in the particular circumstances, especially the public interest in the proper administration of justice and note 2.4 which states that compliance with the Principles is subject to any overriding legal obligations.

The Court of Appeal in The Attorney General for Zambia v. Meer Care & Desai and others [2008] EWCA Civ 1007 noted in paragraph 234:

> ... it is plain that he was providing the service of a bank account, albeit only in credit... with almost none of the payments through the client account being related to any legal work done by the firm. It is equally plain that this was not a proper thing for a firm of solicitors to do.

Recent High Court judgments

In the past two years, two High Court judgments have upheld the Principles underlying Rule 14.5:

Premji Naram Patel v. SRA [2012] EWHC 3373 (Admin)

Mr Patel was a sole practitioner who acted for a company importing high value motor vehicles from Europe at a reduced price, to be sold in the UK for a substantial profit. Two significant investors were unwilling to pay funds directly to the company's owner because of past business failures. Instead investors paid money into the client account operated by Mr Patel. Mr Patel then transferred the relevant funds to the vehicle manufacturers directly.

We alleged that Mr Patel 'permitted his bank account to be utilised by a client and/or third parties to receive and pay monies where there were no underlying legal transactions'.

The Tribunal imposed a fine of £7,500.

Mr Patel appealed to the High Court. He argued that the second sentence of Rule 14.5 had to be read disjunctively: payments into and out of a client account have to relate to either (a) an underlying transaction or (b) a service forming part of the solicitor's normal regulated activities. He submitted that solicitors must not permit their client account to be used as a banking facility but will not be in breach of the rule if its use occurs as a consequence of a client's instructions in relation to an underlying transaction, albeit not a legal transaction.

The Court rejected that argument and upheld the fine imposed by the SDT commenting that 'movements on client account must be in respect of instructions relating to an underlying transaction which is part of the accepted professional services of solicitors'.

Fuglers & Ors v. SRA [2014] EWHC 179 (Admin) (QB)

Fuglers LLP acted for a Football Club. The Club's bank account was withdrawn after a winding-up petition was brought by HM Revenue & Customs (HMRC). The Club was insolvent.

Over a period of 4 months, approximately £10 million of the Club's money passed through Fuglers' client account.

The SDT fined Fuglers £50,000 and its two managers £5,000 and £20,000.

They appealed against the amount of the fines that were imposed. The High Court dismissed the appeal and confirmed the seriousness of the misconduct that had been found by the SDT.

At paragraphs 39–43, the Judge sets out three reasons why client accounts must not be used as banking facilities for clients:

- Objectionable in itself

> 'The first strand is that it is objectionable in itself for a solicitor to be carrying out or facilitating banking activities because he is to that extent not acting as a solicitor. If a solicitor is providing banking activities which are not linked to an underlying transaction, he is engaged in carrying out or facilitating day to day commercial trading in the same way as a banker. This is objectionable because solicitors are qualified and regulated in relation to their activities as solicitors, and are held out by the profession as being regulated in relation to such activities. They are not qualified to act as bankers and are not regulated as bankers. If a solicitor could operate a banking facility for clients which was divorced from any legal work being undertaken for them, he would in effect be trading on the trust and reputation which he acquired through his status as a solicitor in circumstances where such trust would not be justified by the regulatory regimen.'

- Risk of money laundering

> 'The second strand is that allowing a client account to be used as a banking facility, unrelated to any underlying transaction which the solicitor is carrying out, carries with it the obvious risk that the account may be used unscrupulously by the client for money laundering. This was the danger referred to in paragraph 58 of the Tribunal decision in Wood and Burdett (8699/2002) which is referred to in note (ix) itself. That this was one of the dangers at which the rule was aimed is reinforced by the express mention in note (ix) of the criminal sanctions attaching to money laundering.'

- Insolvency or risk of insolvency

> 'The third strand arises in the particular context of insolvency or risk of insolvency. In such context, to allow a client account to be used as a banking facility is objectionable for several reasons. In the first place, it allows the client to achieve that which the client will normally be unable to achieve from any bank. It is the common practice of banks, as happened with the Club's bank in this case, to withdraw facilities upon notification that there has been a winding up petition. The solicitor is therefore giving the client a commercial service which would otherwise be unavailable to it through the device of using a solicitor as if he were a bank. Secondly there is the risk of disaffection and opprobrium which is involved in favouring one creditor over another. This exists in the absence of any risk of insolvency, but becomes more acute in the event of insolvency or potential insolvency. This arises irrespective of whether dispositions would or would not be subject to invalidity by the operation of section 127. A third reason is the risk of section 127 (of the Insolvency Act 1986) applying so as to require creditors to reimburse payments from the client account in a subsequent liquidation. A solicitor who knowingly makes or facilitates such payments may be subject to a personal liability, quite apart from the liability of the payee to reimburse the amount transferred.'

Risks

You should therefore be aware that:

- **Providing banking facilities through a client account is objectionable in itself**

For the avoidance of any doubt, our view is that you should only receive funds into client account in relation to an underlying transaction that you or your firm is advising on. It is not sufficient that there is an underlying transaction if you are not providing legal advice to one of the parties.

- **There must be a reasonable connection between the underlying legal transaction and the payments**

Whether there is a reasonable connection is likely to depend on the facts of each case but where the legal services are purely advisory, it will clearly be more difficult to show a reasonable connection. The fact that you have a retainer with a client does not give you licence to process funds freely through client account on the client's behalf. Throughout a retainer, you should question why you are being asked to receive funds and for what purpose. You should only hold funds where necessary for the purpose of carrying out your client's instructions in connection with an underlying legal transaction or a service forming part of your normal regulated activities. You should always ask why the client cannot make the payment him or herself. The client's convenience is not the paramount concern and, if the client does not have a bank account in the UK, this considerably increases the risks. You should be prepared to justify any decision to hold or move client money to us where necessary.

- **Significant aggravating factors include the risks of insolvency and money laundering**

The seriousness of the breach will be aggravated by indications that the funds were paid into, or transferred out of client account, to avoid responsibilities imposed by insolvency legislation or to perpetuate suspected financial crime or tax fraud. In the case of Simms SDT 8686/2002 the Tribunal noted at paragraph 76:

> A solicitor who involves himself in transactions which he knows or suspects or should have known or suspected could involve illegality or impropriety or who gives such transactions credibility cannot but appreciate that his behaviour will be perceived as affecting his integrity and trustworthiness and so affect the reputation of the Profession. The duties of a lawyer as an officer of The Supreme Court are not simply owed to the client but also involve the respect which the Profession owes to the law itself and to justice.

You should be aware that criminals often target solicitors' client accounts to lend credibility to fraudulent schemes or to launder the proceeds of their criminal activity. You must not allow money to move through client account unless it is in connection with a genuine transaction about which you are providing legal services. You should ensure that you undertake proper due diligence before accepting any funds into client account and you should not act if you do not fully understand the transaction on which you are advising.

Compliance with Rule 14.5 offers an important 'first line of defence' to clients who may seek to take advantage of your client account to launder money. It also helps you to secure professional independence from your client in compliance with Principle 3.

You should make sure that you and all members of your firm are familiar with the warning notices and guidance we have issued in relation to high yield investment fraud and money laundering.

Other related issues/considerations

Use of escrow accounts

Firms may hold funds 'in escrow' or subject to professional undertakings in circumstances where they are advising a party to the underlying legal transaction; for example, funds for the purchase of an asset (e.g. an aircraft) might be held pending the completion of a purchase.

The decision of the SDT in Wilson-Smith (SDT 8772/2003) (para 60) was unequivocal that a solicitor should not act as 'escrow only' agent:

> It can be described as nothing other than crass stupidity to accept a role as, for example, an 'escrow agent' when the solicitor cannot know what that means as, indeed, that expression has no meaning in English law.

The use of escrow accounts is a serious risk if they do not have a reasonable connection to an underlying legal transaction (which you are advising on) or are not in association with the recognised 'professional duties' of a solicitor. For the avoidance of doubt, if you are instructed only to advise on the terms of an escrow account in the absence of being instructed on an underlying legal transaction or the provision of other professional duties (such as probate services), this is likely to involve a breach of Rule 14.5.

In each case you must therefore carefully consider all of the relevant circumstances and the risks involved before you agree to hold funds in escrow. You should be prepared to justify your decision to us where necessary.

A possible alternative: If parties want funds to be held independently in escrow, they could appoint an independent trustee company or bank regulated by the FCA and authorised to provide banking and/or escrow services.

Private Client Services

Historically, some solicitors have agreed to receive and hold funds for clients to enable them to pay routine bills and invoices on their clients' behalf. This has been predominately for the clients' convenience as they may be based abroad or because they are incapacitated so that operating their own bank accounts is problematic.

In view of technological advancements, in particular the ease of internet and telephone banking, we consider that allowing client account to be used in this way is no longer appropriate. Clients can now operate their bank accounts from their own homes or indeed from anywhere in the world. Allowing clients to hold anonymously what might be significant funds in a client account gives rise to significant risks in relation to potential money laundering or other breaches of the law, such as exchange control consent regulation. The anonymity of client accounts is attractive to criminals.

In each case, you must therefore carefully consider all of the relevant circumstances and the risks involved before you agree to hold funds in this way. You should be prepared to justify your decision to us where necessary.

This guidance is not intended to affect your ability to make reasonable and proper payments on your client's instructions when related to an underlying legal transaction on which you have been instructed, for example, upon completion of a house purchase on your client's instructions under Accounts Rule 20.1(f). Once a transaction is complete, we would remind you that Rule 14.3 provides that client money must be returned to the client promptly, as soon as there is no longer any proper reason to retain those funds. If you retain funds in client account after completion of a transaction, the risk of a breach of Rule 14.5 increases. Risk factors of laundering in particular would involve the payment of substantial sums to others, including family members, or to corporate entities, particularly overseas, since there is no reason why the client could not receive the money into their own account and transfer it from there.

Enforcement action

Failure to comply with this warning notice may lead to disciplinary action.

Further help

- High-yield investment fraud: Warning notice. Issued on 10 September 2013
- Money laundering and terrorist financing: Warning notice. Issued on 8 December 2014

Further assistance

If you require further assistance with understanding your obligations in relation to anything please contact the Professional Ethics Guidance Team.

APPENDIX C3

Money laundering and terrorist financing

WARNING NOTICE

Issued on 8 December 2014

Status

Whilst this document does not form part of the SRA Handbook, the SRA may have regard to it when exercising its regulatory functions.

Who is this warning notice relevant to?

This warning notice is relevant to all regulated persons who have alegal obligation to ensure that they:

- **do not** facilitate money laundering or terrorist financing; and
- **do report** any suspicious transactions.

This notice highlights warning signs which you should be aware of, and which may require you to take action in order to avoid committing a criminal offence or breaching your professional obligations under the Solicitors Regulation Authority (SRA) Handbook.

Our concerns

The SRA supervises those it regulates for compliance with money laundering legislation. It has identified an increasing number of firms failing to have adequate systems and controls to prevent, detect and report money laundering.

The Financial Action Task Force (FATF), an independent inter-governmental body, issued a report in 2013 highlighting the vulnerabilities of legal professionals to money laundering and terrorist financing, in which it identified 42 'Red Flag Indicators'. Being aware of these indicators or warning signs of money laundering and terrorist financing should assist you in applying a risk based approach to meeting your obligations under the Money Laundering Regulations 2007 and other money laundering legislation. If red flag indicators are present in your dealings with a client, you should ask further questions of your client, or make a suspicious activity report to your firm's nominated officer or the National Crime Agency (NCA), as appropriate.

Our expectations

We expect all firms and individuals regulated by us to comply with money laundering legislation including taking appropriate steps to conduct customer due diligence (CDD) when required to do so by the Money Laundering Regulations 2007. We expect firms and individuals to be aware of, and act properly upon, warning signs that a transaction may be suspicious.

The warning signs highlighted by FATF (and expanded on in Chapter 11 of the Law Society's Practice Note on Money Laundering) include:

If the client:

- Is secretive or evasive about who they are, the reason for the transaction, or the source of funds.
- Uses an intermediary, or does not appear to be directing the transaction, or appears to be disguising the real client.
- Avoids personal contact without good reason.
- Refuses to provide information or documentation or the documentation provided is suspicious.
- Has criminal associations.
- Has unusual level of knowledge about money laundering processes.
- Does not appear to have a business association with the other parties but appears to be connected to them.

If the source of funds is unusual, such as:

- Large cash payments.
- Unexplained payments from a third party.
- Large private funding that does not fit the business or personal profile of the payer.
- Loans from non-institutional lenders.
- Use of corporate assets to fund private expenditure of individuals.
- Use of multiple accounts or foreign accounts.

If the transaction has unusual features, such as:

- Size, nature, frequency or manner of execution.
- Early repayment of mortgages/loans.
- Short repayment periods for borrowing.
- An excessively high value is placed on assets/securities.
- It is potentially loss making.
- Involving unnecessarily complicated structures or steps in transaction.
- Repetitive instructions involving common features/parties or back to back transactions with assets rapidly changing value.
- The transaction is unusual for the client, type of business or age of the business.
- Unexplained urgency, requests for short cuts or changes to the transaction particularly at last minute.
- Use of a Power of Attorney in unusual circumstances.
- No obvious commercial purpose to the transaction.
- Instructions to retain documents or to hold money in your client account.
- Abandoning transaction and/or requests to make payments to third parties or back to source.
- Monies passing directly between the parties.
- Litigation which is settled too easily or quickly and with little involvement by you.

If the instructions are unusual for your business such as:

- Outside your or your firm's area of expertise or normal business, or if client is not local to you and there is no explanation as to why a firm in your locality has been chosen.
- Willingness of client to pay high fees.
- Unexplained changes to legal advisers.
- Your client appears unconcerned or lacks knowledge about the transaction.

If there are geographical concerns such as:

- Unexplained connections with and movement of monies between other jurisdictions.

- Connections with jurisdictions which are subject to sanctions or are suspect because drug production, terrorism or corruption is prevalent or there is a lack of money laundering regulations

The SRA Principles

You have a duty to ensure you comply with money laundering legislation. Failure to do so may result in you breaching one or more of the SRA Principles, including:

- Principle 1 – Uphold the rule of law and the proper administration of justice.
- Principle 2 – Act with integrity.
- Principle 3 – Not allow your independence to be compromised.
- Principle 6 – Behave in a way that maintains the trust the public places in you and in the provision of legal services.
- Principle 7 – Comply with your legal and regulatory obligations.
- Principle 8 – Run your business or carry out your role in the business effectively and in accordance with proper governances and sound financial and risk management principles.

The SRA mandatory outcomes

You should have regard to the specific outcomes under the SRA Code of Conduct 2011, in particular outcome 7.5 – to comply with your legal obligations under the Proceeds of Crime Act (POCA) 2002, the Terrorism Act (TACT) 2000 and the Money Laundering Regulations 2007. You must ensure that you do not facilitate money laundering, even when money does not pass through your firm's accounts. Your firm should have appropriate policies and procedures in place to protect it from being used for money laundering or terrorist financing outcomes 7.2 and 7.3.

Enforcement action

Failure to comply with this warning notice may lead to disciplinary action, criminal prosecution or both.

Further guidance

From us

- For guidance on making requests to proceed with suspicious transactions, see our Warning notice: Money Laundering and Terrorist Financing – Suspicious Activity Reports (SARs)
- For guidance on conduct issues, contact the Professional Ethics Guidance Team.

From others

- FATF report on the vulnerabilities of legal professionals
- Detailed guidance on your obligations and on the warning signs of money laundering is available on the Law Society website.
- Law Society practice note: Anti-money laundering
- For advice on anti-money laundering, contact the Law Society Practice Advice Service.

APPENDIX D

Sources of help

APPENDIX D1

Useful contacts and publications

USEFUL CONTACTS

- Law Society (**www.lawsociety.org.uk**).
  - Practice Advice Line: support for solicitors on a wide range of areas of practice (tel. 020 7320 5675, 9 am to 5 pm on weekdays).
  - Law Society Consulting: expert and confidential support and guidance, including face-to-face consultancy on risk and compliance and finance and accounting (tel. 020 7316 5655, or email consulting@lawsociety.org.uk).
  - Lawyerline: advice to solicitors on client care and complaints handling (tel. 020 7320 5720 or e-mail lawyerline@lawsociety.org.uk).
- SRA (**www.sra.org.uk**).
  - Contact Centre (tel. 0370 606 2555 or +44 (0)121 329 6800 for international callers, 8 am to 6 pm on Mondays, Wednesdays, Thursdays and Fridays, and 9.30 am to 6 pm on Tuesdays).
  - Professional Ethics Helpline: (tel. 0370 606 2577 9 am and 5 pm on weekdays, or email professional.ethics@sra.org.uk).
- Legal Ombudsman (**www.legalombudsman.org.uk**).
- Information Commissioner's Office (**www.ico.org.uk**).

Other membership organisations

- Chartered Institute of Legal Executives (CILEX) – the professional body for Legal Executive (**www.cilex.org.uk**).
- Institute of Chartered Accountants in England and Wales (ICAEW) Solicitors Group (**www.icaew.com/en/technical/legal-and-regulatory/solicitors/solicitors-group**).
- Institute of Legal Finance and Management (ILFM) – education authority and membership body for legal finance, administration and practice management professionals (**www.ilfm.org.uk**).
- Institute of Paralegals (IoP) (**www.theiop.org**).
- National Association of Licensed Paralegals (NALP) (**www.nationalparalegals.co.uk**).

USEFUL PUBLICATIONS

- *Law Society Gazette* (**www.lawgazette.co.uk**).
- *Legal Compliance Bulletin* – up-to-date, practical information on every aspect of legal compliance and regulation for solicitors, barristers and practice managers (**www.lawsociety.org.uk/support-services/risk-compliance/legal-compliance-bulletin**).
- Law Society books – see p.ii (**www.lawsociety.org.uk/bookshop**).

- Law Society e-newsletters – including Professional Update, Anti-Money Laundering Update and Junior Lawyers Update (**www.lawsociety.org.uk/news/newsletters**).
- SRA Update – an e-newsletter sent to all regulated individuals but others can subscribe by e-mail (**SRAupdate@sra.org.uk**).
- SRA's Compliance News – an e-newsletter sent automatically to COLPs and COFAs but others can sign up to the mailing list (**www.sra.org.uk/compliancenews**).

Index